CHILD PSYCHIATRY: A PRIMER FOR THOSE WHO WORK CLOSELY WITH CHILDREN

CHILD PSYCHIATRY: A PRIMER FOR THOSE WHO WORK CLOSELY WITH CHILDREN

R. DEAN CODDINGTON, MD
Professor Emeritus
Department of Psychiatry
Louisiana State University School of Medicine
New Orleans

MOLLIE M. WALLICK, PhD
Professor
Department of Psychiatry
Louisiana State University School of Medicine
New Orleans

DEO VERITATI INTELLIGENTIAE

WARREN H. GREEN, INC.
St. Louis, Missouri, USA

Published by

WARREN H. GREEN, INC.
8356 Olive Boulevard
St. Louis, Missouri 63132, U.S.A.

ISBN No. 87527-361-0

Printed in the United States of America

CONTRIBUTING AUTHORS

STEPHEN R. COCHRAN, MD
Clinical Assistant Professor
Department of Psychiatry
Louisiana State University School of Medicine
New Orleans

KATHARINE N. DIXON, MD
Clinical Associate Professor
Department of Psychiatry
University of California at San Diego

CAROL J. LARROQUE, MD
20 Brookfield Avenue
Barrington, RI 02806

DOUGLAS S. POOL, MD
Clinical Assistant Professor
Department of Psychiatry
Louisiana State University School of Medicine
New Orleans

ELSA RAE POOL, MSW, MHA
New Orleans

WILLIAM C. SZE, PhD
Associate Professor
Department of Psychiatry
Louisiana State University School of Medicine
New Orleans

PREFACE

As a child psychiatrist interested in community psychiatry, I have worked with teachers, child care workers, both in hospitals and in group homes, nurses, counselors, speech pathologists, occupational and physical therapists, and foster parents—a variety of people who choose to work with children. Most of them have had personal experiences as parents, baby-sitters, camp counselors, or with younger nieces, nephews, and siblings but have had few opportunities to work closely with child psychiatrists. We have had many very interesting conversations which were, in fact, mutually satisfying. I learned much from these dedicated persons and contributed, I hope, to their understanding of the complex world of children.

Thirty years ago when I was a young pediatrician, the normal development of children was viewed as a rather dull subject. I recall my consternation when a faculty member predicted that I would come to love working with infants once I got into practice, because at that time well-baby care didn't seem the least bit challenging. It was the rare diseases and emotional disorders that fascinated us all. But things have changed! I have discovered what my teacher knew then and his teachers knew before that: every child is unique. Identical twins are not always identical; the intrauterine environment has a major influence on egg, embryo, and fetus. And, of course, everyone knows today that the extrauterine environment affects almost every aspect of physical and emotional development. Eye color is determined solely by genes, as far as I know. But hair color can be changed by environmental manipulation, and sex can be altered by the surgeon and significantly affected in terms of gender identity by patterns of rearing. Only a portion of intelligence is genetically dependent, perhaps 75% under the best of conditions. We can no longer view child development as a predetermined, fixed sequence of events but must think in terms of feedback mechanisms and child-environment interaction.

The environment plays an ever-increasing role as the child grows. The vicissitudinous results are at once fascinating and mind-boggling—gratifying when we understand and humbling when we do not. The examination of the child alone does not suffice; information must be gathered from parents, too, and from teachers, observers, and specialists in all child-oriented disciplines. No one professional group has a corner on the market. But most of all, we must listen to the child and try to help him articulate his thoughts. It's in this area that I have been able to aid the counselors, teachers, and other front-line soldiers with whom I have worked. And it is to this end that this book is directed.

Putting the content of innumerable conferences, staffings, group meetings, and discussions into writing is not an easy task. It became apparent very soon that I needed the help of a skilled communicator. Mollie Wallick obtained her PhD in Special Education after more than 20 years' experience in early childhood education, which included work with some very disturbed children and with many representatives of other disciplines. She thus became the logical choice as collaborator in this work.

The book is divided into three sections. The first is an overview of normal child development that can serve as a guide to the newcomer to the world of childhood and a brief refresher for the more experienced. References for further reading have been provided for those who wish to pursue the subject. Some readers may wish to skip this section and proceed directly into the area of psychopathology.

The second section contains the real theme of the book. It is designed to teach the reader what to look for when assessing a child and how to recognize anxiety, depression, and internal conflicts. It is hoped that study of this section will lead to increased understanding of troubled children and will help the reader become more empathic. This part should not be skipped.

The final section is devoted to the description of specific emotional or psychological disorders of childhood and may be used to acquaint the reader with the domain of pathology. It can also serve as a ready reference for the student who is puzzled about the behavior of a given child.

We are grateful for the help of several contributors: Carol Larroque, a pediatrician particularly concerned with the attachment of mother and infant, Stephen Cochran, a child psychiatrist who wrote the chapter on development of the preschooler, William Sze, a social worker who knows and understands families, Katharine Dixon, a child psychiatrist with a special interest in eating disorders, and Douglas and Elsa Pool, a child psychiatrist and social worker who collaborated on the chapter on substance abuse.

We would be remiss if we failed to acknowledge the efforts of Beverly Magee, Anita Harris, Nell Hawkins, and Sue Schneider, who typed and retyped the manuscript amidst their many other duties. We are also indebted to Constance Deck, proofreader par excellence. The index could not have been completed without the able assistance of Charles Chapman and the secretarial help of Dee Bonvillian.

RDC

Contents

CHILD PSYCHIATRY: A PRIMER FOR THOSE WHO WORK CLOSELY WITH CHILDREN

Chapter 1

INFANCY

CAROL J. LARROQUE, MD

It is late afternoon. Terry collapses on her bed, closes her eyes momentarily, and breathes deeply. Feelings of exhaustion, exhilaration, and frustration flood her simultaneously. It has been a rough week!

Just four days ago, Terry returned home from the hospital with her newborn son, Stephen. Since then, days and nights have merged as she has worked to meet the unexpected demands of her new baby. She just never realized that it would be this difficult. However, as her thoughts linger on her newborn, Terry smiles to herself. She then yawns, stretches, and decides to take a quick shower while little Stephen sleeps.

Terry moves rapidly as she anticipates the feel of warm water over her fatigued body. What a luxury it will be to freshen up! Stepping into the cool shower stall, she is about to turn on the faucet. Suddenly, Terry's heart accelerates! She can hear Stephen screaming in the next room.

What should she do? Stephen just doesn't seem to follow any schedule—except to breast-feed every two hours. The telephone, the doorbell, and the voices of neighboring children all awaken him. Terry wonders if she is doing something wrong with her son. Could her relatives be right when they say that Terry and her husband, Bill, are spoiling Stephen? Relatives warned them that, if they pick up their baby each time he cries, he will soon run their lives. Is Stephen spoiled or does he just need his mother? Can he really see and hear? Is he aware of all that is going on about him? What does Stephen feel at this young age? Terry is confused. She loves her little son and wants to do what is best for him.

***

It is 7:30 on a cool October morning. Alice and Bob are breathless as they bring 9-month-old Rachel to the baby sitter's home for the first time. This will be Alice's first day back at work since she took maternity leave ten months ago. She has enjoyed the months with her delightful baby. At the same time, she is excited, though somewhat apprehensive, about getting back to the office.

Alice and Bob feel uncomfortable as Mrs. Greene opens the door to her home. Even though Mrs. Greene is a wonderful woman with many grandchildren of her own, Rachel's parents feel a bit guilty about leaving their daughter with a sitter all day. Inside the living room, the adults chat and Mrs. Greene gently reaches out to take Rachel into her arms. Rachel stiffens, her face wrinkles up, her eyes widen. Rachel then bursts into a lusty cry, even though Mrs. Greene is speaking softly to her.

Alice is emotionally distraught as she wonders if there is something she and Bob could have done to make this easier for Rachel. Both parents wonder if they are doing the right thing.

***

Hand-in-hand, David and 22-month-old Jason walk together to the corner grocery store to buy some bread for the evening meal. The father is amused by the chatter of his little son. He feels proud as he hears Jason mutter excitedly, "Daddy bye-bye, Jason bye-bye." David enjoys watching Jason smile and say "Hi" to Mr. Reynolds in the grocery store. The father is impressed by his personable young son.

David purchases the loaf of bread and, as they are about to leave the store, Jason grabs several packages of bubble gum. David tells him to put the gum back, adding that "Gum is not for little boys." Jason refuses. "My gum," he says, "Mine!" David struggles to take the gum from Jason's hand. He tells Jason that the gum belongs to Mr. Reynolds. Again Jason holds the gum tightly, emphatically screaming, "Mine!"

Within seconds, Jason is in the midst of a full-fledged tantrum: lying on the ground, crying, and refusing to let go of the precious possession in his little hands. The father is bewildered and embarrassed by his son's behavior. David feels helpless and angry with Jason. He just can't believe that this has happened. What brought on this sudden behavior? What should he do to stop it?

Many parents and many professionals who work with young children will be able to relate to the dilemmas illustrated in the previous vignettes. For centuries, parents and other "experts" in the field of child care have theorized over the ideal approach in raising infants and children. While we still flounder in our attempts to make the most appropriate decisions in guiding infants and children into happy and successful adulthood, we are now able to consider the results of some remarkable research conducted within the last 15 years.

A generation or two ago, it had been the common belief that it is best not to "spoil" infants. Authorities believed that by not attending to a crying baby (who was fed and whose diaper was dry), parents could teach the infant not to be too demanding. Therefore, mothers were told not to pick up their babies each time they cried, lest they become unruly, demanding adults.

Since attitudes regarding child rearing are passed down from generation to generation, many parents may find themselves thinking in the same way today. However, recent research has shed new light on early infant development.

In 1972, Silvia Bell and Mary Ainsworth published a study regarding infant crying and maternal responsiveness. Upon completing their longitudinal study of 26 infant-mother pairs, the authors concluded that consistency and promptness of a mother's response correlates with a decline in the frequency and duration of her infant's crying. They noted that, by the end of the first year of life, individual differences in crying reflected the history of maternal responsiveness; that is, the mothers who responded to their infant's crying by interacting with their babies from birth, generally had toddlers who cried less at one year of age.

The information about infant crying patterns fits in well with other current data about newborns. We are now aware of the marvelous capacity of a newborn infant to show visual preferences, to hear, to communicate, and to relate socially. The recent work of T. Berry Brazelton further supports the earlier work of Alexander Thomas and Stella Chess by demonstrating that, right from birth, infants relate to their environment differently. These individual differences are related to the infant's cultural and genetic endowments. It is, therefore, not surprising that infants have emotional needs as well as physical needs. It is also not surprising that different infants will relate to stimulation differently: while some babies respond to an unpleasant source of stimulation by withdrawing from it, others may respond by actively demonstrating their disapproval.

In the initial vignette, Stephen is much more sensitive to external stimuli than some other babies. He requires the frequent, soothing intervention of his mother, especially during the first two months of life when his own immature body systems are not yet regulated. As a breast-fed infant, Stephen, indeed, may be hungry every two hours. In breast milk, the lactalbumin:casein ratio (60%:40%) makes for small curds and easy digestibility. The breast-fed infant experiences a more rapid emptying time of his stomach, as compared to the infant fed a commercial formula. Therefore, infants who are breast-fed often sense hunger two to three hours after feeding, whereas a formula-fed baby may feel satisfied for longer periods of time.

Stephen's mother would probably be comforted to know that the technique of lifting a baby to one's shoulder and holding him close, in an upright position, works wonderfully to soothe a crying baby. This technique not only stimulates the infant's vestibular system, but also allows the infant to visually scan his environment when looking over his mother's shoulder. This scanning is thought to enhance the infant's cognitive development.

While some of this information may appear new to us today, our primitive ancestors, by their lifestyle, were able to meet their youngsters' needs. As hunters and gatherers they continually carried their babies with them, stimulating them with their movements and bodily contact, and breast-feeding their young promptly, as often as needed.

ATTACHMENT

At birth, the human infant is totally dependent on the adults of his species for his continued survival. The infant's perception of the world as warm and secure—or as cold and rejecting—depends on the care he receives from others. According to Erik Erikson, infancy is the time of learning "basic trust" or "mistrust." Reciprocal interaction between the newborn and his primary caretaker enhances attachments of each to the other. This "attachment," in turn, assures the infant of the continued nurturance and nourishment needed for his growth and development.

Parent-to-Infant Attachment

The attachment of parents to their infant may occur at different times during the perinatal period. Some parents experience a sense of attachment during the pregnancy, others at the time of delivery, while others experience it only after they have had the opportunity to get to know their baby, a few days after his birth. Many mothers report that the special feeling, that their infant really belongs to them, occurred at a time when their infant looked at their eyes.

Attributes of both the infant and the parents, as well as external circumstances, can affect the attachment process. The very appearance of the human infant (as with others mammals such as kittens, puppies, and bunnies) enhances parental attachment. The head of the newborn is large in proportion to the rest of the body, the nose less prominent, the coiled arms and legs are proportionately short as compared to those of an adult. This "cute" appearance triggers a desire in adults to hold and cuddle the young of its species. In the case of sick, deformed, or very premature infants the typical "cute" appearance may be jeopardized and this may contribute to the disruption of parental attachment.

Some authorities in neonatal behavior, such as John Kennell and Marshall Klaus of Case Western Reserve University, have demonstrated by their research that there appears to be a "sensitive" period in human mothers. During this period, extended contact of a mother with her newborn will foster a special attachment of the mother to him. This special attachment is called "bonding." Bonding appears to affect the mother's subsequent behavior toward her baby. Mothers who experienced bonding demonstrated more eye-to-eye contact, fondling, soothing, and other affectionate behavior toward their babies. They also demonstrated a different pattern of linguistic behavior while interacting with their children: two years after delivery they used more questions, more words per proposition, fewer content words, more adjectives, and fewer commands than control mothers.

Since human beings are complex physically and psychologically, many authorities in human development feel that bonding is not crucial for a mother to attach to her newborn, though it may enhance the attachment process.

While there are no comparable studies evaluating the father-newborn relationship, a process similar to bonding, termed "engrossment," is thought to occur in adult males.

It may be more difficult for parents of a premature, sick, or deformed newborn to attach to their baby. These parents are frequently separated from their baby during the first few days of life and, therefore, are not given the opportunity to bond. They may be fearful that their baby will die and, thus, may be afraid to engage in an intimate relationship with him. Finally, they will be grieving the loss of the "healthy baby" they had been expecting. While in such an emotional state, it is very difficult for parents to attach appropriately to their newborn. In such circumstances, the assistance of sensitive personnel can be invaluable to the future relationship of parents and child.

Infant-to-Parent Attachment

During the first few weeks of life, an infant is unaware of his separateness from his mother. Prior to birth, he rested securely in her body—in a warm, fluid-filled, amniotic sac. Effortlessly, he received adequate nutrition via the umbilical cord, as he rhythmically swayed with his mother's movements. The process of birth then brought about a dramatic change! But the neonate still strives for the homeostasis he experienced prior to his delivery. He appears most comfortable "swaddled" or snuggly wrapped, and often assumes the same position as when he was a fetus. He enjoys gentle swaying movements and is intolerant of hunger pangs. He is incapable of delayed gratification at this young age and wishes to be satiated immediately, giving out a lusty cry to have his needs fulfilled. He may also communicate by tensing or relaxing his body, wiggling, grimacing, and sucking. A sensitive mother who is appropriately preoccupied with her baby during these early weeks will quickly learn to read her infant's "cues" and efficiently respond to his needs. The infant's demonstration of satisfaction, as well as his remarkable growth and development, will be very gratifying to the primary caretaker. Thus, a marvelous reciprocal relationship between mother and child is established.

As the infant's needs are consistently met, he becomes aware of "cause and effect." Hunger regularly sets in after a couple of hours and the baby cries; this alerts his mother, and the ultimate result of his crying is that he is fed and satisfied. The baby thus begins to learn the "messages" of his own body, and will begin to gain a sense of control in meeting his physical needs.

If, on the other hand, a caretaker is truly negligent and is guided by personal whims rather than the baby's needs, the infant will have difficulty sensing the connection between his hunger cry and his satisfaction with milk. If feeding is totally contingent on the needs of the caretaker rather than the newborn, the newborn as an adult may continue to look to outsiders to tell him how he feels. Basic trust of others, as well as a sense of security, will be violated.

The newborn infant is sensorially well equipped to initiate an attachment to his mother. It has been shown that by two weeks of age an infant can distinguish, by smell, the breast pad of his mother from that of other women. His sense of hearing matures even sooner, probably in utero, because at birth he is capable of distinguishing his own mother's voice. Goren, Sarty, and Wee have demonstrated that at only nine minutes of age, infants will turn their heads and eyes significantly more to follow a face-like stimulus than either of two equally bright and complex stimuli consisting of the same facial features. This phenomenon suggests that there is an innate predisposition at birth to respond selectively to faces. This marvelous predisposition sets the stage for the social interaction that is to take place between an infant and an adult.

Gradually, the young baby begins to sense itself as a separate being. By 6 weeks of age a social smile is beginning to emerge, and by 3 months of age most mothers will report that their babies recognize them and are responsive to them.

The baby's attachment to a primary caretaker and the caretaker's reciprocal emotional investment are crucial to the baby's continued development. In the security of a warm and trusting relationship, an infant between 3 and 6 months of age will learn to roll over. Between 6 and 9 months of age, he will begin to crawl and learn to get into and out of a sitting position, while maintaining good balance. At approximately one year, the emerging toddler will take his first steps unassisted; however, the range of independent walking may vary from 9 to 17 months. We may also expect the infant to say his first word meaningfully about the time of his first birthday and two-word sentences at the time of his second birthday.

While there is marked variation in the timing when infants achieve these milestones, an infant will sequentially develop motorically, verbally, and socially within a normal range, if given the warm encouragement of his primary caretaker. However, in situations in which a loving primary caretaker is not available to an infant (as may be the case in certain institutional settings), or if the primary caretaker is not emotionally available to the infant due to causes such as severe depression or negligence, the infant will be severely developmentally delayed. In some instances the infant will also be deprived of adequate calories and will thus "fail to thrive" (to grow and gain weight). In such a case the infant's very life is threatened, and emergency care is necessary.

STRANGER ANXIETY

By 8 months of age, most infants are expressing discomfort when confronted by a stranger. They may attempt to withdraw from this new person, cling to their mother or another familiar caretaker, or may cry lustily as the infant Rachel did in the previous vignette. To a child this age, a "stranger" is anyone, even a grandparent, with whom the child does not regularly interact. While most infants will experience some form of stranger anxiety, there is much individual variation in its time of onset, as well as the degree to which it is experienced.

The discrepancy principle hypothesis is a popular explanation for this phenomenon. By 8 months, an infant is clearly capable of distinguishing that which is familiar to him, such as his mother's face. He thus behaves in a comfortable manner in her presence. However, that which is strange or novel (ie, a face discrepant from his schemata) arouses a state of uncertainty in the infant who is not yet able to assimilate differences. The 8-month-old child, with his limited repertoire of coping responses, as well as his inability to escape from the situation, will respond to a stranger with fearful behavior.

While much is still unknown about the genesis of stranger anxiety, observations of infants placed in situations in which they are precipitously cared for by a strange adult, demonstrate that the infants are most uncomfortable and some even traumatized. Therefore, if any infant must be placed in a new caretaking situation during this developmental stage, it would be wise to gradually ease the child into the situation. For instance, in the case of Rachel, she and her mother might visit Mrs. Greene together several times the week before Alice returned to work. After two or three visits to Mrs. Green's house, with Rachel permitted to explore both her new environment and her baby sitter in the security of her mother's presence, Alice might leave Rachel alone with Mrs. Greene for a brief period of time. Thus, the transition would be a gradual one for Rachel, and the first day of her mother's return to work would be less upsetting for all.

Emerging in infants during this same time period and reaching its peak at about 15 to 18 months is another type of behavior termed "separation anxiety." During this stage a youngster becomes upset or cries over a parent's departure from him. If the separation is gradual, for brief periods only, the entire process of separation will be facilitated and less traumatic for the child. Separation anxiety may be present well past the child's second birthday.

AUTONOMY

As the infant moves into his second year of life, some marvelous things are occurring. The baby gradually develops into a toddler with independent upright mobility and the ability to communicate through spoken language. The young child is exhilarated with his new independence. While he continues to need the ever-present emotional support of his mother, he is also ready to protect his newly acquired autonomy.

It is during this stage that the toddler appears negative and stubborn as he insists on doing things his way. "No" is a prominent word in his newly acquired vocabulary. He may enjoy messing with his food and playing in water, mud, and sand.

During this time parents may think that their youngster understands more than he really does, especially in a situation in which their toddler is able to say some relevant words. Because the toddler's use of language is still so limited and his needs for autonomous expression so strong, temper tantrums occur at this time.

Temper tantrums during the second year of life are not the same as the willful expressions of an angry adult. They are a discharge of emotion which the youngster is unable to express in any other way. At this age the toddler has little control over his tantrums. As in the situation with Jason, the tantrums are more likely to occur when the youngster is fatigued and hungry. The best way of dealing with temper tantrums is to avoid them: Preventing the child from undue physical or emotional stress is helpful. At times, an adult may be able to distract a toddler from a potential struggle which may lead to a tantrum. When a tantrum does occur, it is best to remain supportive of the child, acknowledging his feelings but not giving in to them. Some children relax if held snuggly; others may kick and punch under such circumstances. At times, it may be necessary to ignore a tantrum altogether (if the child is not harming himself), so as to prevent the tantrum from becoming a means of obtaining parental attention. For the parent to remain calm and understanding, yet firm, is helpful in diminishing an ongoing tantrum and avoiding the occurrence of new ones.

It is helpful to parents to know that temper tantrums are a normal response for children during the second and third year of life. If handled properly by an adult, a youngster will indeed "outgrow" this mode of communication and develop more sophisticated and socially acceptable ways of expressing his negative feelings.

CONCLUSIONS

The first two years of a child's life are demanding and exhausting for parents, but also a time of immeasurable pleasure. To see a young infant gradually blossom into an independent, world-exploring toddler is indeed a marvelous thing.

BIBLIOGRAPHY

Bell SM, Ainsworth, MS: Infant crying and maternal responsiveness. *Child Dev* 43:1171-1190, 1972

Chase RA, Rubin, RR: *The first wondrous year.* New York, Macmillan, 1979

Greenberg M, Morris M: Engrossment: The newborn's impact upon the father. *Am J Orthopsychiatry* 44:520-531, 1974

Kagan JH: *Psychological research on the human infant: An evaluative summary.* New York, William T. Grant Foundation, 1982

Kaplan D, Mason E: Maternal reactions to premature birth viewed as an acute emotional disorder. *Am J Orthopsychiatry* 30:539-552, 1960

Klaus KH, Kennell JH: *Parent-infant bonding.* St. Louis, C.V. Mosby, 1982

Korner AF, Grobstein R: Visual alertness as related to soothing in neonates: Implications for maternal stimulation and early deprivation. *Child Dev* 37:867-876, 1966

Mahler MS, Pine F, Bergman A: *The psychological birth of the human infant.* New York, Basic Books, 1975

Rubin RR, Fisher JJ, Doering SG: *Your toddler.* New York, Macmillan, 1980

Solnit, AJ, Stark MH: Mourning and the birth of a defective child. *Psychoanal Study Child* 16:523-537, 1961

Steele BF: The effect of abuse and neglect on psychological development, in Call JH, Galenson E, Tyson RL (eds): *Frontiers of infant psychiatry.* New York, Basic Books, 1983

Chapter 2

EARLY CHILDHOOD

STEPHEN R. COCHRAN, MD

By 2 years of age, the child has made major developmental advances. He has changed from a helpless and totally dependent infant to a child who is able to move about on his own and to use language to ask questions and make requests. He not only knows that there are separate and important people in his world, but also can recognize and, usually, name them. He is becoming aware of the multitude of things in the world; he recognizes that things have an existence of their own and wants to know their identity.

In order to understand the development of the child from 2 to 6 years of age, it is necessary to look at various paths of development: (1) physical and motor, (2) cognitive and language, (3) a sense of self, and (4) relationships. The latter two categories depend to a great extent on the first two. For example, the development of a sense of self in a child with a handicap may be altered: A child with retarded intelligence develops a sense of self more slowly. A hearing impaired child may develop language more slowly and this, in turn, may affect his developing relationships with significant others. But it also works the other way around. For example, in the case of children who "fail to thrive" and must be hospitalized for malnutrition, a common finding is an inappropriate mother-child interaction. In the latter case, it is the failure in the development of relationships that has a marked impact on physical and cognitive development.

It is important to remember that the development of the child is an interactive process. Changes in one developmental area can have major impact on another. Lines of development are interdependent, with the interdependence also occurring on several levels. First, there is the interaction which occurs within the child himself. In dynamic theories, this is often referred to as the intrapsychic process. However, this process does not occur in a vacuum. It requires a setting or context in which to occur. Initially, it is the family that provides the setting in which the most important aspects of growth take place. The foundation or bedrock needs to be loving and caring, reflected in behavior. As the child grows, so does his world. By the age of 6, the child's world will have expanded to include friends and school.

A final area which affects the development of the child is the larger social or cultural context. It is beyond the scope of this chapter to examine all of the issues involved in this broader area. It is obvious that there are differences in the way a child from the ghetto and an upperclass child from the suburbs look at the world; fear of going out to play in a child raised in the ghetto may be related more to reality than to intrapsychic conflict. We must be aware of the sociocultural contribution and consider its effect on the various lines of development.

THE 2-YEAR-OLD

The child at 2 years has made great strides in motor development. He is as apt to run as to walk. He no longer needs external support to get around. The typical 2-year-old thoroughly enjoys his ability to move about, often to the concern of his parents who must keep an eye on his behavior in order to keep it within safe limits. The 2-year-old is able to kick a ball on request. He can walk up and down stairs in an erect position; he often has to hold onto a railing, but he brings both feet to the same step, while maintaining an upright position. He can make a primitive attempt to throw a ball and can throw it in the direction requested; this is an example of the combination of motor (throwing) and cognitive (in the direction requested) development.

In the area of fine motor development, the typical 2-year-old can turn pages one at a time, make a tower of six or seven blocks, and line up two or more blocks to make a "train." He can hold a crayon and imitate a circle; to be sure, the circle is a primitive scribble, but it is a clear attempt to imitate "roundness." By 2 years of age, the child has the imitative ability and the fine motor ability to unscrew the cap from a bottle. Thus, a new need in packaging (the child-proof cap) developed.

Cognitive and Language Development

By 2 years of age, the child has become a "person" in his own right. Now he can request things, using a newly acquired tool: language. This is a major advance for the child whose wants and needs were previously expressed by crying or through gestures (such as pointing). It is a welcome change for the parents, who, by this time, are eager to talk with their child instead of trying to figure out his needs from gesture, cry, or babble. It is much more enjoyable to respond to "more milk" than to a whine or a gesture.

The relationship between language and cognitive development is a complex one. In general, language development (represented by the ability to communicate using words) lags behind cognitive development. In other words, the child is able to understand more than he can put into words. However, in general, language development reflects cognitive development in the normal child. The reverse is not necessarily true, however. Delayed language development may occur in children with normal cognitive abilities. Some reasons for this will be discussed later.

The basis of cognitive function, the ability to make distinctions, appears very early in infancy. As the child develops, these distinctions become internalized and are no longer dependent on the presence of the external object or person. That is, the child is able to represent in thought the existence of something outside of himself. Furthermore he is able to do this without the object or person being present. The development of the ability to internally represent external objects or persons begins around 18 to 20 months; this is known as object permanence. This opens the door to the world of play and "make-believe." The little girl, for example, is now able to play like the mother and feed the baby doll—or spank it because "it's bad." It also opens up to the child the world of "things" and the ever present question, "What's dat?"

Some of the signs of normal cognitive and language development in the 2-year-old include the ability to ask for things. Typically, the child of 2 uses two- or three-word sentences and often verbalizes immediate experience using his name ("Johnny fall down"). He begins to use the pronouns, "I," "me," and "you," and is beginning to understand "my" and "mine." He can identify objects by name. He knows up to six body parts and can usually name them. It is now possible for him to follow simple commands, such as "Bring daddy the ball." The typical 2-year-old has developed a vocabulary of from 20 to 50 words.

Development of a Sense of Self

One of the most important tasks for the child is to answer the question, "Who am I?" Answering the question is a process which goes on both internally and in relation to others. It is a process in which the child both creates and discovers himself, while being created and molded by his family and, later, by the world. To proceed optimally, the process requires normal physical abilities (including normal cognition) and an environment that allows these abilities to grow and develop. A sense of self does not develop in a vacuum, even if physical abilities are normal. The extreme examples are severely neglected children who stare vacantly into space with blank, expressionless faces. For these children, the question, "Who am I?", was answered by neglect that said, in effect, "Nobody."

One of the central processes in the development of a sound sense of self is identification, in which the child internalizes his parental figures. Identification is reflected in such actions as mimicry: The child imitates the domestic chores of the mother and "helps" her cook dinner. The child "models" the parental figures and in the process uses them as a sort of template on which to form his own unique sense of self. Here again, this is a two-way process in which it is just as important how the parents see the child as how the child sees the parents. To have an identity, it is necessary to have an identifier. For the child, the principal identifiers are his parents. To develop a sense that one is important, worthwhile, and worthy of love, there needs to be an environment that reflects back these feelings. Even in children who have been abused or neglected, the process of identification is a powerful one: the children often show very strong attachments to the abusing parent; it is as if the loss of the abusing parent threatened their own identity.

By 2 years of age, the child is well on his way toward independence. He can express his independence motorically by running away or, when frightened, by running back just as quickly. Independence can also be expressed verbally. The favorite word of the 2-year-old may well be "No!" The issue for the 2-year-old (and also for the parents) is control. This struggle for control spawned the name, "terrible two's." Often toilet training (the "battle of the bowels") becomes a central theme. While this battle is a trial to parents, it is very important in the child's developing sense of self. Optimally the child will emerge from this stage of development with a new sense of mastery. The dilemma for the child is that the path toward independence and ultimate self-sufficiency must lead away from the omnipotence and helplessness of infancy.

At about this time, he realizes that "mama" and "dada" don't always respond to his demands. It is no longer sufficient just to cry to get his needs met. Now the child is expected to say what's wrong. On the other hand, mothers are tired of the total dependency of infancy and welcome the move toward independence (as long as it is within bounds). It is the setting of these boundaries that makes this an important developmental stage. The boundaries cannot be so rigid as to stifle the creative aspects of the child's developing sense of self; at the same time, they help the child with his first lesson at dealing with limits and set the stage for future interactions involving give-and-take.

Development of Relationships

As the child develops and grows more independent and sure of his identity, he gradually becomes more aware of relationships. The 2--year-old is still in an in-between stage. He is interested in other children but is not yet sure what to do with them. The first rule in relationships is that relationships require relationships. The primary relationships are of course those with parents and significant others (grandparents, caretakers, close relatives, close friends of the family). The rule may at first seem redundant. However, it must be remembered that, for the child, relationships are seen as a matter of survival. Because the child is dependent on parents or significant others to supply basic needs (such as food, protection, and relief from pain), these relationships or bonds are extremely strong. It is these bonds which form the model for future relationships. While the recognition of these relationships occurs from infancy, their understanding and "working out" may take a lifetime.

One of the most important ways of working this out (probably the most important) is through the medium of play. It is through play that the child explores, works out, and "tries on" ways of behaving that he has observed in the world around him. The 2-year-old imitates, talks to himself, and pretends. In play with other children, he engages in what is called "parallel play." In other words, the play tends to be alongside another child, rather than with him. While 2-year-olds mirror each other, they do not cooperate in the sense of developing play with give-and-take or with a common goal, such as "building" something. Nevertheless, they are attentive to the play of other children and interested in what they are doing and, especially, in what they have. The primary end point of play is the attainment of mastery. Play gives the child a chance to practice behaviors, as well as to deal with the feelings or emotions which they express.

By 2 years of age, the differences in play between boys and girls are beginning to emerge. Boys tend to be more aggressive in their play; they tend to crash cars or to build towers and knock them over. Some of this behavior is thought to be the result of a biological component within males, but much of it is culturally or environmentally determined. By the end of the second year, gender identity has been established; this refers to the balance between masculinity and feminity in the child. By 3 years, the child can usually tell you whether he is a boy or girl. The formation of gender identity is a combination of the biological sex of the child and the shaping and modeling of the parents, as well as the child's own experimenting (in play) with sexual roles and stereotypes.

The handling of aggression is another task of importance to the child of 2. The basic mechanism for the expression is found within everyone, though the way in which anger is expressed is learned. Much of this learning occurs in the home—a result of both the child's own interactions and what he sees or observes occurring between other members of his family and significant others. The child must learn appropriate means of expressing his anger, as well as a suitable time and place for its expression. Anger can be used in many ways: as a means of communication, for need fulfillment, and—as in the "battle of the bowels"—for purposes of control.

There are two important defenses which begin to develop during this period. The child is often trying to deal with angry or hostile feelings—feelings which are prevented from being destructive by the child's small size and by the parents' imposition of limits on the expression of anger. But the feelings are very intense, nonetheless; to deal with them, the child denies or displaces the feelings. The development of ways of dealing with feelings is a normal part of development. Here again, it is how they are used that determines whether or not they are healthy. The little girl who spanks her doll because "she is bad" is most probably using an appropriate displacement to work out her angry feelings. (It would not be appropriate to slug her infant or toddler sibling.) The displacement of feelings in play (within limits, of course) is one of the normal ways in which a child deals with aggressive feelings, just as a hard game of racquet ball serves a similar function for an adult.

The overuse of denial as a way of dealing with feelings can be problematic. The goal of growth is to understand and appropriately control feelings, and not to deny their existence. To deny a feeling which is a part of oneself is, in a way, to deny one's own validity. In the developing child, to deny feelings of anger prevents their being "worked out." It is this working out or resolution of feelings that allows the child to grow and to pursue relationships and friendships. For example, the anger that develops out of one child's desire to have the toy with which another child is playing is often seen in children of this age. Learning to share is one resolution. For the child, watching the way his parents resolve their disagreements is another way of learning. This is not to say that parents should fight in front of their children. But it is in everyday expressions that the child learns that feelings of anger can be resolved and that they are not necessarily destructive.

Common Problems

Delay in speech production. In evaluating a speech delay, it is important to determine whether the delay is due to organic or environmental causes. The evaluation of organic cause of speech delay should be done by trained specialists. These include physicians (pediatricians, family practitioners, child neurologists, child psychiatrists) and speech pathologists who work with children. Some useful questions to ask in screening a child with a speech delay of organic origin include:

(1) Can the child hear? (Even if the child responds to sound, an audiological exam should be done to rule out the existence of a hearing loss in the frequencies related to spoken sound.)

(2) Can the child understand? Is the child able to respond to simple requests? The question here is whether the areas of the brain responsible for understanding language are working adequately: Is there a problem with the reception of language, or a receptive aphasia? Or is there a problem of understanding because of poor cognitive ability?

(3) If the child can understand what is said, is he able to produce the sounds necessary for speech and to arrange them in order to make sense? In other words, is there a problem with expression, or an expressive aphasia?

(4) Is there a problem with the child's basic ability to relate, such as is found in autistic children?

Speech problems related to the milieu include: (1) an environment which lacks language stimulation, such as an environment of neglect; (2) an environment which punishes language development, such as a home in which there is physical, emotional, or sexual abuse (delayed speech development occurs when there is a high degree of physical or emotional trauma); and (3) an environment in which talking is used to resolve the power struggles of the 2-year old.

Problems with toilet training. Common complaints from parents of 2-year-olds involve problems with toilet training. In evaluating these complaints, it is imperative to remember that toilet training is an important part of normal development. In fact, approximately 20% of children are not fully toilet trained by 3 years of age. Most often, problems can be dealt with by educating the parents (assuming that they are intelligent and caring). When this approach is not successful, an evaluation of the child and of his environment is necessary.

Problems with behavior. This is a complex area, because the range of behaviors which can be defined as problematic is so large. Also important is who is defining the behaviors. A clear, detailed, and concise description of the problem is necessary.

Often the source of the problem becomes clear when one examines the answers to basic questions. What is the behavior, described in concrete descriptive terms? For example, if the problem is temper tantrums, the tantrums should be described in detail and the following questions should be answered: (1) When did the problem begin, and did anything special happen at that time? (2) With whom does the problem occur? (3) Where does it occur? (4) When does it occur? (5) How long does the episode of problem behavior last? (6) Does anything make the problem better or worse? (7) How are the episodes resolved, or how do they end?

Perhaps the most important question is one that the evaluator must ask himself: "What function does the behavior serve?" (This will be discussed in more detail in chapter 5.) It is important to keep in mind that almost all behavior serves some function. If it did not, it would disappear. The function may not always be obvious. The behavior may be a "cry for help." It may be a "smoke screen" to obscure other problems within the family or individual.

THE CHILD FROM 3 TO 5

Physical and Motor Development

The typical 3-year-old moves about with ease. He is able to walk up the stairs, while alternating feet; by 4 1/2, he descends the stairs, alternating feet. The 3-year-old can stand on one foot, balancing momentarily; by 5, he balances on one foot for 8 or more seconds. The 3-year-old can pedal a tricycle and his movement has become much more purposeful: now when he moves, it is most often with a goal or destination in mind. The typical 3-year-old is beginning to dress himself and can pull on shirt, pants, and shoes; by 4 years, he dresses and undresses with some supervision, even distinguishing the front and back of clothes, while by age 6, he ties his shoes. The 3-year-old can feed himself with little spilling and can pour from a pitcher. In a game of "catch," the 3-year-old tries to throw overhand but is unable to control the throw, still catching by pulling the ball into his chest with both arms; by 6 years of age, the child has control of the throw's force and direction, and the catch—with two hands—is fairly coordinated. Also by about age 6, the typical child rides a two-wheeled bike.

Fine motor developmental milestones also include the ability to copy figures and to "build" on a small scale. The typical 3-year-old can copy a circle and imitate a cross, and his drawing improves by practice in tracing things; by 5 to 6 years, this ability has expanded to primitive human figure drawings with body parts which are recognizable, and the typical 6-year-old copies the shape of a diamond. By 3 years of age, the child can build a tower of ten cubes; by 6 years, this ability has advanced to "building" more complex figures, such as bridges or steps two to three high.

Cognitive and Language Development

As noted in the discussion of cognitive development of the 2-year-old, the central theme of cognitive development is the ability to represent an external object internally in thought. This representation—in play—allows the child to "work out" themes dealing with conflict, mastery, and understanding. It is in this period that we see the rapid emergence and increasing complexity of symbolic play. The child imitates both language and action of significant others in his environment. Furthermore, he can defer his play: the actual presence of an event or of the role model is not necessary. Thus, the little girl may bathe, feed, or spank the baby doll, all the while repeating phrases that she heard her mother or father use. She may do this on her own or with a friend, long after the original event.

By this time, the child's language reflects an increasing understanding of the world. Furthermore, questions are now asked for clarification: "Is this right, mommy?"; by 5 years, the child will be asking the meaning of words and not just what an object is. The typical 3-year-old can name objects, use plurals, and describe what is happening in a picture; by 4 years, he names at least one color, and, by 5, knows all the primary colors. By age 4, he understands prepositions such as "on," "under," "in back of," "in front of," and "beside." During the period from 3 to 5, the length of the child's utterances increases from three-word sentences to complex, compound sentences, and short-term memory (as reflected by digit span) increases; by 5 years, the child usually repeats four or five digits correctly in sequence. At 3 years, the child is just beginning to deal with the concept of numbers; by age 4, he counts to three while pointing correctly to the objects being counted; by 5, he counts to ten, demonstrating one-to-one correspondence.

One important aspect of the thinking of the child of this age is that he is not yet able to deal with more than one property at a time; his thinking is unidimensional. At this age, if a child is presented with two glasses of equal size, containing equal amounts of water, and if the child then watches someone pour the contents of one of the glasses into a taller, thinner glass, he will say that the water is no longer equal and that the taller glass contains more water: the child is able to focus on only one dimension, ie, height.

In addition, the child at this age is egocentric: he sees things and assumes that other people view things in the same way. It is for this reason that objects are often seen by children as having intent; when the child falls and hits himself on the coffee table, he reports that "the table hurt me." The combination of egocentric thought and unidimensional thinking often leads to problems in communication between adults and children. Parents often forget that the child is unable to handle explanations with multiple factors or consequences. It is probably for this reason that the parent's standard explanation, "just because," developed.

Development of a Sense of Self

By 3 years of age, the child is well on his way to effecting a sense of self. Gender identity is established; but while the child knows which sex he is, the understanding of what this means and what role this plays is not as clear. In the previous stage (called the "anal" stage because of its emphasis on issues of control, particularly around bowel training), the relationship was primarily a dyadic one, a one-to-one struggle for control and autonomy, with the child struggling to establish a separate sense of self; by 3 years of age, this is fairly well established (reflected, for example, in the child's ability to use personal pronouns, such as "I" and "me"). The 3-year-old knows his full name.

There is a transition at this time from dyadic to triadic relationships, characterized by an alternation back and forth between the parents in an attempt to gain an exclusive relationship. The child is well aware of sexual differences, but is unsure of their meaning and of how to deal with them. Every child has elements of identification with both parents; there are both masculine and feminine elements in each of us. But because the sexual differences are real, there will be a pull toward behaviors characteristic of the sex of the child. It is during this period between 3 and 5 that the child attempts to gain the exclusive attention of one parent, leaving the other parent out.

The 3-year-old boy is full of himself: He likes to show off how big he is and how strong he is. He likes to identify with superheroes. He wants to impress mom with his great prowess and abilities. He becomes a rival with the father for her attention. He recognizes that father has a special position or relationship with mother that he would like to have. At the same time that he would like to take his father's place, he is also identifying with his father and learning about relationships and "masculine" behavior. Soon, the boy begins to realize that "he is not as big as he thought." He becomes concerned that his father may become angry with him and take away his masculinity as punishment. The threat of bodily harm is a very real one to the little boy who, at this age, often makes a huge production of a small cut or scrape.

But the boy is also very attached to his father. Remember that it is the father who demonstrates the behaviors of the masculine role. It is also the father who interjects reality into the boy's fantasy of having the mother exclusively. It would be just as frightening for the boy to attain the goal of displacing the father: it is one thing to displace the father in fantasy; reality is another matter, and much more frightening. This is one reason why boys of divorced parents often have so much difficulty. They not only feel responsible for the divorce (because of their fantasies), but also feel small and inadequate to take the father's place. In addition, once again, there is the primary attachment that boys have to their fathers.

For the girl the situation is reversed. However, because sexual roles are different, the girl's development is not a mirror image of the boy's. This disparity is also a result of cultural differences. In traditional families, the mother is usually the child's primary caretaker. She is the one who does most of the feeding, comforting, and raising of the child. For the child, the mother usually becomes the primary love object. Thus for the little girl, competing with the mother for her father's exclusive attention means that she must risk losing her mother's approval and caretaking. In addition, because she is already aware of sexual differences, she realizes that she cannot take the father's place and have mother exclusively. (The boy, on the other hand, fantasizes the possibility of possessing the mother, who is the primary love object and caretaker.) The girl also uses her mother as a role model for identification. In families where the differences in roles are strongly distinguished, the girl sometimes feels "cheated." In families where there is more equality in childrearing, the sexual differences are not as important, since it is the person who is valued, and not the sex of the person.

The Development of Conscience

An important part of the development of the self is the development of a superego, or conscience. The beginning of this can be seen in early signs of empathy displayed by toddlers. A toddler who sees another child or person in distress will often attempt to give comfort. However, a major part of conscience comes from the parents: (1) There is the identification with the parents and with those values which are displayed in their behavior; it is important that the values which are articulated are also demonstrated in behavior. (2) Conscience develops from the interaction between parents and child. Initially the child distinguishes right and wrong on the basis of parental approval or disapproval; gradually these values are internalized by the child. Initially the child behaves for fear of the disapproval of the parents or significant others; the disapproval is external to the child. When children internalize and identify with their parents, these injunctions and values become a part of them, and external disapproval is no longer necessary to produce a feeling of discomfort; on their own, they feel guilty. By 6 years of age, the child has developed an effective superego.

Problems of the Period

Nightmares. Children from 3 to 5 have nightmares; these often take the form of animals chasing them or trying to bite them. Sometimes, children have fears of someone coming after them. Comforting bedtime rituals become an important way of dealing with these fears.

Excessive separation anxiety. Some children from 3 to 5 have difficulty separating from their parents. They are excessively frightened, and may withdraw or cry for long periods when left. In many of these situations, it is the mothers who have trouble separating and who may need support. Often getting the father involved serves to break the overinvolved mother-child interaction. In general, excessive separation anxiety signals a problem in the mother-child and/or family system. However, one must also take into consideration the intellectual age of the child.

Enuresis. From 7% to 10% of children still wet the bed at 6 years. Causes of enuresis are multiple and may be either organic or functional. Enuresis sometimes runs in families. Most often, if enuresis is the only symptom, it will eventually resolve itself or can be treated with behavior modification or medication (Tofranil). (For an in-depth treatment of the subject, see chapter 16).

SUMMARY

This chapter considered development during the "magic years" of early childhood, tracing such paths of development as physical and motor, cognitive and language, a sense of self, and relationships. The child's development was viewed as interactive; emphasized was the interdependence at different levels of the various lines of development. Also considered were common problems typical of the 2-year-old and of the child from 3 to 5.

BIBLIOGRAPHY

Erickson EH: *Childhood and Society*, ed 2. New York, W. W. Norton, 1963
Fraiberg SH: *The Magic Years*. New York, Charles Scribner & Sons, 1959
Lewis M: *Clinical Aspects of Child Development*, ed 2. Philadelphia, Lea & Febiger, 1982

Chapter 3

THE ELEMENTARY SCHOOL CHILD

R. DEAN CODDINGTON, MD

All development occurs in a rather gradual way, although there is a lot of variation from one child to another, with some children maturing more rapidly than others. Nevertheless, some rather distinct changes take place which distinguish 6- to 11-year-olds from their preschool counterparts. Elementary school children seem less anxious and more secure, and think and behave differently. Our forefathers may well have recognized this shift when they designed our educational system, since the obsessive thinking seen in 9- and 10-year-olds is a real asset to a learning process based on rote memory. Children learn at much earlier ages, of course, but more flexible techniques are needed for the preschool child and for children in kindergarten, first, and second grades.

This chapter will address developmental changes in the way children think, in their relationships to others, and in their ability to control impulses. The importance of the expression of emotion will be emphasized, as the discussion of personality formation continues.

MENTAL ORGANIZATION

A useful way of conceptualizing the distinction between preschool and elementary school children is in terms of the way in which they think. The younger child can be viewed as having a phobic organization, characterized by anxiety over separation from mother, masturbation, and oedipal wishes. In contrast, the 6- to 11-year-old can be viewed as having an obsessive mental organization: he is learning to control impulses regarding both sexuality and aggression. This obsessiveness facilitates learning, memory, speech, and conceptualization. This type of thinking is very realistic and concrete, leading Piaget to call this, in his developmental scheme, the period of concrete operations.

This shift in thinking can be seen in children's play. The ease with which a child between 4 and 6 uses fantasy gives way to more realistic games, often involving counting or scoring. A 3-year-old playing hide-and-seek will hide in plain view and cover his eyes, convinced that no one can see him. The 5-year-old will hide but can't resist peeking, confident that he won't be seen as he ducks back into his hiding place. The 8-year-old, however, is much more realistic: he knows he'll be discovered if he makes the slightest sound. Of utmost importance are the rules of the game—eg, the extent of the count before the one who is "it" can begin searching, the boundaries of the game, and so on.

Because of the capacity of elementary school children to control their impulses, they appear less interested in sexuality. Unlike the 4-year-old who masturbates without shame or embarrassment, the 9-year-old masturbates secretly. This appearance of having put aside such childish things led psychoanalysts to call this period "latency." They believed that sexual impulses and wishes were repressed into the unconscious, where they remained in a dormant state, only to reappear with the advent of puberty. Now we know that sexuality remains very much alive and well in the conscious mind, though suppressed by the child's newfound ability to control his impulses. He now has a superego. You will still see references in the literature to "latency-aged" children but the term is not very descriptive and, gradually, is being abandoned.

RELATIONSHIPS

One's capacity to relate to other people is referred to by the term "object relations," and is viewed as an important—perhaps the most important—function of the ego. In our complex society it is hard to think of a person as truly independent; everyone must relate to other persons in a way that permits mutual dependence at times. Obviously, the infant's earliest object is its mother; equally as obvious is the importance of the family during the early years. Even though nursery school experiences and playmates are significant stimuli for the growth of the ego, the preschool child can always—or almost always—retreat to his home when the going gets rough. As one 5-year-old put it, "When the children tease me, I get homesick." The freedom to retreat diminishes with school entry. The 7-year-old with an emotional need to go home may learn the effectiveness of stomachaches and headaches, as opposed to the simple truth. Mandatory education and peer pressure force others to "tough it out." Most children at this age are ready and willing to broaden their horizons and enlarge their circle of friends.

Imaginary Playmates

Sometimes children conjure up an imaginary playmate in the late preschool period and use this imaginary friend to help cope with different situations. Most commonly, it is a friendly playmate with whom the child either discusses problems or works them out through practice with a safe ally. Occasionally, the imaginary playmate may be used as a scapegoat who advises the child to engage in some forbidden act and who, therefore, deserves the blame. As the child reaches school age, this relationship with an imaginary playmate may be continued, although the child knows the playmate isn't real.

The intensity of this object relationship may be so great as to seem "real" to observers. That is, the child may appear to be hallucinating, actually hearing and/or seeing the object, rather than fantasizing. Does the child think the playmate is real? With this question we are assessing another ego function, "reality testing." On the one hand, a child who seems able to distinguish reality from fantasy in every other way should be viewed simply as a normal child with a strong relationship with an imaginary playmate. On the other hand, poor reality testing may indicate the presence of a psychosis. The hallucinations and delusions of some schizophrenic adults are pretty well limited to a single object—a voice, for instance. The voice tells them to do things or they discuss problems with it, but are fairly well organized in other respects. This pathological thinking seen in adults is called "primary process thinking," referring to the child's prelogical thought processes.

Imaginary playmates are not indicative of psychopathology in 4- through 9-year-olds with good reality testing and should not be viewed as predictive of schizophrenia in later life. Their existence may indicate a child's difficulty in talking with his parents, but may also occur in perfectly normal, healthy families.

Broadening Sphere of Influence

Other adults—scoutmasters, teachers, and Little League coaches—take on added importance to children in fourth and fifth grades. These adults are often seen as ideal parents, more tolerant, understanding, and wise than real parents. The child's own parents become less romantic and seem to develop "clay feet." "Johnny's parents let him go to the movies; why don't you?" After his parents' response, the child may continue with "Oh, that's stupid." Nevertheless, strong ties with the parents are retained. In fact, when a child feels confident enough to risk derogating his parents in this way, it is indicative of the strength of the relationship and should not be taken as a sign of disrespect.

This willingness to challenge a parent may seem to be a relatively insignificant developmental step. It becomes more significant in view of the fact that many children around the age of 10 are referred to child psychiatry clinics because of behavior problems in which a difficulty with the expression of anger is central.

Peers

Another major change in object relations is the increasing importance of peers. The child wants to be accepted by others and will alter his or her behavior to accomplish this aim. The family remains the primary source of cultural values, but peers assume an ever increasing role as the child broadens his horizons. His society is no longer limited by the boundaries of the family, neighborhood, or kinship and will never again be so restricted. This acculturation process is both necessary and healthy. It promotes growth and facilitates learning. But it also has its traumatic moments when the child is confronted by a fact of life from which, previously, he had been protected.

IMPULSE CONTROL

This enlargement of the child's environment, the widening of his horizons, presents an increased need for him to exercise control over his emotions. Heretofore, the parents were the predominant controlling force as the child developed his own superego. Much progress has been made by age 6 as described in the preceding chapter. The process continues as the child relates to others, adults and children alike, but his capacity to control his own impulses without parental supervision is put to the test in the elementary school years.

Freud said that we are born with two instinctual emotional forces, sex and aggression, and he was right. These two biologically based emotions are apparent in all cultures, races, and societies, though some sociocultural groups may be more aggressive than others. These forces have obvious survival value and their absence would very likely result in extinction of the group. Though aggression is more pronounced in males than females in many animal species, and probably in humans, too, it is hard to separate instinctual aggressiveness from that resulting from sociocultural influences. We encourage certain behaviors and discourage others in very young children and differentially raise boys and girls.

As we have said already, sexuality is generally suppressed during the elementary school-age period but reappears in adolescence. In contrast, the control of aggressive impulses is the major emotional task of 6- to 11-year-olds.

It is important to distinguish between the terms "aggression" and "assertion." Although they are synonymous, aggression implies a desire to dominate, often in disregard of others' rights; assertion suggests bold self-confidence in expression of opinion. In our adult society we value assertiveness, while denying aggressiveness. We are fascinated by very aggressive sports, even by news reports of war, but claim to be a peace-loving nation. We partake of a daily diet of television violence, while attempting to teach our children not to fight. We seem to be saying that aggression is alright when confined to a sports arena or to someone else's battlefield or to a television program, but unacceptable in real life.

At the same time we don't want our children to be shy and timid, teaching them instead to stand on their own two feet and to stand up for their rights. They are not only to defend themselves when attacked, but assert themselves even when unprovoked.

Thus, as a society we expose our children to much violence and aggression: we elevate the most aggressive persons to hero status on occasion, while telling our children to be assertive but nonaggressive. Or, to put it another way, we try to teach them to be aggressive only under certain conditions. It isn't difficult to see the confusion that may arise in a child's mind, particularly in view of the tendency of elementary school children to be obsessive and concrete. They like to have everything spelled out, but we aren't spelling with precision. Just when they are learning to control their impulses, they are struck with the unfairness, ambivalence, and subtle—and sometimes not so subtle—dishonesty of our society.

Anger is an emotion common to all stages of development, from infancy to senility. Occasional temper tantrums of a 2-year-old are easy to tolerate and are expected to be more frequent in the third year of life. Parents of preschool children have developed a set of rules, a structure, to help the child control his behavior. The elementary school child must learn other sets of rules; some apply to him, but others apply only to his friends in their homes. He finds that there are different structures and begins to question the genesis of his family's body of rules.

The child learns that behavior that is tolerated in his home is not tolerated in school—a frustrating experience. His attempts to collate the different sets of rules, one set integrated with another, requires practice and will be punctuated with many errors. Modification of his family's rules is also necessitated by his growth; every year or so, his role in the family and his responsibilities change. Inevitably, clashes between child and parents occur, with the child attempting to assert himself while avoiding excessive retaliation. Desired goals for parents are to give as much responsibility as the child can accept without overwhelming him and to tolerate his inept attempts at assertion without overt aggression, in return.

Accepting Anger

All children need to express anger from time to time, though the expression itself is often ineffective. In my view, three criteria must be fulfilled for the expression of anger to be a profitable experience. First, the emotion must be directed at the one for whom it's intended. Second, to be effective, the method of expression must hurt a little bit. When a parent shrugs off an angry outburst like water flowing from a duck's back, the effort—that is, the attempted expression of anger—has gone for naught. The child will be both frustrated and embarrassed, thereby increasing, rather than decreasing, the pent-up anger. The third criterion is that the mode of expression must not exceed the parents' tolerance and result in retaliation so great that the child regrets the attempt.

Parents rarely have trouble understanding this reasoning but, when the time comes to formulate guidelines, they inevitably become mute. When asked what they want their child to do when he's angry at them, parents usually respond with a list of "don'ts": "I don't want him to be disrespectful . . . I don't want him to kick the dog . . . I don't want him to talk back . . . I don't want him to slam the door." Then, after listing 10 to 15 "don'ts" and with a very understanding tone of voice, they may say, "I want him to tell me why he's angry." It makes a lot of sense, except for the fact that the child's immaturity precludes his behaving in such a grown-up manner.

What are some effective, yet acceptable, ways in which, for instance, a 9-year-old can express anger? Games, of course, are great but not easy to get going in a situation of anger; checkers and other table games can be very helpful when a child is more or less chronically grumpy, but aren't of much use in an acute situation. Active, outdoor games—such as shooting baskets or playing catch with a baseball—can be effective in father-son confrontations. In the latter case, the father can subtly encourage the child to throw the ball harder or over his head, stinging the father's hand or making him run to retrieve the ball. The father can acknowledge the anger with a comment like, "Wow, you're really burning it in; you really must be angry."

It is not uncommon for a 10-year-old to talk back to a parent. Must such a child be considered disrespectful? Isn't it conceivable that the youngster would have more respect for a parent who listens, even when it hurts? If we want our children to be assertive, we must provide an opportunity for practice. What better practice than for a child to stand up and tell his parent what he thinks of him? It might be a heated and awkwardly worded tirade; it might even be inappropriate but, the next time, the youngster may be able to choose his words a bit more carefully. Gradually, over the years, a child can profit a good deal from such opportunities. Admittedly, it would be hard for any parent to tolerate such confrontations on a daily or even weekly basis. But if they are tolerated once in a while, the child will find their necessity less frequent.

The end result of this rather accepting approach to anger is often quite satisfactory to everyone in the family and is also conducive to normal psychological growth and healthy interpersonal relationships.

PERSONALITY DEVELOPMENT

Although we view the growth of one's personality as a continuous process extending well into adolescence, certain personality traits become quite apparent in the preadolescent, the 10- to 12-year-old. Patterns of behavior seem to become firmly established and are likely to continue as the personality coalesces during adolescence.

Imitation of Hysterical Behavior

A little girl, not yet showing any physical signs of sexual development, may become very interested in sexuality and the rather hysterical, overly dramatic, feminine behavior she views on television. She may mimic the behavior and get considerable positive feedback for her cute, coquettish mannerisms. This reinforcement may come from parents, friends, and strangers alike, and may serve to establish this way of dealing with other people (nonverbal communication) as a permanent part of her developing personality. As she learns to use this coping mechanism effectively, she will, on occasion, overuse it and may be viewed by others as a seductive and manipulative woman. Sexuality itself may be the farthest thing from her mind, though her behavior seems "sexy." Unless she learns to broaden her coping repertoire, this hysterical trait may lead eventually to an hysterical personality disorder.

A note of caution is indicated here. Sometimes little girls exhibiting seductive behavior have, in fact, been the victims of child molestation or incest. The professional worker must not overlook this possibility; but he must proceed slowly in exploring the situation, since the area is such a sensitive one. A consultation is very likely indicated.

Manipulative Behavior

Boys, and girls as well, sometimes manipulate others in a different way, more like that of the con artist. They lead one to believe an untruth without actually lying.

> A 10-year-old boy announced one morning to his somewhat new foster parents that his bike was gone. "It must have been stolen," he said. The parents, somewhat suspicious of this boy they had known for only two months, responded with, "That's too bad, for we know how much you liked to ride it. We have no intention of buying another, even though we realize yours was rather old. Maybe you left it at a friend's house and forgot." The boy went out to look for the missing bicycle and was seen walking in a direction opposite to that of his friend's house. He soon returned

> with his bicycle, saying his foster parents were right: "It was at Harry's house, and his mother had put it away." Later the foster parents discovered that Harry and his family had been out-of-town for three days. When confronted with this new finding, he admitted hiding the bike in a vacant lot, hoping it would be replaced with a new one.

In this case, the con game was unsuccessful; the behavior was not reinforced. If the boy had gotten away with it on this and subsequent occasions—and there was considerable reason to believe that he had succeeded previously—it is likely that this method of coping would become a well integrated part of his personality.

Passive-Aggressive Behavior

More commonly occurring than either hysterical or manipulative behavior is passive-aggression. This term is used when a child behaves aggressively, but in a very nonassertive manner: He doesn't do something he should do. He forgets. He doesn't hear a person call. Everyone has run into a child like this and has probably found the youngster most exasperating.

> A 10-year-old boy was playing with his 6-year-old brother. They decided on a game in which they took turns chasing each other, much to the delight of the younger child who loved being chased even more than being the pursuer. But the 6-year-old, laughing with the anticipation of being caught, looked over his shoulder while running at top speed and tripped over a tree root. Loud crying brought the game to a halt and the mother to the rescue, furious at the older boy whom she considered guilty of initiating a game which he always won at the younger boy's expense. The 10-year-old merely shrugged his shoulders and innocently exclaimed, "I never touched him."

If this occurs once or twice, it can be considered normal childhood play. But if it becomes a frequent pattern, we would have to look upon it as rather aggressive behavior (the other person always gets hurt, whether intentionally or not), carried out in the context of a game which the younger child wants to play (passive acquiescence to the desire of the 6-year-old, even though the older boy knew from experience what the outcome would be).

The elementary school child is developing patterns of behavior that may remain as part of his personality. It therefore becomes important that he be aided in the development of a variety of coping mechanisms, rather than any single pattern that may be acceptable at this age but maladaptive in adolescence and beyond.

SUMMARY

The chapter on the elementary school child opened with a discussion of developmental changes in mental organization. Functions of the ego were addressed in sections on object relations and reality testing. The child's broadening sphere of influence includes that provided by other adults and peers. In considering behavioral patterns, aggression and assertion were differentiated, followed by a consideration of clashes with parents over the control of behavior and the expression of anger. The chapter ended with a discussion of personality development, including imitation of hysterical behavior, manipulative behavior, and passive-aggression.

BIBLIOGRAPHY

Lewis M: *Clinical aspects of child development*, ed 2. Philadelphia, Lea & Febiger, 1982

Pulaski MAS: *Understanding Piaget, an introduction to children's cognitive development.* New York, Harper & Row, 1971

Sarnoff C: *Latency.* New York, Jason Aronson, 1976

Chapter 4

ADOLESCENCE

R. DEAN CODDINGTON, MD

Many parents look toward the adolescent years with fear and trepidation, reluctant to enter a period which, once begun, they would like to get through as soon as possible. Preadolescents tend to balance fear, which they also have, with the positive emotion of eager anticipation for all that awaits them. They are often quite ambivalent about what lies ahead.

The biological and psychological reasons for these attitudes will be discussed in this chapter, with the goal of enhancing the reader's understanding of normal adolescence. Such an understanding is the foundation upon which a rational and objective assessment of an adolescent is based. A major pitfall in working with teenagers is the tendency to empathize either with the parents or with their youngsters, based on the clinician's recall of his own adolescent years. Because our world is changing so rapidly, this approach is invalid even for the youngest professional. No teenager today is living in the same world of 5, 10, or more years ago. If one has any doubt about the validity of this statement, he should read Alvin Toffler's *Future Shock*.

COGNITIVE GROWTH

Jean Piaget used the term "formal operations" to describe the thinking of adolescents. They are able to think in a logical and scientific manner and to understand abstract constructions. This may seem like a relatively minor advancement compared, for example, to the infant's acquisition of language; indeed, it may be. On the other hand, when we take into account the vast amount of knowledge available to adolescents and their impressive prior education which must be integrated with new knowledge, the formalizing of cognitive function becomes a prodigious task. Take religion, for instance, and a child raised in a rather ordinary family in which religion plays a significant role. Such a child has learned the tenets of that particular religion more or less matter-of-factly over a period of from 4 to 8 years. As an adolescent, he begins to question the reason for various doctrines and, at the same time, comes to the realization that members of other religious sects are as devout as persons he has known from childhood. Many adolescents become very interested in comparative religion as they seek independence from family; they like to think of themselves as making new and logical decisions about religion, politics, and all the other value systems to which they were exposed throughout childhood.

When we recognize the intellectual context in which adolescence takes place, we see the tremendous amount of rethinking required. Rather than simple change, the cognitive growth of the adolescent parallels the physical growth spurt we have long accepted as the hallmark of adolescent development.

DEVELOPMENTAL TASKS OF ADOLESCENCE

Three achievements face the adolescent: he must leave the safety of his family and become at least semi-independent; he must deal with his newly acquired sexual drive and establish mature heterosexual relationships; and he must define himself in terms of identity and begin to make realistic career plans. It is obvious that these objectives are all interrelated and that mature adulthood will not be achieved until all three objectives are met. Nevertheless, we shall discuss them separately, for convenience.

Independence

It is as hard for parents to relinquish control as their children mature as it is for their children to learn to accept responsibility. Mothers often give permission to go to a friend's home and ask to be alerted if plans should change; later, they become irate when they call the friend's home, only to find that the youngsters have gone elsewhere. The mother describes her concern for the child's welfare, making the child feel guilty for not having called. From the adolescent's viewpoint, however, there may have been no intent to deceive or disobey. As it happened, two friends joined the dyad and suggested a trip to the local pizza parlor. If the adolescent should call home, his peers would perceive him as still dependent (and rightfully so); should he not call home, his mother would worry. He must make a decision: to call or not to call, that is the question.

There is no way for caring parents to avoid this anxiety. Just as it's hard to watch through the kitchen window while an 8-year-old climbs his first tree, similarly, it's hard to sit home when a 15-year-old is "out" for the evening. But watch and wait we must! If the parents have achieved a sense of security in their own identity, they can be comforted by the fact that their children have been introjecting their moral and ethical values for 12 to 15 years and cannot readily set them aside; such parents have little to worry about. On the other hand, parents with poor impulse control—and those parents who, in the past, experienced considerable difficulty with interpersonal relationships—have more to worry about. Their children have not had the benefit of consistent positive modeling and, therefore, have a less integrated superego. When faced with the need to make a moral or ethical decision, the outcome will not be as automatic or predictable as it would be, were the inhibitory function of the superego well established; the outcome would depend more on ego function. If the ego is strong—and this is related to the adolescent's sense of identity, which will be discussed presently—the decision can be made with little difficulty; if not, the outcome is in doubt. (For a more thorough discussion of ego and superego function, the reader is referred to chapter 8.)

Parents must establish the rules in a way that allows sufficient, but not too much, freedom. They must provide the opportunity to make mistakes, but the mistakes must not be too costly. Adolescents can be allowed to determine a reasonable curfew following a basketball game. Without any discussion, the teenager will know that his parents will begin to worry at a certain time; his decisional process should encompass his potential guilt over causing his parents excessive concern. When he gets home, he may find that he overdid it and, consequently, may feel more guilt than he anticipated. But he can learn from his mistake.

Punishment should be short and to the point, just as with younger children. "Grounding" for a month or more seems to imply subnormal learning ability. It is unlikely that more will be learned in the second, third, or fourth week than was learned in the first.

> A 15-year-old boy avoided a traffic accident by jumping an 8-inch curb, but in so doing damaged his father's vehicle. It couldn't be driven, so he abandoned it for the night but did not tell his father until morning. The parents gave their son no credit for avoiding the accident and, in fact, refused to believe that part of the story; they deprived him of his driving privileges for a year. The boy admitted that he should have called his parents right away but, understandably, resented the prolonged punishment. More important perhaps, the absence of driving privileges precluded an opportunity for the youngster to demonstrate his ability to handle the responsibility.

If parents want to help adolescents gain independence, they must give them some responsibility regarding their own punishment. If they take away the use of the car as in the case above, they should then ask, "Now how can you demonstrate your readiness to drive more carefully, avoiding near collisions?" The adolescent should contribute to the dialogue in which this question is answered. Some very rigid rules could be set down, such as, "You must log thirty hours of driving time with a parent present." Or an alternative decision to give the boy a second chance could be made. The point is that by his inclusion in the decision-making process, the adolescent is assisted in gaining a feeling of responsibility.

The development of independence is as difficult for youngsters as it is for their parents. Adolescents want to be as free as their most independent peers but—though they'll never admit it—still want to run home to mama when the going gets tough. They want the use of the family car but know that some of their peers will tempt them to play risky games; they are not certain how well they will handle temptation. Inwardly, they would appreciate their parents' limitation on the use of the car; such limits solve their problem. Many adolescents have a sort of insight as to their level of maturation. That's why we can safely include them in the decision-making process.

Adolescents strive for independence erratically. At 12 or 13 they may look ahead with awe, then suddenly demand new rights and privileges. At 14 and 15 they may become very introspective, quiet, and thoughtful; religious values and comparative religion are areas of interest. Youngsters in their midteens are trying to disengage themselves from the family. It is difficult to do this gradually, and even more difficult to do so with diplomacy. Independence is gained little by little, in fits and starts.

Sexuality

The familiar and dramatic growth spurt during adolescence occurs, on the average, around age 12 to 13 in girls and 14 to 15 in boys. The tremendous individual variation from these average figures is also very familiar, some teenagers starting the spurt two years earlier and some not for another two years. Dramatic growth of the reproductive systems also occurs. The ovaries and uterus begin a period of rapid growth at age 10 or 11 and continue to grow throughout adolescence; menarche occurs at the mean age of 13. The penis begins to become pigmented and larger at age 13, give or take 2 years, and reaches maturity at 15 ± 2 years. The testes start a year sooner and reach maturity a year later.

It is most likely that these physical changes occur automatically when endocrine levels reach predetermined concentrations, with the entire sequence of events established by genes. However, this may be too simplistic an explanation; sociopsychological factors may also play a role.

In anorexia nervosa (see chapter 15), the psychodynamic picture apparently includes a strong reluctance to reach sexual maturity; menarche is often either delayed for several years or, if it has already begun, it is blocked. It looks for all the world as though the girl's psychological inhibitions regarding sex control her biological development.

During the last century there has been a marked tendency for the time of adolescence to begin earlier and earlier and for adult height to be reached sooner. The magnitude of these trends, which have been documented in many geographic regions, cannot be explained by social class differences. Menarche has occurred earlier by some 4 months per decade since 1860, both in Europe and in the USA (see Figure 4-1), too rapid a change to be explained by inheritance alone. There is little reason to believe that the trend has stopped and that girls are now reaching puberty at the earliest possible age. Furthermore, it has been suggested in the literature that menarche occurred around the age of 14 in the civilized parts of Europe during medieval times but rose to age 17 at the beginning of the nineteenth century, possibly due to factors surrounding the industrial revolution.

The difference in the size of children 50 years ago and today is attributable both to an earlier growth spurt and to an increase in mature adult height. Maximal height was not reached until about

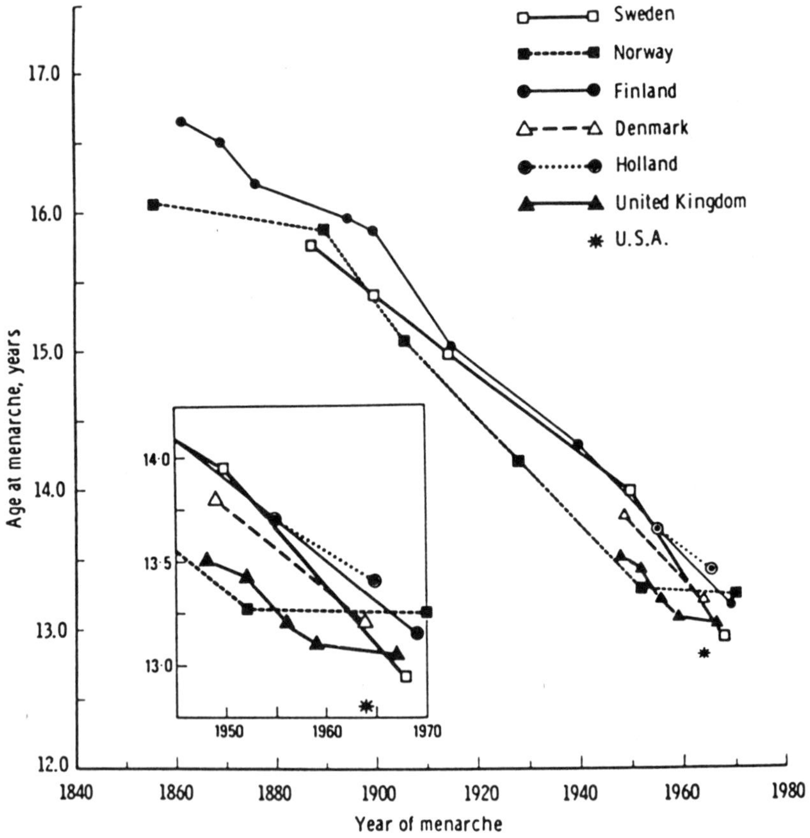

Figure 4-1: Secular trend in age at menarche, 1860-1970. (From Tanner, J.M., Foetus into Man. Cambridge, Mass, Harvard University Press, 1978.)

age 26 in the early part of the century but now is attained by age 16 to 17 in girls and 18 to 19 in boys. There has been an increase in adult height of about 1 cm (0.43 inches) per decade over the last 100 years.

In some animals, a variety of external stimuli, acting through the central nervous system on the hypothalamic region of the brain, affect the onset of estrous, that period in which the female is subject to impregnation. The hypothalamus controls the release from the pituitary gland of hormones that induce ripening of ovarian follicles. Normally, in human and other primates, the hypothalamic mechanism is independent of external stimuli, so that menstruation takes place periodically.

If sexual and physical maturity in humans were subject to influence by psychological (ie, external) as well as genetic and endocrinological forces, the marked overemphasis of sexuality by the entertainment and publishing industries would take on new and greater significance. Enticing as this hypothesis may be, the evidence is weak and the hypothesis can only be viewed as intriguing.

The biggest problem adolescents have concerning sexuality is the control of their behavior. Early adolescents are unable to form mature heterosexual relationships and, yet, often feel compelled to become sexually active in order to mature. It is as though sexual activity produces psychological maturation, rather than the other way around.

> A 15-year-old black girl, about to deliver her third baby, was describing the events preceding her first pregnancy three years earlier. Her parents had been divorced for some time, and she and her mother lived next door to her grandmother. An older boy in the neighborhood started paying attention to Alecia, a development that concerned her mother a great deal—so much so, in fact, that she sent Alecia to live with her father on the other side of the city.
>
> A few months later, Alecia's grandmother died. In her grief, Alecia's mother asked her daughter, now 12 years old, to return home, even though the undesirable boy still lived nearby. Alecia was pregnant within three months!

Alecia had been recalled to her mother's side to help her mother cope with the loss of her own mother. The risk of pregnancy in that neighborhood was apparently very high but, despite this, Alecia was summoned. Or could it be that, because of the risk,

Alecia's presence was requested? Is it possible that, on an unconscious level, Alecia's mother wanted a grandchild to fill the void left by her mother's death?

Identity

The third major task of adolescence is the development of an individualized identity. Teenagers have considerable trouble in this area, as is so apparent when one considers the clothes they wear, emblazoned with signs proclaiming their membership in a gang, their athletic prowess, their musical ability, or their sexuality (with provocative words written across their breasts). Some wear clothes that make them look 3 or 4 years older, while others wear the most outlandish combinations imaginable and cut their hair in equally weird styles. It seems as though any identity is better than none at all.

Activities also serve as indication of the adolescent's identity. Athletics, music, drama, work on the school newspaper or yearbook, academic achievement, membership in youth groups, and religious activities are just a few that a teenager can use to characterize himself. Long-term goals are commonly used, as well. Identification as "college bound" or as a "welding student" or a "business major" serves admirably to help the student feel secure in his world. When one knows where he is going, he knows where he is.

It is often helpful, when attempting to assess a youngster's sense of identity, to ask what about himself he is proud of. If suitable rapport exists with the examiner, a healthy adolescent will name several assets in response to encouraging leads. He may be proud of his physical coordination, intelligence, ability to select color-coordinated clothes, to make friends, or to strum a guitar—and even, as one girl said, proud of not being pregnant. Teenagers who have not yet succeeded in this task will sit and ponder the question; very attractive, bright kids who seem to have plenty of assets may be mute. If various assets are mentioned, they will shrug and say, "Yeah, I guess so," in a very unconvincing way. Some will say that they are proud of their parents or proud of their school, responses which are somewhat impersonal and cannot be interpreted as evidence of a strong identity.

It becomes clear that the establishment of an identity is closely associated with the attainment of independence from the family. One achieves independence as one develops a solid sense of identity. Sometimes an adolescent will make a desperate attempt to gain independence when he has not yet established an identity of his own. It will appear as if he wants very much to go, but doesn't know where he is going. It will seem more like simple rebellion against the parents than a responsible move.

THE DOUBLEBIND OF ADOLESCENCE

In the mid 1950s, Bateson and his associates advanced the concept of a doublebind pattern of communication that evokes disturbed behavior. Weakland elaborated the concept; he defined it as significant communication containing two related but incongruous messages to which a person is forced to respond, since leaving the situation is not feasible. The example sometimes used to illustrate the doublebind is as follows:

> A wife commands her husband to "stand up and be a man!" If he obeys the message transmitted by the tone of voice and stands up, he is being subservient and not being a man. If he obeys her expressed wish that he be more masculine, he will remain seated—disregarding the command and, therefore, not acting according to his wife's definition of manhood. Two incongruous messages were given, one by the tone of voice, the other by the verbal statement; two messages of a different sort were uttered in the same breath.

Now think of what we as a society are communicating to adolescents. On the one hand we are telling them to grow up, to be sexually active, aggressive, and responsible, while simultaneously telling them to behave themselves and to respect the dictates of their elders.

During childhood, rather clearly defined roles are assigned and children have the opportunity to develop physically and psychologically through a series of graded experiences. They are not thrown into deep water until they have learned to swim. The onset of adolescence is usually defined in biological terms as the occurrence of puberty. There is, then, a sudden widening of their world. With puberty, children encounter new ideas, concepts, values, and types of people; quite suddenly, responsibility for self-determination and self-sufficiency is imposed. Adolescents are forced to adjust rapidly, though they are comparatively inexperienced in dealing with issues with which they are faced. They have no defined roles of their own in society but, rather, are caught in the ambiguous overlap between more clearly defined roles of childhood and adulthood. Teenagers are simultaneously treated like children and expected to act like adults—a doublebind, to put it mildly.

Adolescence terminates when a society says it does, not with the attainment of a specific developmental milestone. Laws determining the right to drive a car, to buy alcoholic beverages, to serve in the military, and to vote vary considerably and are neither bestowed in a graded fashion nor based on physical or psychological growth. The mass media do much to make matters worse. The sexuality displayed by adolescent heroes and heroines exceeds normal adult behavior. Teenagers may feel that they should pattern their own behavior on that of a television or film star but, inwardly, may be very fearful of doing so. There was once a vague gradation of sexual behavior from dating in a public setting or at home, to "petting" or "making out," to "going steady," to exchanging class rings, to becoming engaged, and, finally, to getting married—with frequent regression due to change of partners. Now the goal seems to be "to score" on the first, second, or third date. Recent studies have shown that 50% of girls have lost their virginity by age 15 and 75% by age 18. There is much bragging among midadolescent males about their sexual conquests.

In many states, adolescents can obtain a driver's license at age 15. What kind of habits result when, on the one hand, the anticipation of a crisis is taught in safety-conscious driver education courses while, on the other hand, dramatic stunt driving is flaunted by the media? We admonish the teenager to be a good driver but then marvel at how "good" the stunt driver is.

In so many ways, we expect teenagers to act like adults while we, as adults, act like children. We are often irresponsible in our dealings with adolescents: Some parents serve alcoholic beverages to young adolescents at a party in their home. Some fathers take their sons to a prostitute in order to teach sexuality. Some fathers rape their daughters. We flaunt marriage commitments right and left and break promises and lie almost routinely.

"Grow up. Do as I say, not as I do" is not a double-bind communication but, rather, very bad teaching. Children who have introjected much from their parents and who identify with them are conflicted by such a message but are left to their own devices as to how to behave. Should they do as they've been taught, obeying their own superego restrictions, with the risk of being considered immature or afraid? Or should they do as they see others do—movie idols, peers, and even parents?

Despite their vociferous objection, adolescents want clear-cut limits. They do not want the freedom they demand, at least not all at once. Setting the rules must be accomplished with the teenager's needs in mind.

SUMMARY

Often viewed as a tumultuous period characterized by frequent rebellions, adolescence is not difficult to understand when we take into account the developmental tasks which teenagers must accomplish. The task of the parent is to allow the adolescent freedom to make mistakes, while remaining available to offer guidance and support afterwards. The youngster must be able to try his wings, but must not be kicked out of the nest altogether. This parental task is made many times more difficult by societal pressures. Our society says, in effect, that adolescence begins and ends with puberty. But adolescents are simply not ready for adulthood. Rome wasn't built in a day.

We have described the developmental processes—physical, emotional, and intellectual—which define this phase of life, in order to provide the framework within which we can evaluate individual teenagers with whom we work. Without such a framework we cannot expect to be therapeutic, for adolescents will appear to us as they do to everyone else—quite simply, as rebellious teenagers.

BIBLIOGRAPHY

Adams P, Berg L, Berger N, et al: *Children's rights: Toward the liberation of the child.* New York, Praeger, 1971

Bateson G, Jackson DD, Haley J, et al: Toward a theory of schizophrenia. *Behavioral Science* 1:256-264, 1956

Conger JJ, Petersen AC: *Adolescence and youth: Psychological development in a changing world*, ed 3. New York, Harper & Row, 1984

Katchadourian HA, Lunde DT: *Fundamentals of human sexuality*. New York, Holt, Rinehart & Winston, 1972

Tanner JM: *Foetus into Man*. Cambridge, Mass., Harvard University Press, 1978

Toffler A: *Future shock*. New York, Bantam, 1970

Chapter 5

FAMILIES

WILLIAM C. SZE, PhD

There has been a recent upsurge of interest in the functions and dysfunctions of family life. Some argue that, if we wish to have a healthy society, we must begin with the family as the institution in which and through which cultural values and social standards are transmitted from one generation to another.

This chapter will concern itself with family functioning. After tracing the changing structure of the family and considering healthy family function and its converse, the focus of the chapter will be on the concept of role in family therapy.

CHANGING FAMILY STRUCTURE

Since the onset of the industrial revolution, the structural change from the extended to the nuclear family has made it difficult for the family to carry out its functions. The role of grandparents, for example, as significant childcare providers during the parents' working hours has been replaced largely by day-care centers. More elderly are being cared for in nursing homes than at home by family members. In the educational sphere, the nuclear family is responsible only for primary socialization, and formal education is relegated to the school system.

The nuclear family itself is strained further by the high incidence of divorce, alternate life-styles, and remarriages, as reported by Sussman: From 1966 to 1975, husband-wife households decreased from 75% to 66%. From 1963 to 1975, the divorce rate doubled and the number of single-parent families increased from 2.1 million to 4.8 million. The increase in male-headed and female-headed cohabiting couples under age 25 increased 50 and 16.5 times, respectively, from 1960 to 1970. The data suggest significant changes in family composition, character, values, life-style, and role relationships in recent decades in the United States.

Whatever the consequence of the structural changes in the family—the balancing of greater emphasis on individual fulfillment, social mobility, and intimacy with concomitant loss of stability and rootedness—the basic functions of the family remain essentially the same: procreation, sexual interaction, economic support, affection, nurturance, protection of the young and of the infirm, socialization, and transmission of cultural values.

The change in family structure has been of great concern to social scientists. Interpersonal stress among family members and nonreciprocal role conceptions are characteristic of the single-parent and the reconstituted family. For example, in a single-parent family, the custodial right of a child by a possessive parent could cause interpersonal stress among the divorced parents and their children. In a reconstituted family, how a stepchild perceives his position in the reconstituted family and how the stepfamily places him in the family maze are two very complex considerations. Community tolerance toward the broken family is also a significant variable.

Ironically, the three types of family structure—nuclear, single-parent, and reconstituted—represent a sequential process of family development, from marriage, to divorce, to remarriage. But the complexity of multirole linkages has made individual role adaptation very difficult in marital, parental, child, and sibling role systems.

HEALTHY FAMILY FUNCTION

In light of rapidly changing family structure, discussion of the "normal" family has become difficult. Duvall, an early writer on family development, postulated that a typical family passed through an eight-stage life cycle, with the first stage being marriage itself. Many couples today live together as a family without formal matrimony, thereby bypassing this stage. Duvall's second stage is childbearing; increasingly, couples are deciding against having children, either from a lack of desire to alter their life-style or their economic status, or from ideological concerns—eg, the world population explosion. Thus, Duvall's assessment is difficult to apply beyond the 1980s.

However, it *is* possible to conceptualize a "healthy" family. In *How's Your Family?* Lewis describes a healthy family as one that "preserves sanity and encourages the growth of the parents and produces healthy children." He formulates nine factors necessary to maintain family health: (1) the nature of the parents' relationship, (2) the way the family deals with power, (3) the amount and type of family closeness, (4) the way the family talks together, (5) the way the family solves problems, (6) the way the family deals with feelings, (7) the ability of the family to accept and deal with change and loss, (8) the values of the family, and (9) the family's capacity for intimacy and autonomy. A lack of positive evidence of these nine factors is closely correlated with the other extreme in the spectrum of family functioning—eg, troubled family types, as demonstrated in Lewis' study. Most of Lewis' nine factors appear to be relational in nature. Therefore, healthy family function can be defined in terms of the existence of healthy relationships. In short, greater role complexity as a result of multiple family structural changes seen in recent years makes interactional patterns and interpersonal relationships less stable. Furthermore, the phenomenon of "anomie" (normlessness) has become a prevailing problem in many families today.

Social Roles

Most social roles possess the quality of reciprocity; a husband's role can be understood largely in terms of how it relates to that of his spouse. In that sense, one cannot define his role performance as successful if his spouse views it as inadequate or constrictive within the marital context. In their study of therapeutic intervention in families, Tharp and Otis contend that "identifiable psychopathology occurs only when the absence of satisfying role reciprocation produces conflict." In the past, certain unions were referred to as "good, neurotic marriages" when, for example, a chronically but perhaps mildly ill, hypochondriacal man was wedded to an overly materialistic, domineering woman. Either one, viewed in isolation, might be considered psychiatrically ill; but since they complement one another so well in role satisfaction, neither suffers from interpersonal conflict. Or, to put it another way, to take one into individual psychotherapy would, in all likelihood, be disasterous for the other and, consequently, for the marriage.

Role Complementarity and Its Facilitation

In many cases, the focus of intervention to reduce an individual member's stress may have to focus on the family and the reorganization of family role functioning. Facilitating complementarity is the primary concern of family treatment. The observation of stressed forms of behavior during family interaction can provide an understanding of coping devices in the absence of complementarity. Spiegel's list of warning signals is instructive in this process. He identifies two categories of techniques to influence others' behavior—role induction and role modification. Role induction behaviors (coercing, coaxing, evaluating, masking, postponing, and role reversal—a bridge to role modification) represent a one-sided struggle to preserve one's role perception by using maneuvering techniques to persuade one's role counterpart to agree with one's role perception, expectation, or performance. A wife, for example, might use coercion by threatening a divorce, knowing that her husband's emotional, religious, social, or financial situation would prevent such a step. If she feels guilt consequent to such a step she might use evaluation ("Let me think about it a bit more.") to justify her original position. She might mask her true feelings, on the other hand, by flattering, deceiving, or pretending to agree with her spouse. Or she might neutralize her behavior by utilizing passive-aggressive behaviors—by withdrawing or postponing resolution of the role conflict. Hence, role induction is primarily a defensive maneuver.

Therapy would require all parties to reach a point where each could come to recognize and understand the other's point of view. Each would then be in a position to move from role induction to role modification behaviors, which are complementary. Spiegel includes joking, referral to a third party, exploring, compromising, and consolidating as parts of this process. He cites Freud's reference to joking as "the saving of psychic energy coincident with the partial solution of the conflict." The acceptance of a third party usually indicates motivation for therapeutic exploration of the problem, an avenue through which family members can be assisted in recognizing their own cultural biases and defenses and can be led to the compromising and consolidating stages of role conflict resolution.

THE CONCEPT OF ROLE IN FAMILY THERAPY

The purpose of family therapy, no matter what methodology is used, is to help a disturbed or troubled family modify dysfunctional roles or interactions and, thereby, to achieve a more satisfying life. The composition of families, expected behavioral roles, and interpersonal relationships change frequently. The birth of a child, for example, extends the roles of the parents and siblings and complicates interactional patterns. If the child is not wanted or if the parents are not emotionally and financially prepared for his birth, if the mother temporarily drops out of the work force or a grandparent enters the scene to assume part of the child's care, if the child is born with a physical or mental defect or presents feeding or sleeping difficulties, role expectations of family members may be severely strained. Professional help may be needed to assist the family in regaining and maintaining its emotional stability.

The organized family counseling/therapy movement had its beginnings in the United States in the late 1940s and early 1950s. A proliferation of schools of thought stems from this period. Among the approaches and their acknowledged leaders are: Nathan Ackerman's psychoanalytic framework, Jay Haley's and John Weakland's strategic therapy, Don Jackson's and Murray Bowen's expanded systems approach, Salvador Minuchin's structural school, and Virginia Satir's communications perspective.

It should be pointed out that many family therapy approaches have utilized role concept in their therapeutic systems. In *The Psychodynamics of Family Life*, Ackerman devotes a whole chapter to social role and personality. He describes social role as "that aspect of personality that is integrated in social action. The behavioral forms expressed in this are determined by a series of factors: the propensities of personality, the processes of group participation and identification and other temporal-situational phenomena." While Minuchin does not consider himself a role theorist, he does use the role concept in analyzing families; he focuses on age, sex, and generational boundaries vis-a-vis role obligations. In writing of Minuchin, Hoffman states that most of the latter's language seems to derive from organization theory and role theory, drawing heavily on spatial metaphors like boundary, mapping, territory, structure, and role. Role theory, in a spectrum of theoretical schools, has provided a useful clinical framework to help understand interpersonal difficulties within a family context.

Role is best understood as that set of behavioral/task expectations held by relevant others concerning how the demands of a position should be fulfilled. A man, for example, may feel that he has fulfilled his role obligation in a family by working and providing economic sustenance. Changing social mores are currently calling this narrow "male" role model into question. While some men have adjusted to the shift in role expectation, others are experiencing psychological stress. Galoman points out that men in general are spending more time with their children and are doing more of the housework. It is unclear if men generally welcome this shift or feel that it is being forced upon them, with consequent increases in psychological stress and family discord. Even given a willingness to change, such changes are not always easy to accomplish. It has been suggested that the increasing proportion of men admitted to mental hospitals in the 1970s (approximately 10%) is due in part to stress related to the demand for role change.

In many cases role tasks are implicitly rather than explicitly defined. Role concepts may be copied consciously or unconsciously by each spouse from his/her family of origin, with little or no effort to reconcile differences of expectations or to assimilate elements of each other's perceptions. Discord usually arises when other members of the family do not agree with the role holder's perceptions of his/her role, eg, if the wife expects the husband to help fulfill instrumental as well as emotional family needs, while the husband identifies the latter as the sole purview of his wife. The wife may express her dissatisfaction by complaining that her husband does not love her enough or that she feels unwanted or rejected. He may see himself as a good family man working his hardest to provide his best for the family, while his wife and children complain of his neglect and lack of care. The misperceptions may escalate to bitterness, over time.

Role is learned through socialization. In today's industrialized society, there are multiple family models from which to learn, each one with its own role expectations. Models learned from families of origin may not prepare one for the circumstances which present 20 years later. The need for accommodation requires a flexibility for which many are unprepared. The role-making process is one way to compensate for the inherent vagueness in our role conceptions and to lead to modification of existing roles as life circumstances change. Role inflexibility, on the other hand, can lead to resistance, resentment, or depression. Rowe has observed that changing relationships of parents and children at successive stages of the cycle of family development—for example, launching children into the world—often result in conflicts between generations and in the spousal pair, as well.

THE THERAPEUTIC INTERVENTION

If role theory is used in dealing with family discord, the assumption is that the discord is primarily interpersonal in nature and that intrapsychic disturbances are secondary or of minimal importance in the intervention strategy. Following is a description of the intervention procedures I have focused on in my own practice.

I begin by asking each family member to describe the behaviors of his counterrole holder which annoy him most. I then ask the husband, for example, to assume the role of his wife and to play the role in front of her. Finally I ask him to defend the role, as he feels his wife would defend herself. I then go through the family, pairing members in role and counterrole positions. This exercise quickly brings role discrepancies to the surface and creates a state of cognitive dissonance which, in turn, forces each person to reexamine his/her cherished assumptions, beliefs, and values, in terms of interpersonal role relationships. Yalom reports that a state of cognitive dissonance or incongruity is a necessary step preceding change.

At this point, the therapy shifts from role induction to role modification. Joking is frequently present, usually as the first sign that role modification is in progress. Humor is a sign that each party has obtained some insight into the other's feelings and perceptions and is now capable of distance from his/her previous intense involvement in the conflict.

Next I utilize aspects of transactional analysis, specifically the analysis of three ego states, as a basis of interpreting role behavior and the nature of the underlying difficulties. In this mode of analysis, role play and family interactions are labeled "transactions." Berne labels a verbal statement or the acknowledgment of the presence of others as the "transactional stimulus." Any subsequent verbal statement, reaction to the initial statement, or any acknowledgment would be termed the "transactional response." The therapist attempts to understand the meaning of transactions and interprets them in accordance with the principles of role differention and the three ego states — parent, adult, and child. Harris, for example, describes a 34-year-old mother who "during one hour . . . changed to three different and distinct personalities: one of a small child dominated by feelings, one of a self-righteous parent, and one of a reasoning, logical, grown-up woman and mother of three children."

Transactional analysis provides an excellent methodology for observing script dynamics in action. Noteworthy is the appropriateness of the role character which the client assumes. In general there are four role character types: ascribed, achieved, adopted, and assumed. The ascribed role refers to that role given by another in accordance with social criteria, such as age-appropriate behavior, sex-appropriate behavior, or behavior labeled deviant by significant others. The achieved role is earned by an individual through the accomplishment of certain socially valued skills. The adopted role is brought into a given relationship in a quasi-legitimized fashion, eg, a woman acting like a "stepmother" when she is not, in fact, a legitimate occupant of that role. The assumed role is one which the individual takes on in a playful manner, without formal sanctions. Many people wittingly or unwittingly place themselves in an inappropriate and sometimes destructive role position.

> An 18-year-old of average intelligence, incarcerated in a youth facility, had been called "stupid" since his early childhood for failing to meet parental expectation. His parents appeared to be highly driven individuals with very high expectations for their son. The son assumed the role ascribed by his parents and began to play the role of loser both in and out of school. Others around him allowed him to continue this role without challenging it, until the script of loser became the dominant role in his interactions with others.

It becomes apparent that the boundaries between an ascribed role (given by another) and an assumed role (created for oneself) are often blurred. The label of "stupid" or "no good" may be ascribed, initially, but may be assumed by the individual as a way of avoiding schoolwork or interpersonal relations, perhaps out of fear of failure or of being hurt. A teenage girl may initially adopt a parenting or "housewife" role in the face of the illness or death of her mother. The role may be reinforced and extended by her father and younger siblings. She may be reluctant, then, to give up the role, either out of fear of alienating the esteem or love of her father, or out of guilt at leaving her charges alone; or she may cling to the role to avoid the risks of going out on her own. The generational boundaries and role character would be muddled in the process.

In speaking of his structural approach, Minuchin emphasizes that

> "a family is more than the individual biopsychodynamics of its members. Family members relate according to certain arrangements, which govern their transactions. These arrangements, though usually not explicitly stated or even recognized, form a whole—the structure of the family. The reality of the structure is of a different order from the reality of the individual members."

Minuchin's statement personifies the theme of this chapter. If "according to certain arrangements" refers to the role system of the family, the sentence might read: "Family members relate according to the family's particular role system." Therefore, it appears that Minuchin's structural family therapy model is consistent with the role-based therapeutic intervention described. By modifying the role perspectives of the family members, the therapist is able to change their subjective experience and their eventual role behaviors.

SUMMARY

The United States is in the midst of social change. Family structure is changing rapidly, divorce laws are being liberalized, and more women are gainfully employed. All these changes make traditional role models obsolete. New role models cannot be developed overnight but, rather, require a gradual evolving process. New role definitions are needed, along with adaptation to a new set of expectations via education, socialization, or therapeutic means.

From a therapeutic intervention point of view, role conflict often appears to be a major culprit in family discord. Inherent difficulties include (1) defining role concepts, (2) taking for granted the ability to carry out role obligations, and (3) taking advantage of an existing imbalance of the family subsystem to serve one's own purpose. Among the treatment approaches with theoretical underpinning in role theory, role play (specifically role rehearsal), transactional analysis, and techniques of the structural school of family therapy have proven useful therapeutic tools for the resolution of family conflict.

BIBLIOGRAPHY

Ackerman NW: *The psychodynamics of family life.* New York, Basic Books, 1958

Berne E: *Games people play.* New York, Grove Press, 1964

Bowen M: Theory in the practice of psychotherapy, in Guerin PJ (ed): *Family therapy.* New York, Garden Press, 1976

Duvall E: *Family development.* Philadelphia, PA, JB Lippincott, 1971

Haley J: *Strategies of psychotherapy.* New York, Grune & Stratton, 1963

Harris TA: *I'm ok—You're ok.* New York, Harper & Row, 1969

Hoffman L: *Foundation of family therapy.* New York, Basic Books, 1981

Horewitz JS: *Family therapy and transactional analysis.* New York, Jason Aronson, 1979

Lederer WJ, Jackson DD: *The mirages of marriage.* New York, WW Norton, 1968

Lewis JM: *How's your family?* New York, Brunner/Mazel, 1979

Minuchin S: *Family and family therapy.* Cambridge, MA, Harvard University Press, 1974

Rowe GP: The developmental conceptual framework to the study of the family, in Nye FI, Berardo FM (eds): *Emerging conceptual frameworks in family analysis.* New York, MacMillan, 1966

Satir V: *Conjoint family therapy.* Palo Alto, CA, Science and Behavior Books, 1967

Spiegel JP: The resolution of role conflict within the family, in Sze WC (ed): *Human life cycle.* New York, Jason Aronson, 1975

Sussman MB: Family, in *Encyclopedia of social work.* Washington, DC, Nat Assn of Social Workers, 1977, vol 1

Tharp RG, Otis GD: Toward a theory for therapeutic intervention in families, in Glasser PH, Glasser LN (eds): *Families in crisis.* New York, Harper & Row, 1970

Yalom ID: *The theory and practice of group psychotherapy.* New York, Basic Books, 1970

Chapter 6

ANXIETY

R. DEAN CODDINGTON, MD

Anxiety is ubiquitous, leading us to disregard it at times, and yet it may very well be the first signal that something is amiss. In this chapter, anxiety will be discussed, first as a symptom and later as a sign of a specific psychiatric disorder. Since anxiety is often handled automatically by the mind's invocation of a mechanism of defense, some of the more common mechanisms will also be discussed. The purpose of this chapter is to facilitate the reader's recognition of anxiety in its many altered forms—altered, that is, by the mechanisms of defense.

THE NATURE OF ANXIETY

Anxiety is defined as a state of uneasiness and distress about future uncertainties, as apprehension or worry. Everyone has experienced anxiety at one time or another. It can be seen reflected in the face of an infant and is probably the cause of the crying of children who seem unable to explain the basis for their tears. It can be described as a feeling of excitement or anticipation: The mouth becomes dry. The heart beats faster and seems more pronounced, prompting the expression, "my heart was pounding in my chest." The rate of breathing increases. The anxious person may develop a cold sweat, usually limited to the palms of the hands, and may also complain of nausea, vomiting, or "a lump in the throat." The feeling may last a few minutes or several hours. For most people the experience is infrequent and the episodes of mild intensity, but a few suffer from frequent, severe attacks, so debilitating as to make ordinary functioning impossible.

Anyone who works with children should be skilled at recognizing this state when it exists. Anxiety and depression are two common affects or feelings that must be attended to; they cannot be ignored. They are keys to our understanding of the child; if we know the cause of the anxiety, we will know how to treat the problem. To put it another way, if we don't know what is making the child anxious, we will be groping in the dark for a rational treatment program. As a matter of fact, a good many of the children who are classed as hyperactive these days are, instead, overanxious. The current treatment of choice for hyperactive children involves the use of stimulants, medications that ordinarily increase one's alertness and enable him to continue functioning even when very tired. For some as yet unknown reason, these medicines have a paradoxical effect and help the truly hyperactive child but—as you can probably guess—tend to make an anxious child worse. So it is incumbent upon us to become skilled at recognizing anxiety.

Until quite recently most authors distinguished fear from anxiety, defining fear as the response to an external danger, a threat from outside the body; anxiety was defined as the response to an internal threat, some unacceptable impulse or wish arising from the unconscious mind. Because fear and anxiety often occur simultaneously, this distinction is not very useful. Consider, for example, the last time you were about to cross a street and were surprised by a car you didn't see coming, approaching suddenly from around the corner. For a few moments your heart raced and pounded and you were "all a jitter." Was that fear of another auto still unseen, or anxiety caused either by a sudden impulse to kill the discourteous driver or by the reawakening of a long-forgotten fear of castration? Probably the best answer is "all of the above." Thus, distinguishing fear from anxiety has little practical significance.

The recognition of tachypnea (rapid respirations), tachycardia (rapid heart rate), palpitation, dry mouth, cold, wet palms and a worried expression is easy. Even with very limited experience, these signs are readily recognized in children of all ages, though somewhat more difficult to perceive in infants. Much of the time, anxiety doesn't appear this clearly because it is altered by the mind itself. It's as if anxiety is so unpleasant and so ubiquitous that the mind has developed automatic mechanisms to defend against it. If you have a sudden wish to kill, or any wish that is unacceptable to you because of the way you were raised or your own moral standards, a conflict exists which will cause great anxiety if allowed to persist. The mind comes to the rescue and brings into play some defense mechanism it has learned. The anxiety is altered and does not appear in its primitive, physiological form.

DEFENSE MECHANISMS

Projection

One of the most common mechanisms of defense and one that is learned very early in life is projection. For most of us, the wish to kill is unacceptable; we are immediately ashamed if we have such an impulse and restrain ourselves. But this isn't enough to give us peace of mind, because the acknowledgement that we had such a hostile wish labels us subjectively as "bad." Because this classification is also unacceptable, our mind projects the idea onto someone else, as if to say, "I'm not bad but that person thinks I am," or, "I can tell by the way he looks at me that he hates me, because he thinks I'm bad." Most readers will recognize the paranoid flavor of this process for, indeed, projection is the characteristic mechanism of defense seen in paranoid patients.

Although clear-cut paranoia is uncommon in children, projection is often evident. Almost every child has been taunted by a person who called him a name to which he seemed particularly sensitive. An obese child who comes from a family that enjoys food and eating and accepts obesity as more or less natural will probably not be offended when classmates call him "fatso." On the other hand, the child who has been criticised for overeating and taught that obesity is an outward sign of his "badness" is likely to be very sensitive to the same label. It's as if the children are calling him "bad," as well as "fatso." We have then a useful signal; when a child seems overly sensitive to the childhood practice of name-calling, it's almost certainly due to the child's belief that the one teasing him knows the truth and that his secret is no longer private.

Repression, Suppression, and Denial

In the above example, another mechanism of defense was also utilized. There are three methods by which the mind pushes anxiety-provoking thoughts into the unconscious: repression, an automatic unconscious mechanism; suppression, a conscious attempt to forget the idea; and denial, an automatic rejection of the whole idea, as if it did not exist. The sensitive, obese child described above used one or more of these mechanisms to avoid the anxiety associated with his "badness"; but when called "fatso," the previously repressed (or suppressed or denied) material was made conscious again and caused anxiety which accounted for his sensitivity.

Sublimation

Sublimation is defined as the unconscious channeling of unacceptable impulses into some socially acceptable activity. The simplest example of sublimation is that of the boy who occasionally harbors significant hostile impulses — unacceptable to the boy, but relatively appropriate on a football team. Many factors play a role in teaching children which activities can be used as appropriate expressions of various feelings: Athletics can be used for expression of hostile, aggressive impulses. Some religious and social organizations help children express love (and sexual) feelings in an acceptable way. Thus, society, culture, and family work together to establish standards of behavior.

Now, let's look at the possibility that hyperactivity in the classroom may be an example of sublimated anxiety or anxiety-causing impulses in boys. In our society, boys are expected — and even encouraged — to be active, as early as two years of age. There is also considerable evidence that the masculine tendency toward more competitive and aggressive behavior is an inherited trait; it is probably harder for boys to sit still in the classroom for this reason. Consider a family that encourages activity and a young male family member who is anxious over some forbidden impulse (like masturbation). In order to avoid the anxiety through sublimation, he must find a socially acceptable activity. He can sharpen his pencil, go to the bathroom, get a drink of water, ask to participate in the teacher's plan of action, or engage in another expedient project. Too frequent activities of this sort may be termed hyperactivity. We have no idea how many boys labelled hyperactive are really suffering from unrecognized anxiety. (Here is a place for a well-controlled study, using a teacher's rating of hyperactivity and some objective scale measuring anxiety.) The point here is to emphasize the need, expressed earlier, to develop skill in recognizing anxiety in all its various forms.

Rationalization

I have seen hyperkinetic (ie, hyperactive) boys who seemed to accept the diagnosis and their need for medication, who then blamed a missed dose of the medication for some bad behavior that followed. In other words, the boy was saying, "It wasn't my fault: My mother didn't give me my medicine this morning. My brain (with its presumed minor damage) made me do it." The mechanism of defense used here is rationalization. It is readily apparent that, if we want to teach children to accept responsibility for their own behavior, we had better not provide too many rationalizations, such as this. Kids are good enough at finding excuses without any help from us.

Conversion and Displacement

There are other mechanisms of defense that we must understand if we are to recognize anxiety in children. In conversion, anxiety is converted into some physical symptom—as, for example, a headache, stomachache or, more dramatically, the paralysis of a limb. When this defense is used, the child will be remarkably free of anxiety, apparently unconcerned about the headache and even about the paralyzed limb. Closely related to this is displacement, in which the anxiety is displaced from the object on which it is actually focused (perhaps a parent) to some other object or situation (a horse, dog, or school, for instance). One is better off being afraid of dogs than being phobic regarding one's own father. Or, if for some reason, a child is very much afraid of a specific injury (eg, castration), the fear may be displaced to another part of his body; he may panic when the doctor examines his throat. Some people who are very much afraid of an activity or object try to handle it by forcing themselves to be overly involved with the very thing they are afraid of; someone that is afraid of bodily injury might expose himself unnecessarily by joining the football team. This is called "counterphobic" behavior.

Reaction Formation

The last defense mechanism that will be discussed here is reaction formation. When a child has a strong desire or even a need for a close, affectionate relationship with an adult but is anxious about such a relationship, the child may behave as if he hates adults, as if he wants to be left alone. His behavior suggests just the opposite of what he really wants.

BEHAVIORAL MOTIVATION

It is our job to look beyond the overt behavior and to distinguish those cases in which the behavior is driven by anxiety from those cases motivated by other forces. Not all football players are sublimating murderous impulses or are deathly afraid of bodily injury, but some are. Since these mechanisms, except for suppression, are not under conscious control, the child will not be able to explain the reasons for his behavior. When the 6-year-old suddenly appears afraid of the dark and doesn't offer any explanation, our response should be based on the supposition of underlying anxiety over some forbidden impulse, rather than the assumption that the behavior is attention-getting or an attempt to manipulate us into letting him stay up later at night.

I cannot overemphasize the need for those of us who work with children to detect and evaluate the anxiety that underlies behavior. Anxiety and depression (discussed in chapter 7) are the two fundamental emotions that govern much of our behavior. This is not to say that anxiety is all bad, to be avoided at all costs. Quite the contrary, some degree of anxiety stimulates us to study in preparation for an examination and thereby increases learning. But too much anxiety causes the system to break down: defenses are called into play with a resulting decrease in learning efficiency. In modern parlance, we can say that it is advantageous to be "psyched up" for a coming event, but not too much so. This relationship between anxiety and learning is depicted in Figure 6-1.

THE ANXIETY DISORDERS

The reader should know at this point that anxiety occurs in everyone and may co-exist with any mental disorder. There are a few disorders, however, in which anxiety is very prominent—indeed, the most important symptom or driving force. Each of these will now be discussed.

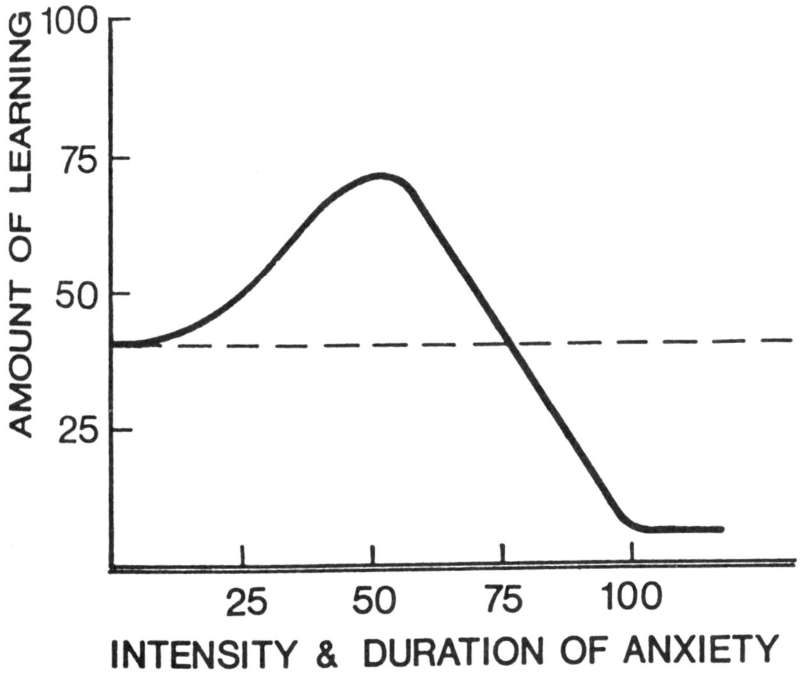

Figure 6-1: The theoretical effect of anxiety on learning.

Separation Anxiety Disorder

By far the most common entity in this group and one which can be severely debilitating is separation anxiety disorder. If children under 4 years have difficulty separating from their mothers, we needn't be too concerned. A 3-year-old, well adjusted to his preschool, might have mild difficulty on occasion—for example, when his father is out-of-town, or when his mother, customarily at home, is away from home for the day. Likewise, a short-lived problem for the first few days of kindergarten or school is not too alarming.* But when the symptoms are marked, or when they occur in third- or fourth-graders as they commonly do, we must give them due consideration.

As the name implies, the child is having trouble separating from his mother; but when we examine the situation carefully, we often find that the mother is also having trouble separating from the child. Not only does the mother worry about the well-being of the absent child, but the child worries about the mother (or father). It seems, at times, that the symptoms are triggered in 10-year-olds, the most common age for this disorder, by the occurrence of some illness in an adult the child knows—a parent, neighbor, or relative. The child becomes unduly concerned about the parent's health, reasoning, it would seem, that, "If Mrs. Jones can catch pneumonia and go to the hospital, so can mommy." The child goes off to school but is overwhelmed by anxiety and can't concentrate. The anxiety is often converted to a socially acceptable symptom such as a headache, or stomachache with nausea and vomiting. (This is a true conversion reaction, not a conscious manipulation to get out of school.) The child reports to the teacher and is usually sent home. Once the child sees that the mother (or father) is alright, the symptoms vanish in an hour or so. Because of this pattern and the rarity of symptoms on Saturdays and Sundays, this disorder was previously—and erroneously—known as "school phobia." However, children with the disorder are usually

*We are making a clinical judgment here as to whether or not the clinical picture is warranted by the circumstances; we must be very careful in this judgment. A history of a mild problem on entering kindergarten is often obtained from third-grade children with full-blown separation anxiety disorders; hence the appearance of mild anxiety at age 5 provides us with an opportunity to prevent a problem later on. We must avoid premature reassurance.

good students who like school. Even though there may have been some incident at school that seems etiologically significant, we should pay close attention to the child's previous experience separating from mother, her possible overprotectiveness, and her health. This approach will lead to a better understanding of the problem than will an exhaustive review of school activities.

The treatment of choice is to gently but firmly insist on an immediate return to school. The child knows that is where he or she belongs and usually wants to be there. We should not accuse the child of malingering, but should discuss the mother's health openly with the child present. We should then call the school while mother and child listen, informing the principal of the child's need to return to school the next day and to stay all day. We can be empathic, appreciating the fact that there will be a lot of anxiety the first day back, while reassuring the child that this will decrease daily.

Physicians often find themselves in a bind, torn between returning the child to school when he may "really have" an acute abdominal condition. In all cases of anxiety that is converted to pain, the pain is "real," not an act. It hurts! The physician must give due consideration to physical causes of abdominal pain even when the picture appears rather clearly to be a separation anxiety disorder. He must be careful, however, not to make the matter worse by a too-exhaustive physical workup that keeps the child out of school; every day the child misses means he or she is further behind in schoolwork, thus creating a new cause of anxiety.

When a separation anxiety disorder occurs in adolescents, it is usually quite a different matter. There is less concern about the parents' health and almost always evidence of more serious underlying psychopathology.

The Avoidant Disorder of Childhood

In contrast with separation anxiety, the avoidant disorder of childhood is rather uncommon. The essential feature is the excessive shrinking from contact with strangers long after the normal separation anxiety of infancy should have disappeared. In addition there are good relationships with family members and a clear desire for affection and acceptance by peers. These children may cling to their parents and become tearful over even trivial demands for contact with strangers. They become very embarrassed and shy in a social situation, sometimes even unable to speak.

The Overanxious Disorder of Childhood

The essential feature of the overanxious disorder is the presence of anxiety, excessive worrying and fearfulness that is not focused on anything particular. It is not concentrated on separation from parents or on contact with strangers; nor is it in response to some specific stressful event. It is free-floating anxiety, even more painful and disturbing than ordinary anxiety, since the child cannot attribute it to any one precipitating cause. Overanxious children constantly seek approval and may seem perfectionistic, overconcerned about their performance and about what people will think.

A brief case vignette will impress the reader with the intense suffering which overanxious children are forced to endure.

> Janie was an attractive, 11-year-old girl with long hair, fair skin, and rather frightened-looking blue eyes. Over the summer, her parents became increasingly concerned about her, as she continued to voice many worries and was repeatedly bothered by fantasies and nightmares. She often worried that she would forget how to do things, such as how to tie her shoes. Although she had been reasonably happy at school in the past, during the summer she began worrying about returning to school in the fall. She found it impossible to take a bath alone, would have to examine the water before she got in, and could not wait to get out. Her mother assisted her in her daily baths. Mrs. B. reported that Janie specifically had difficulty washing around the genital region and would tell her mother that she was afraid "it would fall off down there."
>
> When the school year began, Janie's anxieties accelerated. She did not participate in classroom work and her grades dropped. Janie reported concern about her father's drinking and became extremely agitated and upset whenever her mother took even one social drink. While she considered herself close to her mother, she often worried that something would happen to her. For as long as she could remember, she had slept in her parents' bed between her mother and father. On a few occasions when they locked the door, she became very anxious about "what might be happening to her mother in there." Janie had many anxieties about growing up, starting menstrual periods, and developing breasts. She wished to stay a little girl and particularly didn't want "to get all that bleeding." She had no understanding of the basic facts of life and believed that mothers get pregnant because "it's natural: God puts the baby there." Janie was bothered by her thoughts, and

> her difficulty in distinguishing between her thoughts and her fantasies caused concern that she may have "done something and not remembered it." In particular she confided to her mother her worries that she might touch her "too-too" (her word for vagina) in class and not remember it. On one occasion, when she was rubbing alcohol on her dog's ear, she asked her mother if maybe she "drank the alcohol and couldn't remember it." She was also bothered by thoughts that her mother is "not real and that she herself is not alive."

This is obviously a complicated case of a very disturbed little girl. Many details have been omitted, along with data regarding her development and interpersonal relationships within the family. The intent was to impress the reader with the seriousness of this disorder. It is only fair to add, however, that Janie has responded very well to psychotherapy provided by a very empathic and understanding social worker.

Phobic Disorders

During different development periods, children are prone to a variety of fears, such as fear of the dark, of monsters, cemeteries, and ghosts. A persistent, irrational fear of a specific object together with its avoidance, is called a simple or specific phobia. In children, the object is most commonly an animal. If the phobic object is easily avoided there is little impairment, but a phobia of dogs is quite debilitating.

Sometimes a simple phobia develops after some frightening experience with the animal; at other times the condition results from displacement of anxiety, initially caused by an intrapsychic conflict, onto some heretofore insignificant animal. The only child that Sigmund Freud ever worked with was Little Hans, who was phobic to horses. Freud asserted that the phobia was a compromise between internal and external demands, that Hans had been seductively dealt with by his mother and later threatened with penile amputation when she found him masturbating. The conflict was then displaced onto an external object, a horse. (Freud didn't actually analyze Hans but developed this formulation from information supplied by his father.)

The simple phobias of childhood usually disappear without treatment and are not often brought to our attention.

Adjustment Disorders

Adjustment disorders are discussed in more detail in Chapter 9 but, for the sake of completeness, should be mentioned here. They are defined as maladaptive reactions that begin within three months of some specific psychologically stressful event and are subdivided into several categories, one of which is identified by a predominantly anxious mood. Some children that seek our help and appear to be suffering from anxiety may be reacting to some specific life event, such as the marital separation of their parents, moving to a new school district with the loss of all their old friends, or some other set of circumstances with which they are having difficulty coping.

SUMMARY

Anxiety and depression are the two fundamental emotions to which those of us who work with children must always be alert. We must look for signs of anxiety and depression that may be hidden by one or more mechanisms of defense. These defense mechanisms work in the service of the ego, sparing the pain and suffering that would be expected in the absence of intrapsychic defenses. When we see evidence of reaction formation, displacement, conversion, or any other defense, it is our responsibility to investigate its necessity. Conversely, we must also wonder why a child doesn't seem anxious when in a situation or set of circumstances that often produces it. What mechanism of defense is protecting the child—repression? denial? sublimation? The anxious child cannot sit down and tell us his troubles. It is up to us to meet him more than halfway.

Chapter 7

DEPRESSION

R. DEAN CODDINGTON, MD

This chapter is, from a clinical point of view, one of the most important in this book since it deals with a symptom as well as a syndrome or disease. The symptom is experienced to a mild degree by everyone in society, including children. When its intensity becomes overwhelming, it is a very important mental disorder that, in adolescence, is the third or fourth leading cause of death.

Study of this material will enable the reader to recognize depression as it appears in babies, children, and adolescents. The chapter will act as a guide to the correct diagnosis of different depressive disorders. Finally, it will encourage the reader to initiate treatment appropriately and to obtain additional therapeutic help, when needed.

THE PROBLEM OF DEPRESSION

> Henry was a 10-year-old boy who looked so woebegone and hopeless when first seen that no one could fail to recognize his depression. His uncombed, shoulder-length blond hair covered the outer portion of his face. Tears welled periodically in his eyes as he told his story in a quiet, expressionless voice. An occasional half-smile revealed his attempt to be brave. It seems that for several years an 18-year-old brother had bullied Henry while the parents held firm to their philosophy that Henry must learn to defend himself. They were unmoved by the gradual, four-year decline in Henry's grades, coupled with the increased time spent alone in his room. It was only when he said he wanted to die because there was nothing to live for that the parents were prompted to seek professional help.

It was hard to see how anyone would fail to recognize Henry's depression. His despair could not be denied. But most of the time this is not the case, and we are forced to make a conscious effort to answer the question, "Is this child depressed?" As indicated in the preceding chapter, those of us who work with children must always be on the alert for signs of anxiety and depression, the two most fundamental emotions. We must assess the child's utilization of mental mechanisms of defense: denial, repression, suppression, rationalization, and so forth. But we have, in addition, another tool at our disposal—a skill, if you will—that can be of immeasurable help. That skill is an empathic response to the child.

Lawrence Kolb defines empathy as "a healthy form of identification which is limited and temporary but which enables one person to feel for and with another and to understand his experience and feelings." He describes the empathic individual as one who "possesses a warm capacity for projecting himself into the situations and feelings of others." Empathy is not the same as sympathy; it is much more than simply feeling sorry for the child. It is also more than a "gut feeling" about a situation. To feel for and with another person means—to a limited extent and for a limited period of time—to really share that person's feelings. One comes away feeling depressed, following an interview with a depressed child. But this feeling is healthy and can be used to make an objective evaluation of the child, as opposed to the unhealthy overidentification which is sometimes overwhelming.

Empathy is a tool you can use. Also, your capacity for empathy with children, which may well have contributed significantly to your decision to work with them, can be increased through experience and continued reappraisal of your own feelings.

I recently saw the devoted father of a little girl who was the object of a custody battle between the recently divorced parents:

> The father was well-to-do, so that there was really no financial issue in the settlement. He enjoyed his work, friends, and parents and gave no outward appearance of depression. He spoke in an animated way about his work and things he and his daughter did together, but I came away from our discussions saying to myself, "This man is really suffering." He was trying to keep a stiff upper lip but felt threatened at the possibility of having less time with his daughter as a result of her mother's demands. After two or three visits, he acknowledged his depression and cried openly.

His depression was not, at first, readily discernible but my empathic response forced me to look further.

Suicide in Children

Suicide is rare before the age of 10 and then remains very low through age 14; only one child per year, per 100,000, takes his own life (see Tables 7-1 and 7-2). Suicide becomes nine times more common in midadolescence. The rate doubles again in late adolescence and young adulthood. As children get older, they are better able to obtain more lethal means to commit suicide—drugs, for instance, or the family automobile—and they plan their deaths in a way that is more likely to succeed. Midadolescence is also a time when a person thinks a lot about his own identity and his future; whereas a child of 12 may continue to be hopeful about the future despite a depressing family situation, his hope diminishes at age 17 as he faces the reality of the situation. The fantasies of childhood give way to hopelessness. For this reason we are unable to say that, because the suicide rate is low among preadolescents, depression is also low. To do so would be to offer false reassurance. In fact, the suicide rate is higher in midadolescence because (1) adolescents are thinking more seriously about themselves and the future; (2) they are better able to commit suicide, since society gives them a driver's license and subtly encourages the use of alcohol and drugs; and (3) the prevalence of depression among adolescents may be greater.

To place suicide in perspective, let's look at the causes of death of 15- to 24-year-olds in 1982. Motor vehicle accidents accounted for 35%; 15% were attributed to "other accidents and adverse effects," while 12% were attributed to suicide and 13% to homicide; all other causes accounted for only 25%. Since suicides are always underreported due to the social and religious stigmata attached to them, and since some accidents may have resulted from intentional self-destructive or dangerous behavior, it is conceivable that more adolescents die by their own hand than from any other cause.

TABLE 7-1
SUICIDE RATES FOR MALES BY AGE: 1950-1979

	10-14	*15-19*	*20-24*
1950	0.5	3.5	9.3
1960	0.9	5.6	11.5
1970	0.9	8.8	19.3
1975	1.2	12.2	26.4
1976	1.2	11.4	26.4
1977	1.6	14.0	29.2
1978	1.2	12.6	26.8
1979	1.1	13.4	26.5

TABLE 7-2
SUICIDE RATES FOR FEMALES BY AGE: 1950-1979

	10-14	*15-19*	*20-24*
1950	0.1	1.8	3.3
1960	0.2	1.6	2.9
1970	0.3	2.9	5.7
1975	0.4	2.9	6.8
1976	0.4	3.2	6.4
1977	0.3	3.3	7.1
1978	0.4	3.0	6.3
1979	0.5	3.2	6.3

The suicide rate for midadolescents and late adolescents (age 15 to 24) began rising in the late 1950s and leveled off in the 1980s (Figure 7-1); the death rate from homicide, the third leading cause of death in this age group, has taken a similar course (Figure 7-1). By contrast, the rate of automobile accident deaths has been highly variable (Figure 7-2). To what can we attribute the increased suicide rate? Are today's youths more depressed than they were 20 years ago? In our search for an answer we might look at other data. Figure 7-3 depicts the divorce rate; we are at once struck with the similar appearance to the rates shown in Figure 7-1. We cannot conclude that marital problems cause suicides and homicides, although they are highly correlated. (The correlation between divorce and suicide in this age group over the last thirty years is .97, and between divorce and homicide is .94.) We can conclude, however, that these associations are very strong and not coincidental. All three behaviors may be due to a common cause or set of causes. The turmoil that Alvin Toffler describes in *Future Shock* may be the culprit.

In view of the rising suicide rate, the prevention of suicide is a very important goal; but there must be hundreds of depressed children for each one who attempts to end his life. It is the early recognition of depression that we should strive for. To be more specific, we should strive for the early recognition of clinical depression—the distinction between the everyday, garden variety sort of unhappiness and the dysphoric mood which indicates a significant breakdown of the protective mechanisms of defense. Children of different ages behave differently when depressed, so they will be discussed in three groupings: infants and preschoolers, elementary school-aged children, and adolescents.

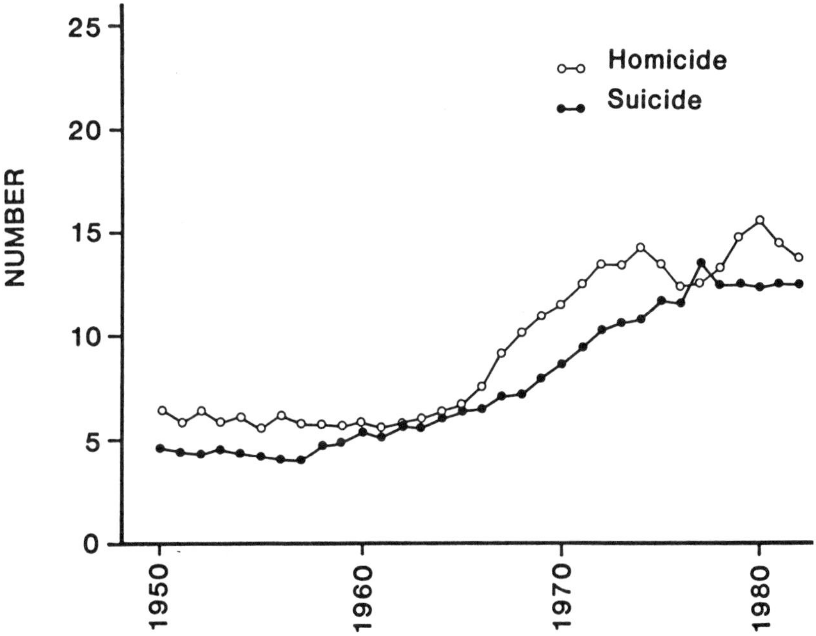

Figure 7-1: Death rate from suicide and homicide for mid- and late-adolescents (age 15–24), 1950 to 1983.*

*Data compiled from publications of the National Center for Health Statistics of the U.S. Public Health Service.

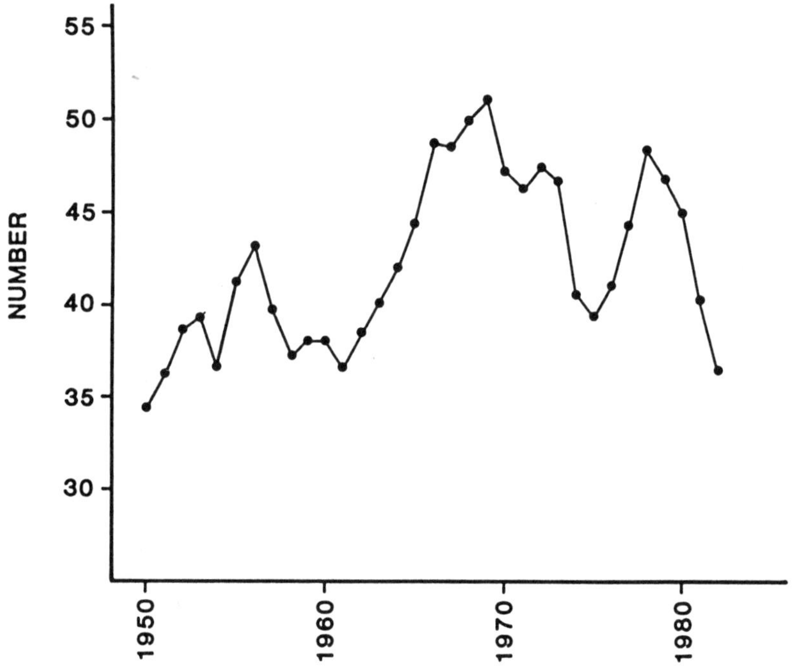

Figure 7-2: Death rate from automobile accidents for mid- and late-adolescents (age 15 to 24), 1950 to 1983.*

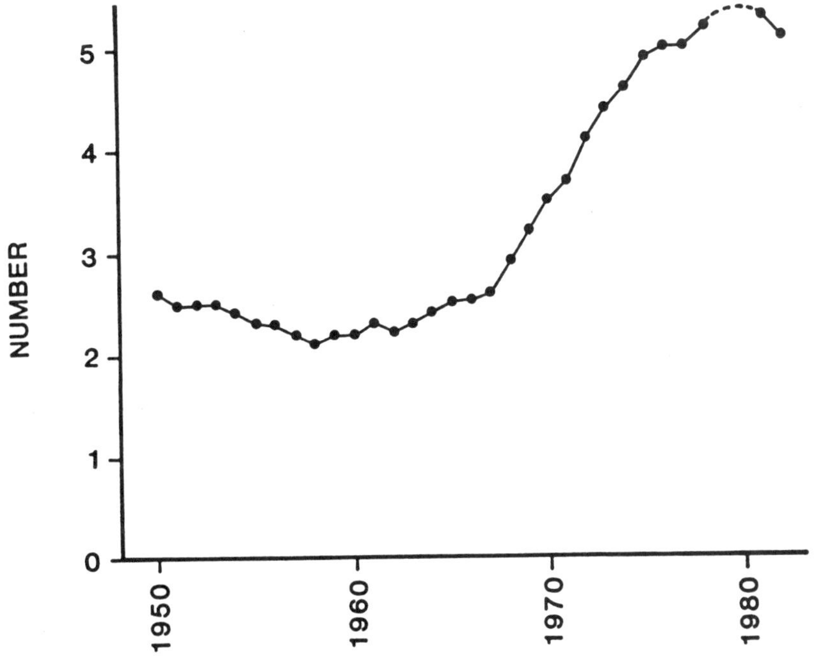

Figure 7-3: Divorce rate in the United States, 1950 to 1983.*

*Data compiled from publications of the National Center for Health Statistics of the U.S. Public Health Service.

RECOGNIZING DEPRESSION

Infants

Rene Spitz was the first to describe the effects of depression in infancy. An advocate of Freud, he decided to make objective observations on those infants cared for in two "hospitals" in the 1940s. One was a home for children who were to be adopted; in the other setting, attached to a prison, pregnant inmates delivered their babies and then returned to prison. Spitz was, therefore, able to control the contact these infants had with their mothers; he demonstrated very clearly that it was separation from their mothers that resulted in depression, which he then described. It so happened that these infants were also deprived of normal visual and auditory stimuli, in that they lay in cribs looking at white walls, with the sides of the beds often covered with white sheets. There were almost no toys, and one nurse cared for eight or nine infants. It has since been shown that, during the first six months of life, visual and auditory stimulation—and, in addition, tactile and motoric stimulation in the form of rocking, bathing, and cuddling—are necessary for normal growth and development. From age 6 months, the child seems able to relate to the mother as a person and to begin to develop his own ego structure. Therefore, the diagnosis of maternal deprivation is used when the mother or a substitute is absent after six months; sensory deprivation refers to the lack of stimulation prior to that time.

Spitz showed that after one month's separation from the mother, a retardation in the child's developmental quotient takes place. After two months, the child shows signs of withdrawal, anxiety on approach, loss of appetite, loss of weight, and cessation of normal development. After three months, the infant seems to regress to an earlier stage of development. Insomnia ensues, along with a particular lack of resistance to infectious diseases. In Spitz's research, the mortality rate from measles and the like was 37% by two years of age. This depressive state was reversible if the mother was reunited with the child, even after three or four months. The term used to refer to the child who regresses to an early stage because of lack of maternal care and other forms of stimulation is anaclitic depression. The word, "anaclitic," means to depend on, or lean on impersonal objects for comfort.

In 1956, George L. Engel and his colleagues had the opportunity to study an infant who was born with an atresia of the esophagus. This congenital anomaly prevents food from reaching the stomach, making immediate surgical intervention necessary to enable the child to be fed through a gastrostomy, an opening directly into the stomach. Although technically it is not difficult to feed such an infant, it *is* difficult to deal with such an infant in a relaxed, maternal way. The infant is unable to reject foods, exhibits unusual cues as to when he is satiated, and the very presence of the life-saving tube, which can become inadvertently dislodged, causes considerable anxiety among most mothers.

> The mother of the infant with an atresia of the esophagus was only 19 years old and had little support from her husband, a truck driver who was home only on weekends. The mother became depressed and was further unable to relate normally to her infant daughter, Monica. At 18 months, Monica was discovered on a pediatric unit, very poorly nourished and, according to the nurses, clinically depressed.

Thus, Engel was able to describe the same type of depression that Spitz had previously described, but with the mother-infant relationship physically intact but psychologically unsatisfying to both.

As Engel and his associates studied Monica's behavior in various situations, they began to expand the concept of depression into the broader construct of helplessness and hopelessness. (These latter ideas were developed over a number of years.) The investigators noted that, if Monica felt threatened and helpless to defend herself, she turned away and sometimes fell asleep; under normal circumstances, in contrast, we would expect a threatened infant to protest very loudly and vigorously.

Preschoolers

Older preschoolers who have had a normal infancy will not ordinarily present as anacliticly depressed, though they may have the same symptoms to a lesser degree. They may sleep more than usual or may suffer from insomnia. They may lose their appetites and withdraw from friends and activities previously enjoyed. It is important to note that you will be given the impression—by the child himself and by his parents or other people who know him—that the child's behavior prior to the onset of current symptoms was quite different. Symptoms should be present for at least two weeks before a formal diagnosis of depression is made. Children under 6 will usually look quite apathetic and sad when depressed.

Elementary School Children

Elementary school children may present with a picture similar to that of older preschoolers but may also exhibit loss of energy, fatigue, feelings of worthlessness, self-reproach, excessive or inappropriate guilt, diminished ability to think or concentrate, and recurrent thoughts of death or suicide. As we think about these symptoms, it becomes apparent that the first signs of depression may appear in the classroom as a decline in academic performance. Moreover, elementary school children have a greater ability to express themselves verbally and may even describe their unhappiness and suicidal thinking. They may report a lack of interest in activities that used to hold their attention for prolonged periods of time.

Adolescents

Adolescents are different only in that they have developed a larger repertoire of coping behaviors, many of which can be self-destructive. A car may be available; some teenagers have a tendency to go for long rides, alone or with friends, sometimes driving too fast and occasionally appearing quite reckless and frankly suicidal. Alcohol, the age-old folk medicine, and now street drugs are often used to ameliorate the unpleasant feelings associated with depression. Not only are they seldom effective, but many are depressants in and of themselves, thereby compounding the problem. Teenagers may write letters or poetry with depressive themes, sometimes giving the impression that they see little hope in the future. As you might imagine, a sense of hopelessness sometimes forebodes dire consequences, so we shall examine the construct in some detail.

HOPELESSNESS

Several unrelated observations will clarify the concept of hopelessness: During World War II a considerable number of unaccountable deaths were recorded of soldiers who died when they were apparently in good health; on autopsy, no pathology could be found. The coroner of the City of Baltimore contended that a number of individuals have died each year after taking small, sublethal doses of poison, or after inflicting minor, nonlethal wounds on themselves. Apparently they died as a result of belief in their own doom.

Similarly, it was noted that young British merchant seamen had a higher mortality rate after being set adrift on a life raft than did their older, seasoned shipmates, even though the older men didn't seem to be in as good physical condition as the young men. The British government asked Kurt Hahn, an educator known for his talent in combining challenging physical activities with academic discipline and community service, to address the problem. He reasoned that old, experienced seamen survived longer on a life raft because they knew, through the accounts of others, that it was possible to do so; but the young men, with few seasoned friends to relate such stories, gave up hope and died.

Hahn developed a rigorous training program designed to teach men that they could run further than they thought they could, swim further, and above all, that they could survive a few days without food or water. It was successful! After the war, the Outward Bound program developed as a direct result of Hahn's success. Camps located in wilderness areas in many parts of the world are used as bases of operation from which adolescents and young adults go on expeditions designed to challenge and to teach coping skills.*

The notion that death may be due to loss of hope has also been studied in the laboratory. Curt Richter, of Johns Hopkins University, compared the behavior of wild rats to that of domesticated rats in a situation from which there was no escape—ie, all the rats would eventually drown. Domesticated rats, subjected to a variety of earlier experiments, lived much longer than the wild rats, some of whom died when they were handled prior to placement in the no-escape situation. It seemed as if either fear or something akin to hopelessness resulted in death.

Richter did two things. First, he taught some of the wild rats that escape was possible, by removing them from the situation soon after placing them in it; he taught them to be less afraid or to have hope, if you will. Then, he attached tiny electrodes to their

*For further information on these highly recommended programs, write Outward Bound National Office, 384 Field Point Road, Greenwich, CT 06830.

bodies in order to record the electrical activity of the heart; if they died from fear, the heart rate should have increased until it became so inefficient that death ensued. He discovered that the opposite occurred: the heart gradually slowed and then stopped, as would be expected if it were due to a "giving-up" process.

Thus, the evidence indicates the need for concern about children or adults who seem to be losing hope.

It should be clear from the foregoing that hopelessness is an extreme example of depression. The vast majority of depressed people have not yet reached this stage of despair and are not ready to give up completely. In fact, it's well known that a number of people who try to commit suicide don't want to die! That's one of the reasons that suicide prevention centers seem to be helpful; the person doesn't really want to die and, at some intrapsychic level, is receptive to alternate suggestions made by someone on the telephone.

Most children and adolescents become depressed when their psychological defenses fail to ameliorate the effect of stressful situations and traumatic events that occur; there is a failure to adjust to or cope with the environment. The diagnosis then would be adjustment disorder of childhood (or adolescence) with depressed mood. (Although there are no statistics to support my contention, I expect that this is the correct diagnosis for 75% of depressed youths.) Another group of patients is classified as having a major depression due, we believe, to some biological or combined biological and psychological process, rather than a purely psychological reaction to external events. Such depressions used to be called endogenous (from within) as opposed to reactive depressions. These two diagnostic categories will be discussed separately.

DEPRESSIVE DISORDERS

Adjustment Disorders with Depressed Mood

A dynamic equilibrium exists between the external environment and the internal milieu of healthy individuals. Our bodies constantly adjust to variations in the environment and are remarkably efficient in doing so. We adapt readily to atmospheric oxygen concentrations varying from sea level to about twelve thousand feet and, given a few weeks, can adjust to altitudes of 20,000 feet where the oxygen is rare indeed. Similar statements can be made regarding our ability to tolerate variations in temperature, light, sound, population density, and caloric intake, but in each case the human body has limitations. Extremes in either direction exceed our capacity to adjust. The loss of ordinary stimulation can be as disruptive to normal psychological and physiological functioning as can overstimulation.

Failure to stimulate babies visually, affectively, socially, auditorily, tactilely, and proprioceptively results in failure in optimal development, as discussed above. Children need to be stimulated in order to achieve optimal learning rates and even to grow. But they can be overstimulated, too, and, consequently, unable to cope. Either situation, too little or too much stimulation, can result in an adjustment disorder with depressed mood. (Adjustment disorders can also be associated with an anxious mood as we saw in chapter 6, or with a mixed mood, involving both anxiety and depression.)

How does understimulation or overstimulation get translated into feelings of worthlessness, self-reproach, or excessive or inappropriate guilt, the predominant depressive symptoms of both children and adolescents? Ordinarily, the psychological mechanisms of defense prevent the unpleasant affects of anxiety and depression through denial, repression, sublimation, conversion, displacement, and so forth; but in some cases they fail to do so. The depressed patient is unable to use his defenses to a satisfactory degree and is left with unresolved conflict for which he takes the blame. An example or two will help to clarify this concept.

> An 8-year-old boy was brought to my office after he ran away from home and was returned by the police—only after being severely frightened by a dog, the onset of darkness, loneliness, and becoming thoroughly lost. His grandmother had died recently after a long illness. The death came as no surprise to the boy or his family; she had been hospitalized for several weeks. On the Sunday prior to her death, the boy was invited to accompany his parents when they visited her, but was allowed to stay home and play baseball with his friends instead. She died before another visit was arranged, leaving the patient with feelings of guilt; he argued, in essence, that she would have died happier if he had made the visit. He was apparently unable to deny her death or to blame his parents by rationalizing that they should have insisted that he visit. Because his defense mechanisms were insufficient,

he was burdened with inappropriate guilt and acted in a rather self-destructive manner—ie, by running away. If he had been a few years older, his defenses might have been strong enough to prevent the self-reproach; if not, the self-destructiveness may have appeared as a serious suicide attempt.

***

In another case, a beautiful 15-year-old girl emptied several available medicine bottles in an effort to resolve a conflict that resulted from overstimulation. She was nominated as queen of her high school and, at the same time, as sweetheart of a high school fraternity. Of course she was thrilled and flattered, but she began to think of some problems. If she accepted the nomination as queen, she would have to be the best-dressed girl in school for the month before the election, and if she accepted the other honor, she would be expected to date all the boys in the fraternity. She didn't know if she could measure up to the expectations, whether realistic or not. She may have been projecting a lot of her own desires or impulses onto others. At any rate, another idea, the "crowning blow" one might say, was the fantasy that she would be elected queen and would be walking across the gymnasium floor in a beautiful, long white dress, catch her heel in the hem, and fall flat on her face. This embarrassment, this feeling of worthlessness (a true queen would never do such a mundane thing as catch her heel in a hem) was beyond her coping ability.

These two examples are rather extreme. The psychological defenses had failed to the point of leaving no alternative other than to turn the feelings inward, with resulting self-destructive behavior. This, of course, is not the usual case. Most of the time the child is successful in partially defending against feelings of worthlessness and guilt. He will blame others for his failures; teachers, peers and parents are prime targets. In addition to this displacement, he will use denial and rationalization, as in the case of the high school athlete, who says that the conditioning program and practice leave him no time for homework and, besides, he no longer wants to go to college; in fact, he can't read well enough to keep up. Or, there are those children from homes where many arguments between the parents are over the child's behavior. These children may deny their guilt and depressive mood and may participate with friends who use mind-altering drugs "for fun."

This capacity of most children to hide depressive feelings through some mechanism of defense led to the term "masked depression." Though popular a few years ago, the term has fallen into disuse as we strive to be more precise in our diagnostic efforts; it still serves as a reminder that we should look carefully for signs of depression even when, for all intents and purposes, the child appears relatively happy.

Major Depression

The term major depression is used currently to denote a depressive episode that does not seem to be reactive to any recent event or situation. It may be the first occurrence of such an episode, or one of several. Theoretically, it is due to a biological condition or to an inherited variation in biochemical function that predisposes to depression. For this reason, one can sometimes obtain a history of depression and/or suicide in other family members.

These endogenous depressions have been recognized in adults for more than 100 years but, until recently, little attention has been given to their occurrence in children or adolescents. There is now considerable evidence that they do occur in childhood. But we are at a loss to describe any specific lesion or biological disease that produces endogenous depression, although we do know that depression as a symptom is associated with a number of illnesses. At this point in time we cannot be sure whether a child inherited a predisposition to depression from his mother or whether he was born as a completely normal individual who developed a tendency to respond in a depressive manner. As explication of the latter alternative, it may be that the mother's chronic or periodic depressions produced a distant and unempathic mother-infant relationship, as described by Engel and Reichsman (see above). It is certainly possible that the infant's neuroendocrinologic mechanisms can adapt to nonempathic parenting just as, when necessary, one's oxygen-carrying capacity can adjust to life at 20,000 feet. If a person learns to live without empathy, without the warm, supportive understanding of others, and cannot profit from such support when it is available, he may be doomed to chronic or periodic depression. In other words, an endogenous depression in an adolescent may reflect either a genetically determined condition or a biological adaptation to one or more anaclitic depressions of infancy.

These major depressive episodes and their causes will become much more clearly understood in the near future, as a consequence of research that is currently under way. I suspect, however, that we will find them to be relatively uncommon when compared to the reactive depressions of the adjustment disorders.

TREATMENT

At the present state of our knowledge, individual psychotherapy must be provided to a depressed child just as soon as we become aware of his dysphoria. The therapist must be empathic to the child's needs; there is no substitute for this capacity. Without it, all the training and education in the world will not suffice. The therapist can be a layman, counselor, teacher, occupational therapist, or child psychiatrist. (When an endogenous depression seems likely, a child psychiatrist with his medical background is needed.) The point is that a depressed patient needs immediate, objective, supportive attention, delivered in a sensitive and understanding manner. Theoretically, his parents are in the best position to provide this kind of help and this is, of course, what usually occurs. Sometimes, however, for a number of reasons, communication between parents and children leaves something to be desired. In such cases, professional help is indicated.

Urgency in providing help is dictated by a need to assess the danger of suicide and prevent it. Once there is no longer concern about suicide, a more deliberate effort to find an appropriate therapist can be made. The secondary goal of therapy is to explore the predisposing or etiologic factors, to get to the root of the problem. Simple reassurance is not enough. The therapist must understand the psychodynamic development of the depression, if relapses are to be avoided. The parents will almost always have to be involved as well. The need to explore precipitating factors cannot be overstressed. Temporary suicide prevention is relatively easy, but elimination of the causative factors, or alteration of the patient's interpretation of them or sensitivity to them is necessary for treatment of the depression. An experienced psychotherapist is needed for this task; treatment may be fairly prolonged, sometimes several months.

Antidepressants may also be used but should not be relied upon at the outset. To prescribe antidepressant medication immediately after making the diagnosis is bad practice because (1) they aren't needed in most cases; (2) relief of the symptoms without gaining an understanding of the psychodynamics involved is counterproductive and may remove the patient's motivation for psychotherapy; and (3) adolescents, particularly depressed adolescents, are too prone to become dependent on medications.

SUMMARY

After highlighting the problem of depression, the chapter concerned itself with the recognition of depression in infants, preschoolers, elementary school children, and adolescents. A section on hopelessness was followed by a consideration of depressive disorders.

It is suggested that those readers who encounter unhappy children in their work attempt to determine the extent of the unhappiness. Is the child depressed? If he seems to be, if his mood reflects something more than the ups and downs of daily life, the reader should provide immediate support in any way possible. Then, he should help the parents arrange for a more definitive diagnosis and, if indicated, for appropriate treatment. It may be a matter of life and death.

BIBLIOGRAPHY

Carlson G, Strober M: Affective disorders in adolescence. *Psychiat Clin N Amer* 2:511-526, 1979

Engel GL, Reichsman F, Segal HL: A study of an infant with a gastric fistula. *Psychosom Med* 18:374-398, 1956

Grossman E: A rough cure for adolescence. *Harper's Magazine* 234(May):69-80, 1967

Kolb LC: *Modern Clinical Psychiatry*. Philadelphia, Saunders, 1977

Puig-Antich J: Affective disorders in childhood: A review and perspective. *Psychiat Clin N Amer* 3:403-424, 1980

Richter CP: On the phenomenon of sudden death in animals and man. *Psychosom Med* 19:191-198, 1957

Spitz RA: Anaclitic depression. *The Psychoanal Study of the Child* 2:313-342, 1946

Chapter 8

INTRAPSYCHIC CONFLICT

R. DEAN CODDINGTON, MD

The subject of this chapter may be the hardest to comprehend, since conflicts within oneself—within one's own mind—force one to consider the possible existence of an "unconscious" that is outside of awareness. Sigmund Freud introduced the concept, defining the unconscious as that portion of the mind that contains repressed ideas, wishes, and affects. During recent reassessments of Freud's work, the concept of the unconscious, in particular, was found useful; it lends itself to an understanding of certain human behavior that is otherwise hard to fathom. The position that there is an unconscious will be defended, and a number of examples of conscious versus unconscious conflicts will be presented in this chapter. The reader should emerge with an understanding of this fundamental principle and, perhaps, with keener insight into his or her own behavior.

THE NATURE OF THE UNCONSCIOUS

The conscious portion of the mind can be viewed as an organized, logical collection of thoughts, memories, hopes, moral guidelines, fears, and everything else that one could use to describe himself in detail. Within the constraints of memory, any one of us could delineate his life, family, education, avocations, and hopes for the future in a well-organized manner. In the process, some long-forgotten memories or wishes might come to light, memories that we could say were just beneath the conscious portion of the mind. The logical thinking associated with the exercise is called "secondary process thinking." But no matter how thorough this biography, unconscious material would remain outside the realm of awareness.

Now let's allow our hypothetical autobiographer to sleep. Upon awakening, he reports a strange dream in which two people, somewhat like his parents, stood laughing as he fell over a cliff and tumbled endlessly into a bottomless chasm. This dream material belongs to our historian (no one else dreamed it), but, no matter how hard he tries, he cannot integrate it into his autobiography. This is called "primary process thinking" because of its primitive, illogical character. Ordinarily, such a dream is immediately repressed—pushed back into the unconscious—and cannot be recalled in the morning. But if it could, along with the affect and other thoughts associated with it, it would begin to fit together with other unconscious material and would fill in some gaps in what we once considered a complete autobiography. Primary process thinking—that is, primitive, raw, earthy, natural thoughts associated one with another in a simple, crude fashion without modification by social or cultural restraints—can be seen normally in very young children; its remarkable innocence and naiveté is especially appealing in dreams of persons of all ages and in severely psychotic adults, in whom the controlling function of the ego has broken down.

Unconscious ideas or feelings occasionally slip out under the guise of humor or in one's misuse of a word—a slip of the tongue, if you will. Sometimes they are projected onto another person, but most of the time they are unavailable to us. The psychoanalytic method is specifically designed to enable unconscious material to come to light. A quiet, relaxed atmosphere is arranged, in which the patient can freely associate one thought with another; in order to reduce the control of the patient's production by verbal or nonverbal cues, the analyst sits outside the patient's view. Freud discovered psychoanalysis, incidentally, through his use of hypnotism, another method of determining what lies beyond the conscious mind.

Perhaps the best way to emphasize the importance of this concept is through a brief case report:

> A young married man sought help because of frequent temper outbursts of which he was ashamed. He described a relatively uneventful childhood in a stable, upwardly mobile Christian home, in which alcohol was taboo. The work ethic was prominent, and the parents expected their children to attend college. John, as we shall call him, met Patricia in high school and maintained contact with her in the next few years, although they attended different schools. John had played football in high school and was offered a grant-in-aid at an out-of-state school. His temper was not a problem during adolescence, presumably because it was channeled into athletics, or sublimated (see chapter 6). But now, after

> only one year of marriage, his temper threatened both his job and his marriage. He irritated others at work and would get so angry with his wife that he would slap her.
>
> John and Patricia were sexually intimate during their college days "because we loved each other," but John really felt that sex should be limited to the marital relationship. Following their marriage, however, he found Patricia less attractive sexually, and continually quizzed her about other boys whom she had dated during their college days. He became furious if she withheld information or if she described some fleeting, intimate experience; she was either a liar or a "fallen woman." He excused her premarital sexual activity with *him* because they were in love, but a relationship with anyone else during that four-year period was viewed as promiscuity. As you might expect, he had a different standard for himself.

On interviewing Patricia, who confirmed the history, including the wife-beating, it was discovered that she was, apparently, rather accepting and was making no move toward a marital separation; she tearfully reported, "I guess I deserve it." She had not been promiscuous in college, although she had been intimate with others when her relationship with John was not going well. She was less active sexually than most of her peers. Then why the statement, "I deserve it"? As it turned out, she, too, was reared in a proper family with high moral standards. During her adolescence she was often at odds with her mother over her desire to start dating, the clothes she chose to wear, the hours she kept, and the boys she dated. She was acting out against her mother's prohibitions and was succeeding. Her father was asked to step in, but was too busy.

Now, at this point in our investigation, we can make an inference if we accept the concept of an unconscious that remains an active force in determining day-to-day behavior. Patricia identified with her loving mother throughout her preadolescent life, so she agreed with her mother's view that she was misbehaving in the high school years. She was behaving as other girls but, nonetheless, felt guilty about it. If her parents had set firmer limits, she would have been angry—but would have had no reason to feel guilty. The guilt was repressed into her unconscious mind but has resurfaced ten years later in behavior that provokes anger in her husband and results in punishment and in her feeling that "I guess I deserve it." Her husband's punishment, however, is in response to some current statement or behavior. If she acts seductively toward him, he is reminded of her "tainted" past and becomes angry. Therefore, her guilt isn't relieved but, rather, remains as an unconscious millstone about her neck.

If we don't accept the concept of an unconscious and are forced, instead, into another formulation, we are left with some rather unsatisfactory explanations. In fact, we would have no understanding of Patricia other than, according to John, as a liar and a cheat; in that case we might "understand" John's abusive behavior, though of course we would not condone it. Alternately, we could disregard her altogether and try to get John to find another socially acceptable outlet for his supposedly innate anger. Our treatment, then, would be rather superficial and ungratifying, since, most certainly, it would fail.

The concept of the unconscious is very useful as we attempt to understand human behavior and is necessary in formulating a meaningful individual treatment plan. Intrapsychic conflicts would rarely exist to any significant extent if all behavior were based on secondary process thinking, unaffected by the unconscious. At most we would debate issues, such as whether or not we want to buy this or that and whether or not we love this person well enough to marry. Most of the time, all decisions would be logical and carefully thought out; the world would be run by the best and the brightest. The very fact that this is not the case can be viewed as evidence of both unconscious drives that motivate some and unconscious inhibitions that restrain others. These forces contribute to our varied personalities and human idiosyncrasies.

COMMON INTRAPSYCHIC CONFLICTS

Erik Erikson described the entire life cycle in terms of conflicts: trust versus mistrust in early infancy, autonomy versus shame and doubt in early childhood, initiative versus guilt in the later preschool years, industry versus inferiority in the elementary school years, and identity versus role diffusion in adolescence, to list those pertinent to the period in which we are interested (see chapters 1-3). For the present discussion, we will concentrate on conflicts in just three areas; an appreciation of these areas will facilitate our understanding of the behavior of children and adolescents. In fact, the concepts are fundamental to clinical child psychiatry.

Dependence Versus Independence

Everyone makes the shift from the total dependence of the newborn to the relative independence of adulthood. But rarely is this developmental process accomplished without some degree of conflict. It is more difficult for males, perhaps, because of sociocultural expectations that boys shouldn't cry but, instead, should be brave, stalwart defenders of the peace. Girls may, on the other hand, remain rather dependent throughout life, without too much difficulty. However, these culturally determined sex roles are changing, thereby allowing us to discuss conflict in this area without regard to sex.

It seems as if children strive for independence from the time they begin to walk. They wander farther and farther from their nurturing parents, returning frequently for comfort and reassurance. The process falters with the idea of staying away from home overnight and, perhaps, at the beginning of school, but it gathers momentum once again as adolescence approaches. The need to behave independently is augmented by peer pressure, additional social expectations, and cultural norms. Rites of puberty and religious values contribute to the acceleration of the drive for independence that becomes so obvious in adolescence. One is expected to leave home in late adolescence and to be capable of independent living. But what happens to the opposite need: to remain dependent on others? Does it simply cease to exist, or is it lurking somewhere in the unconscious mind?

In most cases the defense mechanisms of repression and suppression are used to push these "infantile or childish needs" into the unconscious. Some persons make a very conscious effort to hide the desire to be cared for (suppression); in others, the mechanism itself is quite unconscious (repression). Sometimes, reaction formation is the operative mechanism; the wish to be dependent is not only denied but, rather, is expressed as the opposite desire—in this case, a rather dramatic or inappropriate display of independence.

Conflict arises when largely unconscious dependency needs seek expression but are blocked by the socioculturally determined need to behave in an independent autonomous manner: A 7-year-old who has been developing very nicely expresses some concern when his parents tell him of their planned evening away from home. "I'm still just a little boy," he pleads. The typical adult with a conflict in this area is the producer of a Broadway play who watches the rehearsal while drinking a glass of milk. Outwardly, he is very independent and quite ready to make all necessary decisions regarding the play, decisions upon which many careers may rest. Inwardly, however (ie, unconsciously), he would rather be a little boy, taken care of instead of having to care for others. The conflict contributes to the development of a peptic ulcer; hence the glass of milk.

A large number of adults have conflicts in this area. Dependency needs, ordinarily suppressed, become quite apparent during illness. The sick role allows strong, independent persons to assume a dependent position, with tender care provided by family members, nurses, and doctors. People who drink a lot, overfeed themselves, and indulge themselves in other ways are essentially responding to their desire for succor.

In children we see many instances of normal conflicts in dependence-independence; the 7-year-old described above is but one example. Symptoms of a more intense conflict requiring clinical attention are seen in the separation anxiety commonly identified by the convenient misnomer, school phobia. Here the child, often in the third or fourth grade, feels a strong need for reassurance that his parents are alright and available to him, while, at the same time, knowing he should be in school. The conflict results in loss of concentration, headaches, stomachaches, and sometimes, in vomiting (see chapter 6). Chronically ill children whose progress toward independence has been repeatedly hampered by hospitalization may appear to be very dependent, while consistently demanding autonomy.

Adolescence is, by its very nature, the period in which this type of conflict exists—quite overtly, in fact, since the achievement of independence from family is a major developmental goal. The trap that parents are forever falling into—and it happens to professionals, as well, if they aren't careful—is to assume that this overt drive for independence is conflict-free. It must be remembered that, like the 7-year-old, adolescents are still children. They demand freedom, but need caring, guidance, and limits. The task is to provide the structure in a benevolent, understanding manner, while giving due recognition to each new step toward independence. Do not force independence as one mother did when saying good-bye as her son left on his first date, "Have a good time and keep your zipper up." The poor kid was already scared and had given no thought to sexuality, prior to his mother's implication.

Oedipal Conflict

Oedipal conflict is also ubiquitous, even though it sounds somewhat farfetched at first. Freud chose the term to designate a son's feeling of love toward his mother and jealousy and hate toward his father, although, as we shall soon see, these were not the emotions that motivated Oedipus.

In Greek mythology, Laius, king of Thebes, was warned by an oracle that his son would slay him. Therefore, when his son was born, he exposed the baby on Mount Cithaeron, first pinning his ankles together (hence the name Oedipus, meaning "swell-foot"). Found by a shepherd, the infant was adopted by King Polybus of Corinth and his wife. In early manhood Oedipus visited Delphi and, upon learning that he was fated to kill his father and marry his mother, resolved never to return to Corinth; he believed his adoptive parents were his biological parents.

While traveling toward Thebes, Oedipus encountered Laius, who provoked a quarrel in which Oedipus killed him. Continuing on his way, Oedipus found Thebes plagued by the Sphinx who put a riddle to all passersby and destroyed those who could not answer. Oedipus solved the riddle and the Sphinx killed herself. As a reward, Oedipus was made king of Thebes and married the widowed queen, Jocasta (who was, in fact, his biological mother); they had four children. When the truth of the relationship became known, Jocasta killed herself and Oedipus went into exile.

The psychoanalytic movement contributed to our understanding of child development by pointing out the normal desire of the 3- to 5-year-old child for sexual involvement with the parent of the opposite sex and a concomitant sense of rivalry with the parent of the same sex. This stage is ordinarily resolved when the child identifies with the parent of the same sex. Strictly speaking, the Oedipus complex, as the normal situation is called, doesn't cause any conflict in the child's mind. But when some traumatic event takes place, as, for example, a divorce, in which a boy loses his father and has his mother to himself, he may develop a serious intrapsychic conflict. He may feel he has caused the marital problem, and, indeed, may well have contributed to it by his very presence. The absence of his father makes it hard to resolve the issue, since identification with the father is necessary for resolution. (Although "Electra complex" is sometimes used as the designation of the comparable situation for girls, usually the term "Oedipus complex" is applied to both sexes.)

Other events that disrupt the normal resolution of the Oedipus complex are physical illnesses or death of a parent, significant arguments between parents, and, of course, actual sexual stimulation and abuse of the child. Little children can be very seductive to the parent of the opposite sex and thereby contribute to an overt incestuous act. When they discover society's prohibition, children often suffer the consequence, a conflict of serious proportions.

Passive-Aggressive Conflicts

Aggression presents the third major conflict with which children must deal. As one might imagine, it is closely related to the achievement of independence and to sexuality, as well. There is considerable evidence that aggression is at least partly genetically determined and more prominent in boys than girls. However, this trait is modified by experience: child rearing practices, sociocultural norms, and religious tenets shape aggressive drives, forcing repression or sublimation. An infant boy ever so slightly larger than his peers will stimulate a surprisingly large number of sexist comments like, "He looks like a future football player," or "I'll bet he's all boy," or "Nobody will mistake him for a girl." The type of toys available on the market and presented to children by family and friends and, of course, the exposure to violence on television and in the movies will play a role in shaping behavior. But it's the parental attitudes and their moral and religious beliefs that determine, to a large extent, how much innate aggressiveness is allowed to emerge.

Considering all the conflicting forces that impinge on the child, it should be clear that the development of an unambiguous attitude toward aggression cannot be taken for granted. The superego, or conscience, is the product of the many prohibitions introjected by the child (see chapter 2). Identification with attributes of those persons the child admires or envies also contributes to its development.

A guiding principle of good parenting is the establishment of a home environment that is as clear and consistent, in terms of right and wrong, as possible. Perfection is an unattainable goal, but we should strive for consistency if we want our children to develop conflict-free attitudes about aggression. Unfortunately, we ourselves often have conflicts in this area—a situation that leads to many double standards. What message is transmitted when parents whom the child admires are overheard discussing how they plan to defraud the government of some tax money? What happens when the parents laugh at television violence or overlook a child's obvious cheating in a card game? How many parents teach that "a foul is a foul only if the referee sees it"? The superego develops with some gaps in it, and the inner restrictions are no longer imperatives. Stealing is not stealing if the amount is small or if the victim is wealthy or a big corporation. For example, a father who services vending machines always comes home with a satchel full of coins and fully expects his 9-year-old son to "snitch" a few nickles or dimes every now and then.

It is understandable from the foregoing that some children learn to be aggressive in socially acceptable ways, either through the unconscious mechanism of sublimation or through a learning process. The child may develop a passive-aggressive personality disorder in which aggression is expressed in a passive way; the person agrees to do as he is told but drags his feet, making it clear that he has no intention of doing it. Bureaucracies are full of such persons. (The reader would do well at this point to read chapter 13, Conduct Disorders.)

IDIOSYNCRATIC CONFLICTS

Thus far we have discussed three common sources of intrapsychic conflict. In this section we will be more specific and deal with the individual complexities that cause so many emotional disturbances.

What happens when a young couple has four children of the same sex, despite their wish for at least one of the opposite sex?

Ordinarily the wish is denied and an adequate adjustment accomplished. But in some cases, one or both parents may not resolve the conflict and may continue to harbor dissatisfaction in a way that is subtly apparent to the child, though not readily apparent to others. As the child grows, let's say it's a boy, he introjects many attitudes and feelings of the parents he loves. One of them is the sense of being somehow incomplete or unsatisfying to others. It is quite possible that this introjection remains with him into adulthood and is manifest by his own dissatisfaction with his achievements. He may earn very high marks in high school or college, while feeling discontented and striving for perfection. It is one thing to want to do well, but quite another when the motivation stems from a lifelong dissatisfaction with oneself. This is an example of an internal conflict that is specific to the person. Even though similar circumstances may occur in other families, they will never be precisely the same. Therefore, it is necessary to evaluate each patient individually.

A conflict may develop very abruptly:

> A young adolescent girl who never had a strong relationship with her father was hurt significantly when he falsely accused her of something. She had a sudden impulse to kick him in the face as a karate expert might do, but had always been taught to respect her elders. The conflict, to kick or not to kick, was resolved by the sudden onset of a paralysis of her leg.

The girl's anxiety was *converted*, another defense mechanism, to a somatic symptom. Cure of her paralysis will occur when she acknowledges the unacceptable impulse as her own, or when she represses or suppresses it once again and finds some "face-saving" explanation for the paralysis.

One final example should suffice:

> An attractive 9-year-old girl was referred by her pediatrician because she had lost both her appetite and 25 pounds. She was able to explain on the first visit that she wanted a sister to play with, but was well aware of the fact that her mother had had an operation (ie, a hysterectomy) and could not have any more babies. She thought that if she wished hard enough, she could have a baby for her mother. This presented a problem. On the one hand she believed in wishes and would truly like to have a sister; on the other hand, she was afraid to have a baby and didn't know how to go about it. If she shared her dilemma with her parents, they would probably reassure her that little girls cannot have babies.

> Unfortunately, she had read in her *Weekly Reader* at school that a girl of 5 in a South American country had given birth to a normal child; she was confused, though her belief that wishes come true was not very strong. (Incidentally, there are a number of cases on record of babies born to very young girls.) Her fantasy suddenly appeared realistic. Her knowledge of pregnancy was limited to "the baby grows in the mother's tummy," so the logical conclusion was that "the seed" enters through the mouth. In order to avoid pregnancy, she had to avoid eating.

The conflict of this 9-year-old is obvious, and its expression as a loss of appetite equally apparent and understandable. The solution in this case was quite simple: the youngster was taught the elements of reproductive physiology by the therapist, while her mother reviewed the subject with her daily for a week. The girl's appetite improved gradually and she regained her weight in a month.

SUMMARY

Much of this chapter has dealt with the concept of the unconscious. Conflicts between conscious prohibitions and forbidden wishes that have been pressed into the unconscious often result in intraphysic conflicts that are manifested in psychological or physical symptoms. An understanding of this concept leads to an understanding of otherwise puzzling behavior.

Three very common conflictual areas, dependency, sexuality, and aggression were described. In order to avoid the impression that all children go through the same problems in the course of growing up, a section was devoted to very specific individualized conflicts. Since both common and idiosyncratic conflicts occur in the same child, careful evaluation of each patient is necessary to understand the complex set of psychodynamics that brings the child to our attention.

Chapter 9

STRESS AND COPING

R. DEAN CODDINGTON, MD

In this chapter the child's repertoire for dealing with change will be addressed. The goal is to help the reader distinguish between an adjustment disorder per se and all other situations in which the child's adjustment to a stressor plays an integral part but is not the primary problem. A system for evaluating the stressfulness in a child's environment will be presented, as an aid to arriving at an accurate diagnosis.

Emphasized throughout the chapter will be the role of understanding and support in the prevention of illness subsequent to environmental stress.

CHANGE

Environmental changes are necessary for normal growth and development. Every baby needs a changing, stimulating atmosphere in order to thrive. Young children love to learn new things. They may be reticent at first but, with time, usually try a new activity or explore a new environment. Adolescents commonly accept novelty as a challenge and appear to their parents to take undue risks. Adults, too, like variation in their lives. A certain amount of change makes life interesting, enhances learning, and promotes psychological development. But we also know that too much change is detrimental and disruptive. How much is too much?

Stress is a very popular word these days and its popularity leads to its use in a variety of ways. It is most accurate to use the word "stressor" to indicate any external or internal stimulus which activates psychological or physiological coping mechanisms. Stress is the result of unsuccessful coping. So when does a stimulating change become a stressor? Obviously, this varies from individual to individual, because we vary in our ability to cope. Learning to fly a light plane will be exciting and exhilarating to one person, but very stressful to one who has poor eye-hand coordination.

Because children are at different developmental levels, they vary immensely in their coping ability. A 10-year-old can deal with a family event that would cause considerable stress in his 5-year-old brother. As we saw in chapter 7 in the discussion of depression in infants, loss of the mother during infancy can be disasterous, even fatal; although very stressful in older children, the death is not as devastating as when it occurs earlier. Still later, as the child matures into adulthood and the mother becomes aged, the loss can be handled through the normal grieving process.

Past experience, too, is exceedingly important in determining a child's ability to cope with a particular event. One 15-year-old girl, who had learned to cope with movement from one foster home to another without undue stress, was overwhelmed when she received two offers of a permanent home: a request for adoption by her foster parents and a proposal of marriage. She had never lived in a permanent home, so these positive and flattering possibilities became stressors. Another example of the importance of past experience is the easy transition from home to kindergarten for children who experienced a normal separation-individuation process as 2-year-olds (for an explanation of separation-individuation, the reader is referred to chapter 19). Children without healthy experiences during this phase may suffer from separation anxiety when they enter school (see chapter 6). The anxiety is a signal that stress is occurring.

Anticipation is another significant factor contributing to the determination of whether or not an event is a stressor. The loss of a child—whatever the cause of death—is tragic. But if the death follows a lingering illness such as leukemia where the eventual outcome is anticipated, the death itself is anticlimactic. It was the earlier diagnosis and the acute relapses that were so stressful; death may come as a welcome relief for both the child and his parents. Indeed, the parents tend to go through a grieving process prior to the actual death. A less controversial example is family relocation because of a job change. If there has been time to adjust, to get used to the idea, to say "good-bye" to friends, and to visit the new locale, the event—when it actually occurs—may not be much of a stressor. There has been time to "work through" the family relocation.

This introduces another contributing factor: significant others. It is probable that the most salient factor in coping with stressors is the support of loved ones, friends, relatives, and neighbors. Very often it is their influence that determines whether or not stress will result. Associated with this is the concept of *neutralizing events*, which balance things a bit. A death in the family is less stressful if friends offer their support. Likewise a death may be less stressful if the birth of a new family member is soon forthcoming. The baby cannot replace the deceased, but can help in the adjustment to the loss.

The child's ability to adjust to the slings and arrows of everyday life is of paramount importance in determining whether an event is a growth-promoting, learning experience or a stressor. If the adjustment can be made with ease, we can probably conclude that stress did not occur. But certain events always cause stress, eg, the death of a loved one. Therefore, the event is a stressor, and the efficiency with which the child can cope with the ensuing stress determines the eventual outcome. The outcome may be an enhancement of psychological growth, but it may also be a physical or mental illness.

INVULNERABLE CHILDREN

Many adults seem to remain surprisingly free of illness; 25% of the adult population account for 50% of all illness. Illness among children is more evenly distributed, but it still seems that some children are invulnerable to the effects of stressors. Though this is an area that has not been investigated extensively, we are tempted, nevertheless, to speculate as to the reasons for this phenomenon.

The endocrine system of some people may operate more efficiently, so that adrenalin and noradrenalin levels, associated as they are with anxiety, rise less in response to a stressor. This could result in a lower level of subjective stress. It is also known that the autonomic nervous system is less reactive in some individuals, a distinction that has been found in infants, children, and adults. The immunologic system is responsive to environmental stressors, too, perhaps accounting for the high mortality of institutionalized infants described by Spitz (see chapter 7).

Though these biological variations do exist, it is likely that early experience has the greatest impact on the individual's coping ability. If so, some thought should be given to enhancing the child's natural ability through a well-planned educational program. There has been almost no research in this area, so our comments are purely speculative.

Statistics tell us that 45% of the babies born this year will experience the divorce of their parents before they reach the age of 18. This large percentage, if accurate, poses an interesting question: should we attempt to immunize children, as well as we can, against the effects of this stressor? Again, we know that children who have experienced a healthy separation-individuation phase as 2-year-olds separate more easily when it's time to enter school. Can we establish some additional process that would enhance their ability to tolerate the prolonged dislocation of a parent through divorce? Can we teach children some sort of problem-solving techniques that would stand them in good stead, should divorce become imminent? Can we enable them to cope with a father who travels frequently on business? Can we help them tolerate loneliness or mild depression? In short, can we prevent the onset of an adjustment disorder?

ADJUSTMENT DISORDERS

An adjustment disorder is defined as the presence of a maladaptive reaction to an identifiable psychosocial stressor. The maladaptive reaction must begin within three months after the stressor and is, of course, a sign that stress has occurred. This reaction must exceed what one would judge to be a normal reaction to the stressor, and the overall symptomatology must not meet the criteria for any other diagnosis.

We spoke earlier of coping with a stressor as a problem-solving activity. If the reaction to the stressor is growth promoting, it is an adaptive reaction. Sometimes the activity brought into play to deal with the stressor has deleterious side effects which outweigh any advantages it might have. We would then consider the reaction maladaptive. For instance, a child trying to cope with a marked increase in the frequency and intensity of arguments between his parents may become withdrawn, shutting out the stressful sound of the arguments. In and of itself, this reaction would be adaptive; but when this withdrawal includes distancing himself from friends and teachers, the child loses possible sources of support. His school grades plummet. The reaction is clearly maladaptive, yet no diagnosis other than adjustment disorder seems appropriate.

Care must be taken to avoid ascribing an unwarranted association between a stressor and the onset of symptoms. People tend to recall specific events more clearly than they do some less dramatic occurrences and tend to blame problems that occur later on the more memorable events. This pitfall in history taking happens more often when several months have passed. We've all heard people say, "I never had trouble like this until I left Indiana; it must be the water, or the weather, or. . . ." They can tell you exactly when they left Indiana and they don't recall the symptom being present before that, but it may very well have been there, though nonstressful because of the support of family members living nearby. In chapter 6, the fact that separation anxiety was formerly termed school phobia is another example of how we tend to make this kind of error. The child seems to be avoiding school and may implicate one or more events as the reason for the phobia. But, as was emphasized in that discussion, the child's anxiety is due, in fact, to the separation from mother. This is a case in which an inability to identify the true cause of a reaction leads a person to grasp at straws and to implicate an event that was either not a stressor or of little significance.

It has been shown that many physical and mental illnesses follow some identifiable stressor, although the association may not be recognized for several months. Stressors seem to play a causal role in infectious disease, chest pain, burns, accidental poisoning, speech problems, and behavioral problems in young children, and with academic problems, peptic ulcer, and juvenile rheumatoid arthritis in older children and adolescents. Also in adolescents, stressors have been implicated as contributing factors in psychiatric hospitalization, suicide, delinquency, substance abuse, automobile accidents, pregnancy, and football injuries. Psychosocial stressors may play a role in many other diseases, including cancer, but investigation in these areas has not yet been carried out in sufficient detail to report.

The point we want to make here is that the recognition of early signs of stress may facilitate an intervention that will help the child to cope and, thereby, prevent the development of pathology. One could keep track of those psychosocial stressors that commonly impinge on the lives of children and could then anticipate the need for support, even before any sign of stress occurs.

Using the Life Event Scales described below, parents could monitor stressors just as they do their child's weight, height, and general health.

LIFE EVENT SCALES

The Life Event Scale for Children (LES–C) is reproduced in Figure 9–1 and the adolescents' scale (LES–A) in Figure 9–2. These have been developed by the author over the past ten years and represent an attempt to quantify the stressfulness of events. Fortunately, some of the events are rare; in contrast, others are very common. In a study of fourth-grade, inner-city children, it was shown that almost 90% of all the events that occurred during an entire year were included in the LES–C. Thus, by allowing the addition of a few unlisted events, we can be rather confident that a fairly complete accounting of stressors is made.

The first 17 items on both scales are familial events over which the child has little or no control. The remaining events are more typical of the different age groups, and the child has some control over many of them. The scoring system is straightforward; Figure 9–3 is a reproduction of the reverse side of the actual scales. (If the reader is interested in how the scales evolved, he can read the second citation in the "Bibliography" at the end of the chapter.)

It would take very little time for a family to record the events that occurred over a three-month period; over a period of time, the family would then have a running record of each child's life event score. Any child with a score higher than those shown on the table in Figure 9–3 is coping with stressors sufficiently powerful to produce stress in many—perhaps most—children. A little support here may go a long way toward preventing further disease and may even turn a threat into a profitable experience.

Figure 9-1

LIFE EVENT SCALE - CHILDREN (Age 6 through 11)

NAME:____________________ DATE:_______ AGE: ___ SEX:___ RACE:___

INSTRUCTIONS: 1. If any of the events listed below occurred in the PAST 12 MONTHS, write the weight in the correct column on the right.	WEIGHT	SUMMER June July Aug.	FALL Sept. Oct. Nov.	WINTER Dec. Jan. Feb.	SPRING Mar. April May
The death of a parent	109				
The death of a brother or sister	86				
Divorce of your parents	73				
Marital separation of your parents	66				
The death of a grandparent	56				
Hospitalization of a parent	52				
Remarriage of a parent to a step parent	53				
Birth of a brother or sister	50				
Hospitalization of a brother or sister	47				
Loss of a job by your father or mother	37				
Major increase in your parents' income	28				
Major decrease in your parents' income	29				
Start of a new problem between your parents	44				
End of a problem between your parents	27				
Change in father's job so he has less time at home	39				
A new adult moving into your home	41				
Mother beginning to work outside the home	40				
Beginning the first grade	20				
Move to a new school district	35				
Failing a grade in school	45				
Suspension from school	30				
Start of a new problem between you and your parents	43				
End of a problem between you and your parents	34				
Recognition for excelling in a sport or other activity	21				
Appearance in juvenile court	33				
Failing to achieve something you really want	28				
Becoming an adult member of a church	21				
Being invited to join a social orginzation	15				
Death of a pet	40				
Being hospitalized for illness or injury	53				
Death of a close friend	52				
Becoming involved with drugs	38				
Stopping the use of drugs	23				
Finding an adult who really respects you	20				
Outstanding personal achievement (special prize)	34				
2. List below any events that occured in the PAST 12 MONTHS but were not included in our list and place a check mark in the correct colums.					

Figure 9-2

LIFE EVENT SCALE - ADOLESCENTS (Age 12 and over)

NAME:________________________ DATE:________ AGE: ___ SEX:___ RACE:___

If any of the events listed below occurred in the PAST 12 MONTHS, write the weight in the correct column on the right.	WEIGHT	SUMMER June July Aug.	FALL Sept. Oct. Nov.	WINTER Dec. Jan. Feb.	SPRING Mar. April May
The death of a parent	108				
The death of a brother of sister	88				
Divorce of your parents	70				
Marital separation of your parents	62				
The death of a grandparent	52				
Hospitalization of a parent	52				
Remarriage of a parent to a step parent	51				
Birth of a brother or sister	50				
Hospitalization of a brother or sister	49				
Loss of a job by your father or mother	46				
Major increase in your parent' income	41				
Major decrease in your parent's income	43				
Start of a new problem between your parents	41				
End of a problem between your parents	30				
Change in father's job so he has less time at home	35				
A new adult moving into your home	34				
Mother beginning to work outside the home	28				
Being told you are very attractive by a friend	26				
Going on the first date of your life	42				
Finding a new dating partner	34				
Breaking up with boy/girl friend	39				
Being told to break up with a boy/girl friend	35				
Start of a new problem between you and your parents	43				
End of a problem between you and your parents	35				
Beginning the first year of senior high school	19				
Move to a new school district	41				
Failing a grade in school	47				
Suspension from school	34				
Graduating from high school	33				
Being accepted at the college of your choice	39				
Recognition for excelling in a sport or other activity	24				
Getting your first driver's license	32				
Being resonsible for an automoile accident	36				
Becoming an adult member of a church	25				
Being invited to join a social organization	18				
Being invited by a friend to break the law	21				
Appearance in a juvenile court	31				
Failing to achieve something you really wanted	32				
Getting a summer job	35				
Getting your first permanent job	40				
Deciding to leave home	41				
Being sent away from home	46				
Being hospitalized for illness or injury	50				
Death of a close friend	63				
Becoming involved with drugs	45				
Stopping the use of drugs	30				
Finding an adult who really respects you	22				
Getting pregnant or fathering a pregnancy	Boys 61, Girls 88				
Getting Married	78				
Outstanding personal achievement (special prize)	39				
Other events (describe and check column)					

Figure 9-3

SCORING INSTRUCTIONS:

1. If any events were added at the bottom of the page, a weight must be assigned. Use the weight assigned to some similar event on the list and place it in the appropriate column.

2. Three-month Scores are computed simply by adding the numbers in each column.

3. Six-month Scores must be adjusted to allow for the attenuation of the effect of events that occurred more than three months ago. To do so add the most recent Three-month Score to 75% of the next most recent Three-month Score.
   Example: A child participating in a study in mid January reported the following Three-month Scores: Summer 80, Fall 40, Winter 0, and Spring 50. The most recent Three-month Score is 40 and the next most recent 80. The Six-month Score is 40 + (75% of 80) = 40 + 60 = 100.

4. Nine-month Scores can be determined by adding 50% of the next most recent Three-month Score to the Six-month Score. In the above example this would be (50% of 50) since the study was carried out in January, added to 100. The Nine-month Score is 125.

5. One-year Scores are computed in the same way, adding 25% of the most distant Three-month Score, 0 in this example.

INTERPRETATION OF SCORES:

The table below can be used as a guide, the figures are not precise and may not be generalizable to other geographic locations. The majority of healthy children and adolescents will obtain scores below these figures. Higher scores seem to increase risk of behavioral symptomatology two to three fold.

Approximate upper limit scores for
seventy five percent of a young population

Length of Scoring Period

Age	Three Months	Six Months	Nine Months	Twelve Months
8 -10	50	95	110	110
11 -13	60	115	130	135
14 - 16	75	140	160	170
17 - 19	90	170	195	200

SUMMARY

The concept of environmental changes as stimuli to growth and to learning (and our need for such changes to make life interesting and exciting) was compared to the concept of psychosocial stressors. Factors that are important in determining whether a change will be a positive growth experience or a negative stressful event were considered. When the individual cannot cope with the stressor, stress is said to occur.

The appearance of stress was described first as a maladaptive reaction, then as an adjustment disorder, and finally as any of a number of physical or mental illnesses. With this in mind—ie, the fact that a maladaptive reaction precedes the onset of specific illnesses—the Life Event Scales were suggested as a simple way of keeping track of the stressors a child is facing, so that supportive intervention can be quick and effective.

BIBLIOGRAPHY

Caplan G: Mastery of stress: Psychosocial aspects. *Am J Psychiatry* 138:413-420, 1981

Coddington RD: Measuring the stressfulness of a child's environment, in Humphrey JH (ed): *Stress in Childhood.* New York, AMS Press, 1984

Henry JP, Stephens PM: *Stress, Health and the Social Environment: A Sociobiologic Approach to Medicine.* New York, Springer-Verlag, 1977

James D (ed): *Outward Bound.* London, Routledge & Kegan Paul, 1957

Swogger G Jr: Toward understanding stress: A map of the territory. *Journal of School Health* 51:29-35, 1981

Chapter 10

ALL GOD'S CHILDREN

R. DEAN CODDINGTON, MD

In chapter 6, we discussed anxiety as an emotion that is experienced by everyone at one time or another. It was described as a normal emotion that becomes problematic only when it exceeds in frequency or intensity the expected reaction to a given situation. In a similar vein, in the chapter that followed, depression was described as ubiquitous. In chapter 8, it was established that intrapsychic conflicts are the inevitable result of growing up in a superindustrial society in which values change almost daily. The stressors experienced by every child were discussed as causes of stress, and failure to adapt to change was presented as one cause of physical or mental illness—not the only cause, but a common one.

This chapter will enable the reader to look at the larger picture: an overview, if you will, of the prevalence of emotional disturbance in today's children. The delivery of psychiatric services will also be described, and some of the problems associated with the delivery system addressed. Finally, the need for professionals of all kinds will be presented.

PREVALENCE OF EMOTIONAL DISTURBANCE

Before discussing the epidemiology of psychiatric disorders, we must distinguish between the words "incidence" and "prevalence." Incidence refers to the number of new problems, or new cases, of a particular type, beginning during a defined period of time. Prevalence, on the other hand, includes all the cases that exist at any single point in time.

The title of this chapter and the theme that runs through the last four chapters suggest our contention that all children are subject to emotional disturbances at one time or another. The incidence of an anxiety attack at some time during childhood is 100%. It is difficult to conceive of a human being progressing from infancy through adolescence without trauma sufficient to interfere, at least temporarily, with psychosocial development. So what is the prevalence of emotional disturbance in any one sample of children?

In a study of fourth-grade children conducted by the author, teachers were asked to rate each child's behavior during each nine-week grading period of the school year. A full 42% of the 84 children were rated as behaving abnormally for at least one period; 27% had abnormal behavior for two or more periods. Moreover, among the remaining children showing no behavioral problems in the classroom, 10% had academic problems for one, but only one, grading period. Their success for three grading periods indicates sufficient intellectual capacity; presumably, their difficulty was due to temporary—probably emotional—factors. Thus, 43 of the 84 children, or 52% had some evidence of maladaptation during the year. These findings suggest the presence of much more suffering among children today than we usually anticipate or acknowledge. (The reader should understand that these children were *not* diagnosed as having specific psychiatric disorders, but were viewed by teachers as deviating from the norm.)

On the other hand, 50% of these children had no evidence of maladaptation during the year. Were they invulnerable, as suggested in chapter 9? Were they merely lucky? Or was some preventive force active? We think the latter is the case. We attribute the psychological well-being of most of our nation's young to the millions of understanding and supportive parents, the hundreds of thousands of knowledgeable and sensitive school teachers, and the untold numbers of other helpful adults who reach out to children every day.

No one really knows the true incidence of mental illness in children. In 1969, the Joint Commission on Mental Health of Children estimated that 10% of children were in need of some form of mental health assistance; in 1978, the President's Commission on Mental Health placed the figure at 15%. A survey of scientific studies concluded that the prevalence of clinical maladjustment among children in the United States was at least 11.8%. The 1980 census reported 62.3 million persons under the age of 18; this means, using the 11.8% estimate, that 7.3 million children are suffering from psychiatric disease or disability. We know that these children are not distributed evenly throughout the population. Children of emotionally disturbed or alcoholic parents, and children whose parents were deprived and abused as children, are at greater risk of developing psychiatric illness. Children without permanent homes (ie, foster children, children with only one parent, and those of divorced parents) are also at greater risk. And children in poor families living in high density housing developments also suffer more often.

THE SERVICE DELIVERY SYSTEM

Seven million children and adolescents constitute a very large group. In 1980, the Graduate Medical Education National Advisory Committee carried out a very extensive study of all medical specialties in an effort to determine national needs in the 1990s. Child psychiatry led the list of specialties that, at present production rates, will be most understaffed. There are only 4,000 child psychiatrists in the nation. The report recommended an increase to 9,000 child psychiatrists. But even this number, and there is no chance of achieving this goal, could not possibly accommodate 7.3 million children; there would be 800 children for each psychiatrist. One child psychiatrist cannot care for one tenth of this number, working full time in either hospital or office. There is a very obvious need for other professionals and paraprofessionals, and it goes without saying that these persons must work in close collaboration with one another. All too often, the working relationship leaves much to be desired. There are, of course, some controversial issues and technical matters over which those from different disciplines and varying schools of thought will argue. This kind of disagreement is healthy in the long run, but can also be destructive. Unfortunately, the lack of cooperation is due most often to personal differences, personality conflicts, and territorial disputes.

With 7.3 million children in need of professional (or paraprofessional) help, we can't afford the manpower waste resulting from such pettiness. Perhaps it is only human and we should learn to accept it. But pettiness is very frustrating—a stressor, indeed. This problem must be resolved in a way that enables us to provide the maximum amount of service at the least cost, without any loss of quality.

Residential Programs

We need intensive treatment programs for severely disturbed children in which the therapeutic efforts of personnel from various disciplines are brought to bear in an organized, noncompetitive manner. There is no room for territorial disputes within residential programs. A psychiatric hospital without a strong educational and occupational therapy program is not only inadequate, but also inconceivable. The patient, step-by-step educational principles of teachers meld well with the behavior modification procedures developed by psychologists. Adaptive physical education complements the expertise of occupational and physical therapists, who have gained an understanding of the importance of motoric coordination and vestibular function. And the neurological orientation of the occupational therapist fits well with the medical orientation of the speech pathologist, physician, and nurse. Any of these professionals can effectively aid a child with an isolated problem in his particular field but, as we shall see, many problems are complex and require the combined efforts of many.

There are two reasons why a team approach is needed in the treatment of seriously disturbed children: (1) No one has the ability to develop and carry out a rational treatment plan by himself; he needs the expertise of other professionals. (2) Working with the complex problems of seriously disturbed children is both demanding and emotionally draining; a team is necessary to provide mutual support to its members. A special education teacher would have great difficulty spending more than a few hours in a classroom with six to eight emotionally disturbed children without a teacher's aide by her side. Just as parents of normal children need respite at times and need to commiserate together at other times, a teacher needs an aide. The most competent psychiatrist or nurse needs to feel his or her work is appreciated by other members of the team. Acknowledgement from above is fine as long as it's an informed, and not a gratuitous, compliment. However, a simple statement of respect from an aide, based on some observed behavior, may be far more important.

Nonresidential Programs

At the other end of the spectrum, the mildly ill child rarely requires the help of the child psychiatrist, but may need to consult another professional or a paraprofessional. How do we distinguish between professional and paraprofessional? Our view—and the reader should recall that one editor is a child psychiatrist (RDC) and the other an early childhood special educator (MMW)—is that these terms are relative. The school teacher is just as much a professional in the school environment as the child psychiatrist is in his, but the teacher would be considered a paraprofessional in a strict medical environment. Of course, one can be a very professional psych aide or teacher's aide; it's the attitude and behavior that count. In dealing with the mildly ill child in a professional manner, there are two pitfalls that should be avoided: premature reassurance and exceeding one's capability.

Premature reassurance. Many problems cease to exist in due time. But an appropriate and timely intervention may cause it to disappear sooner. We should not conclude that help is not indicated simply on the basis that the disorder is self-limited: chicken pox will go away by itself, too; a broken leg will heal without treatment, but it may be crooked. An attempt to be reassuring is probably the most widely practiced error in the field of child mental health care. It's fine to be empathic and supportive, but to pat a youngster on the back and tell him that everything will work out, when you have no particular reason to think it will, is not therapeutic. It is much better to listen carefully and to try to understand. Just because we may have had similar experiences that resolved themselves is no reason to feel the situation will work out similarly again. Every child's problem is unique!

As a case in point, think about a child who is about to enter the hospital to have his tonsils removed. He may have had a lot of sore throats but always recovered, and right now has no trouble at all. Do we reassure him that everything will be alright and that he'll be asleep when they take him to the operating room? That's okay if we *know* it to be true. But we don't! In fact, we know this is not exactly the way things will be, and we know he'll have a very sore throat after the surgery.

A better plan would be to describe every possible detail, about a week in advance. Teach the child what the reality will be and give him a chance to adjust a little each day. One pediatrician kept a surgeon's cap and mask in his drawer so that he could show children what the surgeon would look like in the operating room (Figure 10-1). An anesthesia mask was also used as a teaching device. An approach such as this can be a very effective preventative.

Exceeding one's capability. This phrase must not be confused with territoriality. We don't mean to suggest that one professional should never stray across his disciplinary boundary. Rather, we recognize that everyone has limitations. We should do our best to learn what they are and either accept them or find a way to correct them. It's no disgrace to find that you get overinvolved with certain children and are no longer able to maintain your objectivity. There is nothing wrong with being frightened of psychotic children or feeling uncomfortable talking with an adolescent about sex. Take note of the situations that make you anxious as a way of learning more about yourself. The true professional will acknowledge his or her limitations and either ask for an appropriate consultation or refer the child elsewhere.

SUMMARY

We have tried to make a single point in this discussion, namely, that emotional disturbances affect a great many children who need the help of all of us. No profession has a corner on the market. Every paraprofessional who behaves in a professional manner is very much needed.

Chapter 11

MENTAL RETARDATION

R. Dean Coddington, MD
Mollie M. Wallick, PhD

The American Association on Mental Deficiency (AAMD) uses the term " mental retardation" (MR) to refer to significantly subaverage general intellectual functioning originating during the developmental period and associated with impaired adaptive behavior. It is not possible to deal here with the whole field of mental retardation; instead, we must confine ourselves to the interface between child psychiatry and the more traditional area of mental subnormality. We will discuss the assessment of intelligence from a clinical point of view and, in a section on causation, will point out the many postnatal variables that influence intellectual functioning. Several suggestions for further reading at the end of the chapter contain concise information regarding the biological causes of mental retardation.

The objective here is to lead the reader to a better understanding of children with intellectual deficits and, consequently, toward a therapeutic posture.

> A thoughtful high school graduate working in the gift shop at a bus terminal noticed that a group of deaf children returned every Friday afternoon following a week in a special school. She decided to help them make phone calls to their families and worked out a contract with them: She would make a call if the child taught her one "sign." In addition, she kept a book on sign language beneath the cash register to study when time permitted.

Commendable initiative such as this should be encouraged among those who have contact with handicapped children. Retarded children, in particular, need all the help they can get.

ASSESSMENT

Intelligence is most precisely assessed via an appropriate standardized test, administered individually by a psychologist under optimum conditions. There are two fundamental reasons for using psychologists: (1) They receive very careful professional training in accurate test administration. (2) Perhaps more important, they begin with a clinical evaluation of the child and are therefore able to interpret test results in light of the child's comfort, interest, motivation, and cooperation. It is the integration of test results and clinical observation that makes the psychological report so valuable. What we really want to know is whether or not the child is doing as well as he can and, if he is, whether or not the performance is as good as that expected of children his age. It is detrimental to conclude that a child has intellectual limitations simply because he is not measuring up to expectations at a particular point in time.

Upon receiving a psychological report, it makes sense to read first the section that describes the child's behavior during the test procedure. Then the reader should consider the section, usually at the very end, that refers to the child's potential. Having considered the child's basic intellectual capacity, the reader would then turn his attention to the variation in subtest scores, particularly between the aggregate of verbal and performance subtests. This may lead to a better understanding of the child's intellectual performance.

Intelligence Tests

The notion of "mental age" (MA) was introduced in 1908 by Binet as a measure of a child's intellectual development. A specific MA expresses the average intellectual attainment of children of that chronological age (CA). In 1916, Terman introduced the concept of the "intelligence quotient" (IQ), obtained by dividing an individual's MA by his CA and multiplying the quotient by 100. Such an IQ is known technically as a "ratio IQ," since it expresses the ratio of MA to CA.

The most frequently used individual tests for assessing the intellectual development of children are the Stanford-Binet Intelligence Scale (S–B), the Wechsler Preschool and Primary Scale of Intelligence (WPPSI), and the Revised Wechsler Intelligence Scale for Children (WISC–R). These popular tests have bypassed the ratio IQ in favor of the more sophisticated "deviation IQ," introduced by Wechsler in 1944. The deviation IQ is a standard score in which the obtained IQs are converted to a normal distribution with a mean of 100 and the same standard deviation at every age. (The Wechsler scales employ a standard deviation of 15, while the

S-B uses a standard deviation of 16.) Compared to the ratio IQ, the deviation IQ has more stability over time; also, the latter score can be converted easily to a percentile rank.

Significantly subaverage intellectual functioning is demonstrated by an IQ score more than two standard deviations below the mean of the particular test used—or less than 70 on the Weschler scales. But motivational aspects of the testing situation must be considered, along with the child's interest and cooperation. Also, since any measurement is fallible, an IQ score is generally thought to involve an error of measurement of about five points. Therefore, an IQ of 70 may be interpreted as representing a range of from 65 to 75. Treating the IQ with this flexibility permits exclusion from the mental retardation category of individuals with IQs somewhat below 70 if the clinical picture indicates good adaptive behavior and, therefore, the need for a different approach.

It should also be recognized that an IQ assessment at an early age is not necessarily predictive. Studies have shown that the correlation between intelligence scores obtained at age 5 years and those obtained at age 18 in the same children is between 0.5 and 0.7, an association that is only slightly better than chance alone. The correlation is even less for younger children and only rises to a respectable level of 0.8 or more after age 10. We must be very cautious about jumping to conclusions when interpreting test results.

Other Developmental Tests

Many other tests have been devised to measure some aspect of a child's developmental progress. One reference on the subject lists 57 intelligence tests and 54 developmental tests! The Goodenough-Harris Drawing Test is generally nonthreatening and appealing, and is especially easy to administer and to score; a measure of intellectual maturity, it indicates development in the areas of self-perception and body concept. Also critical to an understanding of the retarded child are achievement testing, personality evaluation, and investigation of perceptual and motor difficulties.

Useful in dealing with human variation are other concepts analagous to MA and IQ. In his infant-assessment scale, Gesell used the ratio concept of "developmental quotient." Bayley employed a deviation quotient to report an infant's "mental development index" and "psychomotor development index." In a developmental approach to the assessment of adaptive behavior, Doll used the concepts of "social age" and "social quotient." In interpreting these analagous scores, one should guard against equating them with MA and IQ, which have intellectual behavior as their exclusive domain.

Test of Adaptive Behavior

In addition to documented subaverage intelligence, the reader will recall that the diagnosis of mental retardation requires the presence of some impairment in adaptive behavior. This refers to the child's ability to meet the standards of personal care and social responsibility expected for his age and sociocultural environment. Several scales are now available to measure social competence, with the leader in quality at this time being the AAMD Adaptive Behavior Scales. Among other scales standardized originally on normal subjects are the Alpern-Boll Developmental Profile and Doll's Vineland Social Maturity Scale. None of the scales is considered more reliable or valid than the astute judgment of a well-trained psychodiagnostician. A street-wise kid may score very poorly on verbal tests but have no adaptive impairment; his IQ of 65 would not justify the diagnosis of mental retardation. The correlation between IQ score and adaptive behavior is stronger in the lower ranges of retardation: It would be unusual to find a child with an IQ of less than 55 without a corresponding deficit in adaptation.

It should be recognized that the psychologist's opinion is based on observations made over a short period of time and in a specific setting which may or may not be conducive to the child's best performance; it is, then, but a cross section of behavior. Therefore, your clinical judgment as teacher or therapist is needed, as well. Your contact is far more frequent and may take place in several settings. You may know that a particular boy loves to work jigsaw puzzles, that he enjoys learning new games, and that he learns both puzzles and games quickly. If, for some reason, the boy has poor language skills, you would expect his performance IQ to be higher than his verbal IQ. In other words, his ability to learn in school may be impeded by his depressed verbal skills, perhaps warranting the functional diagnosis of mild mental retardation. Moreover, your observations may suggest the most propitious place at which to start a treatment program is in an area in which the child has some interest and is likely to succeed. Successful experiences are by far the most effective educational tools.

The Degree of Retardation

The term "borderline intellectual functioning" is applied when the IQ is between 70 and 84—that is, between one and two standard deviations below the mean. Of the entire population, 15% are represented in this category; 3% are more severely retarded and 82% more intelligent. Persons with borderline functioning are *not* considered retarded, but may benefit from psychiatric and special educational intervention.

"Mild mental retardation" is a construct delimiting those persons with IQs from 50 through 69; included are about 2.5% of the general population and 80% of the mentally retarded. Mildly retarded children can be educated to about a sixth-grade level, though this may not be achieved before midadolescence. There is usually no evidence of brain pathology in this group and no associated physical handicaps or congenital malformations. The children look normal and often come from impoverished families with other mildly retarded persons (hence the early term "cultural-familial retardation," now more often referred to as "mental retardation due to psychosocial disadvantage"). Because of these factors, the retardation often goes unrecognized until the child enters school and joins the ranks of the "6-hour mentally retarded."

The more pervasive forms of mental retardation, in which the mental age even in adulthood never exceeds 8 years, are rare. Moderately, severely, and profoundly retarded children often have demonstrable brain disease and structural damage, along with other physical abnormalities.

CAUSES OF MENTAL RETARDATION

In considering the causes of mental retardation, we enter the realm of nature versus nurture. Since intellectual capacity is biological (a function of the brain), it is, fundamentally, genetically determined. Intelligence, as measured by IQ, is represented by a normal, Gaussian distribution; in this statistical model, MR is defined as a deviant range on a continuum of intellectual ability, with normal status defined as the average or middle range. Those with mild retardation represent the lower end of the curve; a possible interpretation is that the mildly retarded are simply less well endowed than the majority.

More severely retarded children, who suffer from other abnormalities as well, comprise about 0.5% of the population. Their retardation may be the result of specific genetic, infectious, toxic, or physically traumatic insults, or the result of a metabolic disorder or a chromosomal abnormality. Some children with mild retardation, on the other hand, may have been born with brains capable of average intelligence; because they were never stimulated at home or elsewhere, they do poorly on IQ tests. How much of the deficit was inborn? How much was environmentally induced? Clinical skills combined with appropriate laboratory studies can provide only partial answers; in many instances, our questions will remain unanswered. This puts us in a moral dilemma of having to provide services for some children for whom the services may be inappropriate.

> A young physician was angered when he learned that a 12-year-old boy who had just received a kidney transplant was mildly retarded. The father had chosen not to volunteer the information before the surgery, and the doctor had not elicited it. Having obtained the information, the doctor was incensed at the thought of wasting a good kidney on a mentally impaired boy!

Is it not true that retarded children have as much right to medical and mental health services as anyone else?

Environmental Deprivation

Stimulus deprivation and maternal deprivation, particularly the work of Spitz, were discussed in chapter 7. Spitz demonstrated very clearly that an infant's developmental quotient was influenced by the nurturing care of those about him. Not only was good mothering necessary for normal growth, but infants regressed when the care was not provided.

The newborn infant's body is a marvelous thing. It adapts to the change from an intrauterine environment to the outside world in an amazingly effective manner; given a minimum of food, air, and activity, it grows and develops. The child learns to walk and to mimic sounds in his environment.* He will grow faster and learn

*The reader might be interested in reading an account of the Wild Boy of Aveyron, who was found wandering in the forests, completely unsocialized, at an estimated age of 10 or 12 years. He was taken in by a physician specializing in diseases of the ear, nose, and throat, and was thought deaf. The account, written originally in 1799, is considered the first recorded attempt at child psychotherapy. It is reviewed in the first volume of the *Journal of the Academy of Child Psychiatry*.

to walk sooner, if provided an optimal diet and exercise; with appropriate stimulation, he will learn to communicate with others (see chapter 1). He will not learn to read if left to his own devices, since reading requires the use of symbols, letters, and numbers. Therefore, he will be retarded by most standards and will be unable to function very well in our society.

Beyond infancy, the child needs an environment that values intellectual performance and patiently encourages childish attempts to learn. He needs to be played with, talked to, sung to, read to, and listened to. He needs to be loved and to feel secure—in his home, his neighborhood, and in his school. Parents who fail to provide such an environment, for whatever reason, are guilty of neglect. Appropriate community services must make up the deficit in order to reverse the regressive process and prevent the development of mild mental retardation.

TREATMENT

The objective of treatment is to enable the retarded child to reach his full intellectual potential and to live as independently as possibly. A variety of treatment modalities may be utilized, in response to the child's individual needs; services of a multidisciplinary professional team are essential.

Since the major problems of 80% of the retarded are psychosocial in nature, educational and other psychologically-based approaches (both preventative and rehabilitative) have been useful. Most retarded persons—and especially the organically handicapped—require a highly structured program with an emphasis on language and personality development.

Educational Approaches

Special education techniques should be initiated as early as possible. Current federal law mandates action on the part of public schools for developmentally delayed children from 3 years of age.

An orderly environment, low pupil-teacher ratio, and carefully delineated behavioral goals have proven effective in enhancing cognitive development. Conditions conducive to learning should be arranged: progressing from easy tasks with prominent cues to more difficult tasks; providing multiple, salient cues for problem solving; rote learning and overlearning for retention; and programmed generalization. Retarded children benefit when tasks are broken down into achievable components, when they are afforded ample opportunity for practice, and when they are rewarded for their accomplishments.

Since the 1970s, programs for the mildly and moderately retarded have been guided by the "principle of normalization," in which services are as culturally normative as possible. The pendulum has swung from institutional care to various forms of community services and from special class placement to placement in a regular classroom for at least part of the day.

Independent living skills should be part of the curriculum and the natural drive for independence that we see in adolescence should be used as a motivating factor. Vocational training and sheltered employment opportunities are important for the retarded. Unskilled trades should be taught and the adolescent helped to find work. He will be as gratified as anyone else in our society when he is able to succeed.

Psychotherapeutic Approaches

Perhaps because of their enhanced vulnerability to environmental stress and their unfavorable competitive position, retarded children are more likely than others to manifest emotional disturbances. As a group, they tend to be more anxious and more impulsive; their immaturities, negativism, and regressions are exaggerated. While not all retarded children are disturbed, many would profit from conflict-resolving psychotherapeutic measures.

Techniques developed for other populations may be used to advantage with the retarded. Supportive psychotherapy may aid the retarded child in surmounting primary or secondary personality problems. An approach based on operant principles of learning may be especially effective.

Familial Approaches

In working with the retarded, the cooperation of family members is essential. Parent guidance has proven useful in preventing and ameliorating emotional disturbances in the children. When treated as valued team members, parents can be helped to adapt inappropriate demands to their child's temperament and abilities. Too often the family has accepted the idea that the child is slow:

The family may continually allow for the deficit, instead of seeking ways in which the child can learn. As if ashamed, the family may hide the more severely retarded child from social contacts. Although these attitudes are changing through the efforts of the American Association of Retarded Citizens, the American Association on Mental Deficiency, and the Special Olympics, families still need considerable help in accepting the diagnosis of mental retardation and adjusting to it. Seeing several families together in multiple family treatment may relieve feelings of stigma and isolation.

CONCLUSIONS

Many developments of the past three decades have led to increased interest in mental retardation. These have included the formation of the National Association for Retarded Children (now, Citizens), dramatic advances in genetics and in medicine, and the push toward integration during the 50s; the national War on Poverty and Project Head Start of the 60s; and legislation benefiting the handicapped during the 70s, with programs guided significantly toward integration by the "principle of normalization." Significant progress has been made in psychodiagnosis, and in prevention, treatment, education, and rehabilitation.

Mental retardation poses a chronic reality problem for the family of the retardate. With professional guidance and community support, most families can be helped to adapt positively and to deal effectively with their situation.

BIBLIOGRAPHY

Grossman H (ed): *Manual on terminology and classification in mental retardation, 1973 revision.* Washington, D.C., American Association on Mental Deficiency, 1973

Hunt JMcV: *Intelligence and experience.* New York, Renold Press, 1961

Itard J-M-G: *The wild boy of Aveyron,* G&M Humphrey (trans). New York, Century Co., 1932 (originally published, 1799)

Menolascino, FJ (ed): *Psychiatric approaches to mental retardation.* New York, Basic Books, 1970

Robinson NM, Robinson HB: *The mentally retarded child: A psychological approach,* ed 2. New York, McGraw-Hill, 1976

Chapter 12

ATTENTION DEFICIT DISORDER/LEARNING DISABILITY

MOLLIE M. WALLICK, PhD

Many descriptive labels have been assigned over the years to children now educationally classified as learning disabled. Among the terms used—often interchangeably—were Strauss syndrome, minimal cerebral palsied, brain damaged, neurologically impaired, process disordered, perceptually handicapped, minimal brain dysfunctioned (MBD), hyperkinetic, and attention deficit disordered (ADD). By whatever descriptor, there is still a controversy over the very existence of learning disabilities (LD). Some professionals consider LD no more than a rationalization for school failure; others use the diagnosis loosely to refer to any learning problem.

This chapter will attempt to convince the reader that LD is indeed a distinct clinical entity. A brief historical overview will be followed by an exploration of observable characteristics of the disorder, a review of diagnostic approaches, and a consideration of educational models, remedial programs, and intervention strategies.

HISTORICAL OVERVIEW

The construct "learning disabilities" was born of varied historical crosscurrents and was shaped by members of several diverse fields. Among the earliest contributors to the research literature were physicians—specifically ophthalmologists and neurologists who proposed the correlation of neurological deficits and reading disabilities.

Four decades ago, a report was published of extended behavioral observations on adults who suffered brain injuries during wartime; described was their residual disordered behavior involving perceptual disturbances, distractibility, and emotional lability. An hypothesis followed, offered by a neuropsychiatrist and an educator, of brain-injured children whose behavior was similar to that of the adults with wartime brain injuries.

The existence of an undetected brain insult, sustained before, during, or after birth, provided an appealing explanation of the children's collection of symptoms and consequent learning problems. However, hard evidence was lacking of damage to the brain in many children manifesting the behavioral syndrome, while an equal number of children with known brain damage failed to exhibit the expected aberrant behaviors.

Meanwhile, professionals in several fields other than medicine —psychology, optometry, audiology, speech and language, child development, and education—conceptualized the problem variously, according to each clinician's specific orientation. As would be expected, terminology, definitions, and prevalence estimates varied accordingly.

In the early 1960s the term "learning disabilities" emerged, with its focus on behavior rather than etiology. In order to provide a consensual framework for identification and program development, Congress, in 1968, formally adopted the term "learning disabilities" and accepted a definition recommended by the National Advisory Committee on Handicapped Children. LD was conceptualized as referring to one or more significant deficits in essential learning processes, such as perception, integration, and verbal or nonverbal expression. Excluded from the category were children whose learning problems were primarily attributed to intellectual, emotional, sensory, or motoric handicap, or to lack of opportunity to learn. Both the psychological-educational emphasis of the definition and its exclusion clause were articulated subsequently in Public Law 94-142 (The Education of All Handicapped Children Act of 1975).

But with the swing of the pendulum in 1981, a new understanding was reached by five of the six organizations which comprise the National Joint Committee on Learning Disabilities. Conspicuous by its absence in their definition is reference to psychological processes. Instead, LD is considered intrinsic to the individual—that is, caused by central nervous system dysfunction. An attempt to remediate the presumed internal impairment is the rationale for several current approaches, reviewed below in the section on intervention strategies.

The fact that, in the elementary grades, learning disabled is one of the most frequently occurring exceptionalities attests to the significance of the classification. The National Advisory Committee on Handicapped Children has estimated "hard core" cases at approximately 1% to 3% of the school population. Many professionals consider this an extremely conservative judgment; while figures vary widely, 5% of school-aged children is a frequent report. As in many other conditions in which language problems are central, it appears that four to six times more boys than girls are affected.

OBSERVABLE CHARACTERISTICS OF LD

An exhaustive review of the literature compiled in 1966 listed approximately 100 different behaviors of children then classified as minimal brain dysfunctioned. The ten most representative characteristics will be described in this section; several are not specific to the learning disabled. In order of frequency cited, the behaviors are hyperactivity, perceptual motor impairment, emotional lability, general coordination deficits, disorders of attention, impulsivity, disorders of thinking and memory, specific learning disabilities, disorders of speech and hearing, and equivocal neurological signs and electroencephalographic (EEG) irregularities.

(1) **Hyperactivity** is characterized by persistent overactivity and excessive fidgeting. A hyperactive person may dash about in an apparent non-goal-directed fashion, picking up various objects in quick succession; he may talk incessantly, asking questions but not waiting for answers. Sleep, too, may be restless. In so-called "true hyperactivity," sustained overactivity is observed across varied situations; in situational hyperactivity, in contrast, high activity is observed in one context and not in another.

(2) **Perceptual motor impairment** includes possible dysfunction in visual or auditory perception, eye-hand coordination, and figure-background discrimination. A person with a visual perceptual impairment overlooks relevant details and significant visual stimuli; he cannot process and recall visual sensations. Similarly, a person with an auditory perceptual impairment displays deficiencies in discriminating, integrating, and attending to pertinent sounds; he has difficulty with syllabication and closure tasks (filling in missing sounds), and is likely to have problems with spelling, writing, and arithmetic. While the perceptually impaired child's sensory acuity is adequate, his eyes and hands do not function in synchrony, and he has problems in ball play and in such paper activities as cutting, coloring, tracing, and copying.

(3) **Emotional lability** refers to variability and unpredictability of mood and performance. Both excessive laughter and explosive irritability may be triggered by minor stimuli.

(4) **General coordination deficits** are those manifest in the areas of balance and rhythm, spatial orientation, directionality, body awareness, and laterality. An uncoordinated person may be unable to maintain gross-motor balance, to move rhythmically, to move his body in an integrated way in hopping, skipping, jumping, and running; he may demonstrate anomalies of hand-eye-foot dominance (ie, lacking one-sided hand-eye-foot preference). An uncoordinated person may be deficient in space/distance judgment and in directional orientation, such as right-left and up-down; he may also lack an adequate global perception of his body and of its sides.

(5) **Disorders of attention** include short attention span, distractibility, and perseveration. Unable to maintain focused attention on tasks, the person appears instead at the mercy of extraneous background phenomena—eg, the periodic cycling of the water fountain—usually unnoticed by others. Perseveration refers to inability to shift attention or to stop behavior which is no longer appropriate.

(6) **Impulsivity** is characterized by an apparently unplanned motor response, somewhat inappropriate to the situation. An impulsive person has difficulty waiting his turn and often acts before considering the consequences of his action.

(7) **Disorders of thinking and memory** involve defective abilities to abstract, conceptualize, categorize, and generalize and to assimilate, retain, and recall information. Thinking and memory disorders are closely associated with perceptual deficits in the auditory channel: oral directions pose a problem both in comprehension and recall.

(8) **Specific learning disabilities** include those in reading, writing, spelling, and arithmetic. Among the descriptors used to refer to inadequate reading proficiency are alexia (total inability to learn to read) and dyslexia (impaired development of reading skills). Associated features of dyslexia include dysgraphia (writing disability) and dysorthographia (spelling disability); there may be letter substitutions and reversals, inadequate letter formation and spacing, and bizarre spelling errors. Developmental arithmetic disorder (dyscalculia) includes impairment in such skills as counting

meaningfully, mastering cardinal and ordinal systems, performing arithmetic operations, and perceiving clustered objects in sets or groupings.

(9) **Disorders of speech and hearing** are currently subsumed under the rubric, "developmental language disorder." Expressive dysphasia is an impairment in the encoding or production of language, manifested in immature, ungrammatical, illogical, or incoherent verbalization. Its more severe counterpart, receptive dysphasia, involves impairment of both language comprehension and production. The term "aphasia" suggests a known neurological cause; still other referents for specific language impairment include congenital auditory imperception and word-deafness.

(10) **Equivocal neurological signs and EEG irregularities** refer to soft (nonspecific) indicators of an underlying neurological disorder. There may be neurological developmental lags, such as delayed suppression of primitive reflexes or lateness in developmental milestones. There may be mild abnormalities, such as reflex asymmetries, mild tremors, subtle coordination deficits, and motor overflow (involuntary movements associated with and in addition to a specific requested action).

It is highly unlikely that a learning disabled person will manifest the entire array of symptoms, in spite of interrelationships among many areas of deficit. Also, there is some inconsistency—over time and place—in the occurrence of the phenomena. The behaviors apparently occur least in a one-to-one situation, under conditions of tight structure, and in self-selected activities.

It should be noted that some persons who are not learning disabled occasionally exhibit some of the reported features of the disorder. The difference lies in the number of observed characteristics and in the frequency with which they occur.

DIAGNOSTIC APPROACHES

The purpose of diagnosis is twofold. First, in the case of learning disabilities, it is imperative to distinguish a person with LD from one with a categorical disability, such as—for example—mental retardation, deafness, or emotional disturbance. Second, to be effective, the diagnosis should suggest a course of remediation by delimiting specific deficits along with areas of strength. While multidisciplinary team decision making is mandated by Public Law 94-142, neither composition of the team nor explicit diagnostic activities is described. In actuality, varied expertise is needed from medical, psychological, educational, communication, and movement personnel—along with information from significant family members.

An early LD task force report of the Department of Health, Education, and Welfare offered guidelines which still serve as a basis for diagnosis. Included among the recommendations are comprehensive medical evaluation and extensive behavioral assessment.

Medical

Within the medical evaluation, both history and observation are important. Medical history should include a review of prenatal, perinatal, and postnatal factors which may have affected the central nervous system, along with specific details of childhood illnesses and developmental milestones. Social history should include such information as socioeconomic status, the constellation and dynamics of the family, significant life events, and parental expectations and tolerance.

The function of a physical examination, complete with routine laboratory tests, is to evaluate general health and rule out systemic disease. A neurological evaluation assesses neurologic integration and the possibility of a specific nervous system disorder. A psychiatric examination helps determine if the symptoms are emotional—either primary or secondary—and may be needed to rule out anxiety, depression, and conduct disorder. Finally, referral to vision or hearing specialists (ophthalmologist or otologist) is indicated in the case of inadequate performance on screening tests or when, based on observation, there is concern about acuity.

Behavioral

Behavioral assessment, too, involves history and observation, in both home and school settings. School records—including test results, report cards, teacher conference notes, and assignment samples—should be reviewed. Especially valuable are classroom teacher ratings of activity level, language development, attending, perception, information processing, persistence, and approach to learning. Functional performance of eye-hand coordination, language, and visual and auditory skills is best assessed within the familiar classroom setting. Also readily discernible there are consistency/persistency of behavior patterns and tolerance level for ambiguity, frustration, and failure.

Psychological. Intellectual, perceptual, and personality functioning are of major concern in a psychological evaluation. Intelligence of persons with LD typically falls within the low-average range; an indicator of learning disabilities is a significant discrepancy between mental age obtained on an individual intelligence test and the grade equivalent score recorded on an achievement test. A test battery with several subtests is often used; variability in subtest scores may suggest further testing or a direction for remediation. Also included within the psychological test battery are tests of impulsivity and personality tests, which may be helpful—along with a psychiatric workup—in distinguishing between LD and an emotionally based conduct disorder.

Visual-perceptual-motor. Visual-motor and perceptual-motor tests may be included in the psychological evaluation or may be administered, respectively, by a developmental optometrist or an occupational therapist. A visual-motor perception test measures eye-motor coordination, figure-ground discrimination, form constancy, position in space, and spatial relations; it determines areas of difficulty and suggests appropriate remediation techniques. A perceptual-motor test measures such gross-motor skills as balance, postural imitation, bilateral motor coordination, and right-left discrimination.

Communication. A detailed evaluation of speech and language behavior should include an auditory discrimination test, tests of receptive and expressive language ability, and an assessment of articulation, voice quality, and rate. Impairment in the ability to think in linguistic symbols and to communicate is common among the learning disabled, but is not exclusive to the disorder. Subtest patterns may be more useful, therefore, in remediation than in the differential diagnosis of LD.

Educational. Within the educational evaluation, results of achievement tests covering a variety of academic skills provide a basis of comparison with intellectual functioning level, as previously noted. Other specific tests measure achievement in such basic skills as reading, arithmetic, spoken language, and written language. As example, diagnostic reading tests assess visual closure, sound blending, and retention of nonmeaningful sequences—functions often deficient among the learning disabled. A comprehensive educational evaluation also analyzes how a person approaches a learning task and his strategies for solution, and explores the differential effects of various didactic methods and materials.

DELIVERY OF SERVICES

Educational Models

Variations in degree of involvement of persons with LD necessitate multiple educational models, including regular classroom, itinerant teacher, resource room, and special class. Some communities have special day schools and even residential schools for the learning disabled.

Public Law 94-142 mandates placement of all handicapped children in their least restrictive environment. For those with LD, the regular classroom with additional support appears more desirable—and, except in cases of severe learning disability, more defensible—than segregated special class or special school placement. Educational support may involve part-time assignment to an itinerant teacher or to a resource room, often with individual study carrels to reduce distraction. Support may also include direct or consultative service of a communication specialist, an occupational therapist, or an adapted physical educator. In the regular classroom portion of the school day, modification of teaching and reinforcement strategies, rate of presentation, and materials and their stimulus value may be needed to assure the LD student's successful performance.

Remedial Programs and Intervention Strategies

Recommendations for the learning disabled most often include a highly structured classroom with reduced pupil-teacher ratio and individualized instruction for at least part of the day, some type of perceptual training, medical management, and counseling.

Special education. In order to accommodate the diverse symptoms subsumed under the LD label, a teacher of the learning disabled should have reasonable expertise in a variety of approaches. The resource room orientation may include a visual-perceptual-motor emphasis on patterning exercises (eg, through crawling), walking boards (for balance), and visual targeting (eg, visually following a flashlight beam). Similar training is available privately through the services of a developmental optometrist and often, in the school system, through those of an occupational therapist.

Students with major learning problems in language benefit from the linguistic approach to remediation, with its emphasis on listening, speaking, and reading. Standard techniques used with the auditorily and speech impaired are employed, frequently with the direct services and consultative assistance of a communication specialist. With all categorical approaches, care should be taken to avoid exclusive focus on one modality to the neglect of another.

Psychoeducational or diagnostic-prescriptive teaching (note the melding of medical and educational terminology) involves an ongoing assessment of needs as an integral part of instruction. Goals and objectives are formulated, along with a selection of strategies and an evaluation of their effectiveness. Both end results and the manner in which the student obtains the results are monitored.

In the case of the learning disabled, it is often profitable to use peer teaching and spaced—rather than concentrated—practice. Overlearning may be needed to assure generalization.

Perceptual training/neurological reorganization. Through occupational therapy, some persons with sensory processing or integrative problems can be helped to respond adaptively. Unlike traditional training which deals with symptoms of impairment, sensory integrative therapy attempts to modify the underlying neurological dysfunction. It has as its goal to develop the brain's capacity to perceive, remember, and motor plan. Essentially, the therapy is based on tactile stimulation (with exposure to various textures, vibrations, and touch pressure) and vestibular stimulation (including spinning in a net swing in various positions, along with scooter board, therapy ball, positioning, and movement activities).

Still another approach to neurological reorganization is a biofeedback technique which attempts to regulate sensorimotor rhythm. The use of advanced electronics for LD and hyperkinesis began in 1974; there are a number of centers in the US currently using biofeedback with the ADD population.

Medical management. The physician's multifaceted approach to the management of a patient with learning disabilities should include treatment of medical problems, both physical and emotional, including systemic and nervous system allergies; diet therapy; and a medication regimen, if indicated, to facilitate both impulse control and learning. It should also involve close collaboration with significant family members to foster their understanding of the complexities of the syndrome and of their role in its remediation.

Some physicians propose that allergy to common food often causes such symptoms of nervous system dysfunction as irritability and hyperactivity, alternating with lethargy and listlessness. Characteristic signs of hypersensitivity include a pale appearance, a stuffy nose, and so-called "allergic shiners" (dark shadows under the eyes). An elimination diet, or another test of hidden food allergy, may be used to determine if a child is reacting to a regularly ingested food.

The best known proponent of nutritional intervention in LD is the late Dr. Benjamin Feingold, who reported a decade ago that hyperactive children improve on a diet devoid of salicylates (natural chemicals found in many fruits and vegetables) and free of food additives, such as artificial colors and flavors. Although many studies evaluating the effectiveness of dietary manipulation report improvement in but a small population of children, most researchers, nonetheless, recommend a trial period of intervention.

Conclusions of a recent conference held at the National Institutes of Health disputed the efficacy of dietary modification and pronounced stimulants more effective in calming hyperactive children. Most often prescribed are Ritalin and Dexedrine; for reasons as yet unclear, the medications—both traditionally considered stimulants—have a paradoxical calming effect on hyperactive persons. Considerable improvement in attending behavior and suppression of symptoms which interfere with learning have been reported in the estimated 4% of the US elementary school population using stimulants. However, the method of treatment remains highly controversial. Judicious use of the medications is dictated by an awareness of their potential side effects (irritability, insomnia, headache, stomachache, depression, dryness of the mouth, height and weight suppression), even though apparently reversible when the drugs are discontinued.

Counseling. Children often need help in understanding their need for dietary or pharmacological intervention. Similarly, they often need assistance in appreciating the rationale for special education and perceptual training.

With progress, the learning disabled person views himself as more like other learners and, therefore, in a more favorable light. Substantial gains in personality development may be achieved along with incremental gains in perceptual, linguistic, and academic areas. But any residual problems may require the attention of a psychiatrist or other mental health worker.

A variety of psychotherapeutic approaches has been used to facilitate more positive emotional attitudes and interrelationships. These include individual psychotherapy, training in social skills, family therapy, group therapy, and counseling groups for parents. Through affective reeducation, the psychotherapist enhances all other remediation efforts. The mental health worker serves as a valued member of the multidisciplinary team in its comprehensive approach to learning disabilities.

SUMMARY AND CONCLUSIONS

This chapter opened with a brief historical overview of learning disabilities and an exploration of observable characteristics of the disorder. A review of diagnostic approaches was followed by a consideration of service delivery models, remedial programs, and intervention strategies.

The American Psychiatric Association uses the term "attention deficit disorder," further qualified as with or without hyperactivity, to describe the problem educationally identified as learning disability. For the hyperactive subset of children, a commonly held—though erroneous—assumption has been that frenetic overactivity disappears in adolescence. A recent assessment of young adults identified and treated as hyperactive in childhood reports tentative evidence indicating that around one fourth of the study population appear problem free and no longer hyperactive; one half have some problems but are not considered overactive, while one fourth continue to require treatment for hyperactivity.

In studying the long-term adjustment of ADD young adults, several investigators found them impulsive and socially inadequate. Even more unsettling is a study suggesting a strong association between early hyperactivity/learning problems and subsequent adolescent delinquency. With all learning disabled children, the prompt and concerted effort of a team of professionals is needed to prevent lifelong disability.

BIBLIOGRAPHY

Adelman HS: Diagnostic classification of LD: Research and ethical perspectives as related to practice. *Learning Disabilities Quarterly* 2:5-16, 1979

Ayres AJ: *Sensory integration and learning disorders.* Los Angeles, Western Psychological Services, 1974

Bush WJ, Waugh KW: *Diagnosing learning disabilities,* ed 2. Columbus, OH, Charles E. Merrill, 1976

Cott A: Megavitamins: The orthomolecular approach to the treatment of children with behavioral disorders and learning disabilities. *Academic Therapy* 7:245-258, 1972

Feingold B: *Why your child is hyperactive.* New York, Random House, 1975

Frostig M, Horne D: *The Frostig program for the development of visual perception.* Chicago, Follett, 1964

Gardner RA: *The objective diagnosis of minimal brain dysfunction.* Cresskill, NJ, Creative Therapeutics, 1979

Gottlieb MI: Pills: Pros and cons, or medications for school problems. *Acta Symbolica* 6:35-64, 1975

Hammill DD, Leigh J, McNutt G, Larsen SC: A new definition of learning disabilities. *Learning Disability Quarterly* 4:336-341, 1981

Johnson DJ, Myklebust HR: *Learning disabilities.* New York, Grune & Stratton, 1969

Kephart NC: *Slow learner in the classroom.* Columbus, OH, Charles E. Merrill, 1971

Lerner JW: *Learning disabilities: Theory, diagnosis, and teaching strategies.* Boston, Houghton Mifflin, 1981

McCarthy JJ, McCarthy JF: *Learning disabilities.* Boston, Allyn & Bacon, 1976

Orton ST: *Reading, writing and speech problems in children.* New York, M.W. Norton, 1937

Rosner J: *Helping children overcome learning difficulties.* New York, Walker, 1975

Speer F: *Allergy of the nervous system.* Springfield, IL, Charles C Thomas, 1970

Strauss AA, Lehtinen L: *Psychopathology and education of the brain-injured child.* New York, Grune & Stratton, 1947

Tull D: Assessment of learning disabilities. *Seminars in Speech, Language and Hearing* 2:123-135, 1981

Valett RE: *The remediation of learning disabilities: A handbook of psychoeducational resource programs.* Belmont, CA, Fearon Publishing, 1967

Wallace G, McLoughlin JA: *Learning disabilities: Concepts and characteristics.* Columbus, OH, Charles E. Merrill, 1975

Chapter 13

CONDUCT DISORDERS

KATHARINE N. DIXON, MD

Whereas normal children are expected to show some degree of misbehavior from time to time, stressed and emotionally disturbed children characteristically display disordered behavior as part of their symptom complex, regardless of their diagnoses. Acting-out behavior is especially common in children with depression and transient situational disorders. A diagnosis of conduct disorder, however, applies to those children who show a persistent pattern of antisocial behavior that interferes with the rights of others or that conflicts with social norms.

Conduct disorders are the most frequent diagnoses among the children who come to the attention of mental health professionals and agencies. In addition, many conduct-disordered children become involved in the correctional system rather than the mental health system. The exceedingly high lifetime cost to the affected children and social system is illustrated by the high frequency of criminal behavior, divorce, unstable work histories, and alcoholism evident when these children become adults. An estimated 35% of all boys between the ages of 10 and 18 years have at least one contact with police. Although not all conduct-disordered children become antisocial adults, virtually every antisocial adult has a long history of behavior problems stemming from childhood. The leading causes of death in the 15- to 24-year-old age group are violence related.

Because the mental health and social problems created by antisocial youth are so serious, early intervention is clearly indicated. Less well established, however, are the means for engaging these children and their families in early treatment and, indeed, what constitutes effective treatment. Conduct-disordered youngsters, unfortunately, often present with a long history of increasingly serious behavior problems, school failure, and escalating conflict with parents and authorities. Because mental health resources are so limited, the youngsters must be screened judiciously for ability to profit from intensive residential and inpatient services. Failure to match the behaviorally impaired youngster with the appropriate treatment program contributes to feelings of futility and resentment among staff members, and to anger and discouragement on the part of the agency or parent seeking services.

In this chapter, a clarification of the diagnostic classification and its component subtypes will be followed by a presentation of techniques for screening the conduct-disordered population for admission to a treatment facility. After a brief section on assessment, the remainder of the chapter will be devoted to aspects of the treatment program pertinent to a child-care worker.

DIAGNOSTIC CLASSIFICATION

The cardinal feature of conduct disorder is a persistent behavioral pattern in which the rights of others or age-appropriate societal norms are violated. Conduct disorders are categorized according to the presence or absence of social attachment and aggressive behavior.

These distinctions give rise to four conduct disorder subtypes: socialized, aggressive; socialized, nonaggressive; undersocialized, aggressive; and undersocialized, nonaggressive. These groupings not only describe the nature of the child's conduct problems, but also give an indication of the child's prognosis and ability to use a treatment program. The socialized, nonaggressive child's ability to form relationships and to control aggressive impulses portends for a better adult adjustment than can be expected from the undersocialized, aggressive child.

Attachment to a parental figure in early childhood is essential for later socialization. Youngsters with socialized conduct disorders have developed the capacity for attachment and social bonding during early childhood years but for various reasons—divorce, parental neglect, family instability—socialization in later childhood and adolescence is continued primarily within the peer group at the expense of adult relationships. Their peer loyalty is conducive to joining with a gang or other antisocial youth for antisocial acts. The undersocialized child has limited capacity to form and sustain meaningful peer and adult relationships. Often, serious behavior problems have been present since early childhood. Friendships tend to be superficial and manipulative, while antisocial behavior is usually solitary and furtive. If the undersocialized child belongs to a gang, he tends to function on the fringe. Since the treatment process depends on the child's ability to work in a therapeutic relationship, the child's limited capacity for attachment has serious implications for his prognosis. Progress with the undersocialized youngster tends to occur more slowly, requiring patience and close attention to the development of trust and rapport.

The aggressive youngster's conduct problems involve physical violence toward property or other individuals. Stealing involves confrontation with a victim; other aggressive delinquent behaviors may include assault, vandalism, and rape. The nonaggressive child violates social rules without physical aggression or destructiveness. He is usually involved in such unruly behaviors as truancy, drug abuse, lying, theft without confrontation, disobedience, and defiance.

SCREENING FOR ADMISSION TO A TREATMENT FACILITY

Several questions must be answered thoughtfully in screening conduct-disordered youngsters for admission to a treatment facility. These include:

(1) Is the child unruly or delinquent?

The unruly adolescent has committed a status offense, such as home or school truancy, while the delinquent has committed an act—such as theft or assault—that would be a crime if he were an adult. A small number of adolescent chronic offenders account for the majority of juvenile crime. Since many states do not permit correctional facilities to incarcerate unruly youth alongside delinquent juveniles, mental health settings receive a high service demand for youngsters in conflict with the law or social norms. It is likely that a delinquent would require an environment more secure than that offered in a treatment setting.

(2) What is the level of motivation for treatment, on the part of the youngster and his family?

Since children rarely request admission to a treatment program, they are, at least initially, involuntary patients. Almost without exception, admission is initiated by the parents, agency, or court. While the initial assessment provides important information about the child's and his parents' motivation to work cooperatively in treatment, it should be recognized that the child or his parents often appear uncooperative or unmotivated in the initial stages of evaluation and treatment. Responsibility lies, in part, with program staff to skillfully engage the youngster and his family in the therapeutic process.

Motivation becomes an important consideration, since the nature and expense of an inpatient treatment program necessitate a relatively short stay prior to discharge home or transfer to a less restrictive and less financially taxing setting. Length of stay and ability to profit from treatment services can be influenced by the degree of internal or external distress associated with the behavior problems. Depression, anxiety, or guilt feelings can be viewed as positive indicators that the child will use treatment services. Behavior problems that are ego-syntonic and not viewed as necessitating change are less likely to be influenced by treatment. Even the most skillful staff will find it difficult to engage the unmotivated, nondistressed child—particularly an adolescent.

Not uncommonly, adolescents involved with the court system view entry into a treatment program as an alternative to entering the correctional system or as a means to present themselves in a good light before the court. Without a clear understanding of treatment expectations for progress and change, these adolescents may not only elude the long arm of the law and mental health, but also contribute to creating a milieu more reminiscent of a juvenile detention center.

(3) What is the current unit population?

Unless a treatment program is specifically designed and staffed for a full complement of conduct-disordered children, close attention needs to be given to its "mix." An excessive number of aggressive and conduct-disordered patients creates a volatile and nontherapeutic environment. Acting-out and group conflict can be minimized by a balance of problems in the unit population.

(4) Are there adequate posttreatment resources?

The child's postdischarge placement influences not only the length of stay and treatment objectives, but even whether the child should be accepted for treatment if no subsequent placement is available. Release into an unchanged and inadequate home environment will contribute to rapid regression to pretreatment behaviors.

ASSESSMENT

The initial evaluation of a conduct-disordered youngster entering an inpatient or residential program should include a physical and neurological examination; psychological, intellectual, and achievement testing; and a consideration of social and family background. The reliability of child assessment is increased by obtaining information from multiple sources—including the parent, teacher, and child—along with direct observation.

Behavioral observations by staff members who see the child daily provide invaluable information about the nature, severity, and frequency of the child's behavior problems. A "honeymoon" period occurs characteristically during the initial phase of observation, particularly with the socialized, nonaggressive child, followed by emergence of preadmission behaviors. In contrast, the undersocialized, aggressive child can be expected to present behavior problems soon after admission. In all cases early and extended observations, with the child off all medication, provide baseline data to which future behavior can be compared.

Low frequency behaviors (stealing, truancy, firesetting, sexual perversions) do not lend themselves readily to counting or to behavioral programs. While other problem behaviors can be easily and reliably counted, finding a standard rating scale with which to monitor the conduct-disordered child may be somewhat problematic. At Ohio State University, an individualized Conduct Disorder Rating Scale completed weekly by a member of the nursing staff is used to monitor the child's targeted behaviors over the course of treatment (see Table 13-1). Such measures are important for the systematic assessment of target behaviors and their response to treatment intervention. While a therapist's observations yield important information about the child's psychological functioning, data provided from the observations of those who work with the child daily—in school and in the residential milieu—provide the most reliable observations of behavioral functioning.

In addition to measures of targeted behaviors, a conduct analysis requires attention to the pattern of antecedent and consequent events. An antecedent event is one which occurs just prior to the child's inappropriate or unacceptable behavior, while a consequent

TABLE 13-1
CONDUCT DISORDERS RATING SCALE*

INSTRUCTIONS: Below is a list of behaviors which may be exhibited by conduct-disordered adolescents. Select those items which pertain to your patient and record them on the rating sheet. You may use other behaviors not included on the list if they are relevant to your patient's situation.

After listing behaviors, rate each one according to the following scale: (4) Daily, (3) Often, (2) Occasionally, (1) Rarely, (0) Never.

BEHAVIORS:	DATE WEEK	1	2	3	4	5	6	7	8	9	10
1.											
2.											
3.											
4.											
5.											
6.											
7.											
8.											
9.											
	TOTAL										

SAMPLE BEHAVIORS:

aggressive verbal behavior
aggressive physical behavior
instigating
destructive behavior
runaway
school refusal
refusal to follow limits
blaming
argumentative
suspicious of others
vulgar language
inappropriate touching
drug talk
refusal to participate in therapies or activities
lying
stealing
conflict with authorities
irritability
intrusiveness
explosiveness
threatening
lacks empathy
teasing
other poor interpersonal skills (specify)

*Developed by Ken Calestro, milieu coordinator, Adolescent Psychiatry Inpatient Unit, The Ohio State University event is one which directly follows the behavior. Three components, then, are involved in the sequence of behavior:

	Antecedent Event	Misbehavior	Consequent Event
Example:	Parent asks child to pick up his clothes	Child whines and complains	Parent drops the request and picks up the clothes himself

The value of systematic observations of antecedent events, misbehavior, and consequent events for the design of behavioral intervention becomes readily apparent from this model.

TREATMENT: THE ROLE OF THE CHILD-CARE WORKER

Children with conduct disorders represent a diverse group. As noted, they may be socialized or undersocialized, aggressive or nonaggressive. Additionally, they may have developmental delays, learning disorders, and/or attention deficit disorders; in adolescence, drug and alcohol use may be a problem. An effective treatment approach must address the variety of differences and contributing etiologies in a multidimensional fashion.

The child-care worker's therapeutic role in the child's overall program is extremely important. Shaping the child's behavior occurs through the daily interactions and therapeutic conversations between staff members and youngsters in the milieu. In spite of the sundry differences these children present, there exists a commonality of treatment goals:

(1) to increase self-awareness of maladaptive behavior and associated feelings,
(2) to improve ability to use relationships in a meaningful and constructive fashion, and
(3) to learn age-appropriate and acceptable behaviors, while eliminating maladaptive behaviors.

The remainder of the chapter will address those aspects of the treatment program pertinent to the child-care worker.

Milieu

The therapeutic milieu serves as the laboratory setting in which the child's growth is catalyzed toward positive, age-appropriate, adaptive, and socially acceptable behavior. Trieshman refers to the milieu as "the other 23 hours." In addition to specific, individually tailored treatment programs, an effective milieu requires structure, safety, clear communication, and therapeutic interactions.

Structure. Structure refers both to the schedule of daily activities and the authority structure of the unit (rules, regulations, expectations). Often, the conduct-disordered child's environment has been chaotic, disorganized, permissive, neglectful, inconsistent, or otherwise lacking in those essentials that aid development of "internal" structure—particularly, age-appropriate impulse control and judgment. The external structure of the therapeutic milieu offers a corrective experience through unambiguous and consistently applied rules, behavior guidelines, and therapeutic activities. Clearly delineated rules and guidelines and consistent limit-setting not only contribute to smooth unit management, but also help the child gain control over impulsiveness, chronic infraction of social rules, and failure to consider consequences of his actions. Further, consistent limit-setting provides the child with the self-control necessary to use other aspects of the program. A well-structured therapeutic environment is sufficiently flexible to allow healthy negotiation and to provide opportunities for practicing positive leadership and personal responsibility.

Safety. Adequate personnel staffing to insure the safety of all children and staff members is fundamental for any facility accepting behaviorally disturbed children. A therapeutic environment requires an even higher staff-to-patient ratio to provide the structure, supervision, and individual attention necessary for the child's progress. An excessive number of aggressive children without adequate staffing not only leads to a destructive milieu, but also interferes with the therapeutic program for all patients. Child-care workers expecting to provide therapeutic services become resentful rather quickly when the majority of their time, instead, seems to be spent policing the unit. Should safety become a problem in the milieu, increasing staff size or more judicious screening for admission must be seriously considered.

Communication. Therapeutic programming and consistently applied limits are impossible without extensive communication between and within shifts of child-care workers. Behavior programs, particularly, become ineffective if not administered consistently by all shifts and, when indicated, by all school personnel.

Therapeutic interactions. The relationship between the staff and the conduct-disordered child is critically important to the child's progress. Most child-care workers choose their career because they like to work with children. A behaviorally disturbed child, however, can make himself extremely unlikeable. A child-care worker needs to relate to the child in a warm and accepting manner, while maintaining an objective distance.

Sharing personal information regarding the child-care worker's past (or present) mischief, antisocial activity, or drug and alcohol use is not appropriate and can be countertherapeutic. Respect, understanding, and firmness combine to provide the context within which the child can utilize the other therapeutic techniques offered. The staff member needs to be able to tolerate some acting-out by the children in the program, while also setting firm limits. Encouragement of adaptive behaviors, a positive experience with authority, and the opportunity to discuss the immediate behavior are among the therapeutic repertoire offered by the child-care worker. Redl refers to those interviews that occur between the child and those in his daily living environment as "life-space" interviews. Here-and-now experiences are the focus of these discussions, in contrast to the long-range content of the therapy hour.

Behavior Therapy

While individual and family therapy, environmental support, and educational remediation are important in the treatment of the conduct-disordered child, behavioral management is the backbone of the milieu and its therapeutic approach. Since behavioral intervention is applied primarily by the staff, an understanding of basic behavior principles is essential for the implementation of a behavior management plan. Behavioral programming may be the simple targeting of a single behavior or may extend to programming the entire unit using a token economy or levels system.

The objectives of behavior therapy for children with conduct disorders, simply stated, are to decrease unwanted, socially unacceptable, or inappropriate behavior and to increase desired, acceptable, and appropriate behavior. Insight on the part of the child is not required. Behavior therapy is based on the premise that the child's maladaptive behavior has been learned through reinforcement, and likewise, that more appropriate behaviors can be assumed by the same learning process. The child's individually designed behavior program may combine a variety of techniques, including reinforcement, extinction, punishment, modeling, and teaching prosocial behavior.

Reinforcement. Reinforcement strengthens a behavior by providing a reward contingent on the occurrence of the behavior. The reward is called a "reinforcer." Rewarding, or reinforcing, a specific behavior increases the likelihood that the child will repeat the behavior in the future. Reinforcement is an important part of social learning throughout childhood. Mother's verbal praise of the toddler's successful toileting, for example, will increase the likelihood that the child will produce that desired behavior next time, instead of soiling his pants. A negative parental response, such as scolding, can reinforce inappropriate behavior, particularly if this is a frequent source of attention for the child. Reinforcement, then, can increase both negative and positive learned behaviors. The objective of reinforcement in a treatment program is to increase or strengthen positive and socially appropriate behaviors through a system of rewards. Although praise and attention are the most common forms of positive reinforcement, children in residential settings often need a system of tangible or privilege rewards before they can move on to intangible reinforcers.

Extinction. Extinction is a technique whereby undesired behaviors are decreased or eliminated—that is, become "extinct"—by removing the reinforcing response to the unwanted behavior. As mentioned above, both positive and negative reactions to behavior can serve to perpetuate the behavior. A negative response, such as scolding or threatening, nevertheless provides attention. Likewise, talking with patience and understanding to a tantruming child while he is having a tantrum can function to reinforce that behavior. Eliminating the reinforcing response to the child's negative behavior weakens the likelihood of similar future behaviors. Ignoring the child who is having a temper tantrum is an example of extinction. Extinction is frequently used in conjunction with reinforcement techniques.

Punishment. Punishment provides a negative consequence for an undesired behavior. Commonly used punishments are time-out, forfeiting points or tokens, restrictions, and loss of privileges. Physical punishment is never justified in the treatment of children. Since punishment only serves to suppress a behavior, it should not be used as the sole approach. Punishment does not teach a desired behavior, and, for this reason, should be used in conjunction with positive reinforcement techniques.

It is important to take into consideration the possibility that what appears on the surface to be punishing may actually be reinforcing. For example, time-out procedures may be rewarding to the undersocialized child who tends to isolate himself. Punishment should be administered in a matter-of-fact fashion without lecturing, scolding, or other negative attention. Such negative attention can be reinforcing.

Modeling. Imitation is an important mode of social learning in childhood. The conduct-disordered child, unfortunately, has learned aggressive, antisocial, or maladaptive behaviors from others in his environment. Similarly, he can learn appropriate social behaviors from the therapeutic adults in the treatment environment. Modeling can be facilitated by role playing, discussion of alternative responses to specific situations, and practice with positive reinforcement in the milieu. Modeling is especially important in learning assertive management of daily situations, rather than the usual aggressive or passive-aggressive coping behaviors.

Shaping. Shaping is the gradual process of behavior change through the achievement of smaller objectives. Often, it is unrealistic for the child to achieve a long-range goal without gradual steps in between. With shaping techniques, the child is reinforced for any behavior that approximates the final desired result.

The Severely Impaired Child

An occasional youngster, usually undersocialized and aggressive, persists with behavior so disruptive and unmanageable that he does not respond to ordinary behavior programs. He consumes an inordinate amount of staff time, interferes with the treatment programs of other children, and eventually erodes the staff's positive regard and ability to be therapeutic. At Ohio State University, a behavior management plan known as "The Private Room Program" has shown promise with a number of these children. It serves to provide a high degree of external control, while giving the milieu a reprieve and allowing the youngster a fresh opportunity to earn support and positive regard from his peers and staff members.

After a careful explanation of the plan, verbal and written, the child is assigned to a private room or to a screened living area, if only shared quarters are available. Of each hour, 55 minutes are spent in his room with solitary activities or school work and five minutes are spent with others out of his living area. Unacceptable behavior during out-of-room time earns an immediate return to his room. Five additional minutes are added to his out-of-room time for each consecutive successful eight-hour period. That is, he earns increasing amounts of time out of his room as he is able to demonstrate self-control for increasing lengths of time. Close supervision and support during out-of-room time is directed toward facilitating positive interactions. Most youngsters, even severely behaviorally impaired, are able to quickly earn increasing amounts of time to be with peers and then move into a less restrictive behavior management plan.

Use of Seclusion and Time-Out

Time-out, whether by sending the child to his room or sitting him on a chair, may serve a variety of functions, including punishment, removal from peers reinforcing his negative behavior, or interruption of escalating negative behaviors. Seclusion, on the other hand, refers to placing the child in a special, unfurnished room to allow him to regain self-control, while free of environmental stimulation. The procedure is intended to protect the child and others in the environment; it is not to be used as a punishing technique. The child should be returned to the milieu at once, when he regains adequate self-control. Frequent, documented checks by staff members insure the child's safety and determine when he can be removed from seclusion. The sensory deprivation of an isolation unit may worsen the behavior of a child with already tenuous reality testing. In such instances, it is best to minimize seclusion time or, preferably, to find an alternative means of helping the child with his out-of-control behavior. Additionally, attention incurred during the uproar of taking a child to seclusion unwillingly may reinforce and encourage negative behaviors.

As a special procedure, written facility guidelines are utilized to incorporate seclusion into the child's individual treatment plan.

SUMMARY AND CONCLUSIONS

Conduct-disordered children present a challenge to the child-care worker, both from the unending number of children needing service and the vast array of their presenting problems. The child-care worker offers the youngster assistance toward change by positive role modeling, behavior shaping techniques, confrontation, and insight-oriented "life-space" discussions. Progress in the treatment program and maintenance of these changes depend not only on the expertise of the treatment providers, but also on the youngster's efforts, motivation, and environmental support system.

Guidelines for a behavior therapy program may be found in Table 13-2 and a sample behavior program in Table 13-3.

TABLE 13-2
GUIDELINES FOR BEHAVIOR THERAPY PROGRAMS

DO—

Carefully design the behavior program, utilizing input from all staff members having regular contact with the child.

Systematically choose target behaviors and monitor the child's progress in the program.

Encourage the child's participation in the design and monitoring of his program, to elicit cooperation and increase feelings of control and responsibility.

Select effective reinforcers, based on staff observations and the child's ideas.

"Shape" the child's behavior by beginning at a level at which the child can succeed, gradually increasing expectations as he shows mastery.

Choose time intervals for reinforcement according to the level of the child's ability to delay gratification.

Provide a written copy of the program to the child, posting another copy easily visible to all staff members.

Keep the program fresh by regular review and update of target behaviors and reinforcers.

Apply the program with respect and positive regard for the child.

DON'T—

Hastily design and implement a program without ample opportunity for discussion and communication among staff members.

Design a complicated program beyond the child's level of understanding or ability to be consistently successful.

Allow failure to occur through careless or inconsistent application of reinforcers.

Lecture, scold, or nag the child while applying punishment procedures.

TABLE 13-3
SAMPLE BEHAVIOR PROGRAM

TARGET BEHAVIORS:	Threatening Stealing Lying
APPROPRIATE BEHAVIORS:	Interacts without verbal or physical aggression Follows directions and limits
REINFORCERS:	
Immediate	1 token for each 15-minute period with appropriate behaviors
Long-range	2 tokens earn one pool game 3 tokens earn a group walk or building privilege with staff member 4 tokens earn half-hour gym time with staff member
PUNISHMENT:	
If targeted behavior occurs:	No reinforcer for the 15-minute time period 15 minutes time-out in room 30 minutes time-out if physical aggression is involved

BIBLIOGRAPHY

Graziano AM (ed): *Behavior Therapy with Children.* Chicago, Aldine/Atherton, 1975, vol 2

Kaufman LM, Wagner BR: A systematic treatment technology for temper control disorders. *Behavior Therapy* 3:84-90, 1972

Maloney DM, Fixson DL, Maloney KB: Antisocial behavior: Behavior modification, in Wolman BB, Egan J, Ross AO (eds): *Handbook of Treatment of Mental Disorders in Childhood and Adolescence.* Englewood Cliffs, NJ, Prentice-Hall, 1978

Maloney KB, Fixson DL, Maloney DM, Phillips EL: Behavior technology in child-care: The teaching-parent and the teaching-family model, in Beker J (ed): *The Child-Care Worker in the United States: A Comparative Analysis of Evolving Role Models.* New York, Human Sciences Press, 1982

Marohn RC: Adolescent violence: Causes and treatment. *Journal of the American Academy of Child Psychiatry* 21:354-360, 1982

Redl F: *When We Deal With Children.* New York, Free Press, 1966

Robins LN: *Deviant Children Grown Up.* Baltimore, Williams and Wilkins, 1966

Sachs D: The efficacy of time-out procedure in a variety of behavior problems, in McDermott JF and Harrison SI (eds): *Psychiatric Treatment of the Child.* New York, Jason Aaronson, 1977

Trieshman AE, Whittaker JK, Brendtro LK: *The Other 23 Hours.* Chicago, Aldrine Publishing Company, 1969

White GD, Nielson G, Johnson SM: Time-out duration and suppression of deviant behavior in children. *Journal of Applied Behavior Analysis* 5:111-120, 1972

Chapter 14

PSYCHOPHYSIOLOGIC DISORDERS

R. DEAN CODDINGTON, MD

This chapter is devoted to a most interesting group of ailments that were formerly called "psychosomatic." The term was used to classify a disease in which both psychological and physical symptoms were present, or in which psychic factors seemed to produce physical symptoms. The classification has fallen into disuse: We now recognize that biological manifestations or mechanisms are present in almost all psychiatric illnesses, and we are now aware that psychological stressors can, and often do, precipitate a variety of physical illnesses. Therefore, there are now no specific groups of illnesses that are referred to as psychosomatic disorders.

Then why write a chapter on the subject? We do so because of the importance of the interface between mind and body and because children, inarticulate by nature, have trouble describing their problems and are sometimes accused of imagining pain or disease. The term, "psychophysiologic," is felt to be a bit more descriptive, due to the subtle implication that the physical manifestations may simply be extreme variations in normal—ie, physiologic—reactions.

PHYSIOLOGIC REACTIONS

A pediatrician was called to see a newborn baby, the first born of an intelligent and enthusiastic young mother who had been discharged from the hospital two days earlier. The baby had diarrhea and seemed disinterested in food.

The physical examination wasn't helpful. Since a different pediatrician had cared for the baby in the newborn nursery, the mother was asked how things had gone. Because of a mild anemia, the baby had been given a small blood transfusion, a common practice at the time; the mother remembered the doctor saying, "Be sure to keep his blood up or he'll need another transfusion." That was the only part of the doctor's message that she remembered.

The young, inexperienced mother went about obeying this command in the only way she knew, by making certain her baby ate properly. She felt food was the key to "keeping one's blood up"; she therefore set up a fairly rigid schedule of feedings. The baby's body responded with frequent expulsion of feces, due to the well-known gastrocolic reflex. When the stomach is filled, the colon becomes more active and defecation often occurs, unless consciously resisted. In addition, anxiety was transmitted to the baby via the mother's increased tenseness as she held him. The diarrhea was produced by the combination of the mother's tenseness and the child's colonic stimulation through the gastrocolic reflex, associated with frequent feedings.

> An 8-year-old girl was having an acute attack of asthma when the pediatrician arrived at her home. Judy had had only a few prior attacks and was known to be allergic to certain pollens. Her cyanosis and respiratory distress prompted the pediatrician, who had not seen her before, to send for an ambulance to transport her to the hospital.
>
> An aunt from out of town was staying with Judy at the time, while her mother was in the hospital having another baby and her father was away on business. Since Judy seemed so alone, tended only by a relative stranger, the pediatrician tried to reassure her by explaining that she was going to the same hospital that her mother was in now and that, although she would be on a different floor, in all likelihood her mother could visit her in a day or two.

The pediatrician followed the ambulance to the hospital and was surprised to find his patient essentially well on arrival. She had been given oxygen but no medication; the anticipated reunion with her mother was apparently curative.

It is well known that a child's body temperature may rise one or two degrees as a result of excitement or apprehension. Hospitalization itself can serve as a stimulus for what is sometimes termed "psychogenic fever." Many other, if not all, physiological parameters are also subject to emotional or psychological influence.

NATURE VS. NURTURE

The child is conceived with a genetic template that determines his sex, appearance, and physiological integrity. The status of every organ system is established at the outset by the genetic composition derived from the parents. There is no doubt of the existence of this natural biological predisposition to physiological functioning. Ordinarily the conceptus thrives, bathed in the amniotic fluid of a normal mother who provides it with nutriments through the umbilical cord. But what happens when there is a deviation from this usual state of affairs? What happens if the mother is overanxious, due, for example, to an overly active thyroid? She pours large amounts of thyroid hormone into her unborn baby, affecting his developing endocrine system and altering, perhaps forever, the status of the baby's thyroid gland. The endocrinologic changes associated with a mother's chronic depression may also permanently modify the genetically established fetal endocrine system. Thus, the intrauterine environment combines with nature to establish what are sometimes lifelong patterns of functioning.

After birth, other environmental influences play a role in establishing permanent patterns of behavior—both physiological behavior and behavior that is usually considered to be psychologically determined. A child born with an allergic diathesis, genetically determined, with a few bouts of asthma precipitated by exposure to pollen to which she is allergic, may then be predisposed to respond to a psychological stressor in a manner in which her body is accustomed to respond: with an asthmatic attack. Such is the case in the second vignette in the previous section. The child's respiratory system may not respond consistently in this way, for other coping responses may prove more efficient as she grows. On the other hand, an overbundance of tender loving care during asthmatic episodes may permanently establish this mode of response. So, it's not nature versus nurture but, rather, the interaction of nature and nurture that sets the stage for the occurrence of a psychophysiologic disorder.

It stands to reason that there is a wider fluctuation in all physiologic parameters in the very young, as compared with the physically mature individual. We know this to be true of some functions such as temperature, heart rate, and respiratory rate in the newborn, in comparison with an older child, though we do not know it to be true in many other bodily activities. It has simply not been studied sufficiently. The temperature of the newborn depends largely on the temperature of the environment, with the neonate's control mechanism apparently not working. The control mechanism of the young child responds wildly when microorganisms invade the body, but temperature fluctuations of this magnitude are much less common in adulthood. The temperature of a young athlete rises with the excitement of the contest—not so in adults.

Some of the control that comes with maturity is apparently due to training. Just as Pavlov's dogs were taught to salivate when a bell was rung, control of many physiologic systems can be altered by life experiences. Physiologic functioning is partly a learned phenomenon; genetics and the environment combine to establish mature modes of operation. As a term applied to children, psychophysiologic is, perhaps, meaningless because it is all-encompassing. On the other hand, it is exceedingly important, since the term reminds us that our attitudes toward sick children may play a leading role in determining not only their illness behavior as adults, but the very presence or absence of illness itself.

When children develop hypochondriacal symptoms, the particular symptom they choose (and one should not infer this to be a voluntary or conscious choice) is one with which they have had some personal experience. A child who had rheumatic fever with redness and swelling of a knee at age 6 may get pain in the knee at age 10 when trying to cope with a stressor. A mother's description of her migraine headaches may, under certain conditions, actuate the development of psychogenic headaches in a little girl; in such a case, the child seems to identify with the mother's headaches, as well as with her various personality traits.

ATTENTION-GETTING BEHAVIOR

When children complain of what appear to be psychogenic symptoms, adults immediately question their motivation. To the observer, the connection between an environmental stressor and the symptoms seems to be a cause and effect relationship. The relationship appears so clear that the child is often accused of consciously and willfully seeking attention. The message is, in effect, that the symptomatology is imagined, not real; the child is "lying" to get attention.

The reader is urged to think for a moment of his or her own experience with a headache that was due to a bad day at the office or to mandated attendance at an undesirable social function. The pain in such a situation is real! The headache hurts, just as much when psychologically caused as when due to a viral infection. All pain is referred to the brain for evaluation, which means that there is a large subjective element in what is called "pain." It is unfair to accuse anyone, child or adult, of imagining the pain, except in the rare situation in which the patient is malingering. We should routinely give the child the benefit of the doubt and accept his complaint as a real, bona fide symptom. Once we have gotten to know the child and are certain of a conscious element in his illness behavior, we can deal directly with it, but not before.

When the child describes his symptom to an understanding, empathic adult (and he is, of course, quite selective in choosing adults in whom to confide) and when the situation seems abundantly clear, there is a tendency for the less experienced adult to conclude that the child is simply seeking attention. Not only do we feel the symptom is imagined or a straightforward lie; we reason, in addition, that the child is simply trying to get us to come to his rescue and solve the original problem—some difficulty with friends, perhaps. The fact that the child searches out an empathic adult, combined with the possible relief of symptoms, seems to convince the less experienced adult that the whole scenario was merely attention-seeking behavior. This line of reasoning is not only unfair; it is also, in most situations, grossly incorrect.

PHYSICAL DISORDERS WITH PROMINENT PSYCHOLOGICAL COMPONENTS

It should be apparent at this point that psychological factors play a role in all physical disorders in children. A brief discussion follows of those disorders in which this factor is especially prominent.

Peptic Ulcers

Peptic ulcers sometimes occur in infants and older children alike, after severe burns or injuries. Although these are called stress ulcers, the reference is to physical rather than psychological stressors. The stomach or duodenal ulcer, with a prominent psychological component, is seen in children above the age of 9 or 10 years, and is more common in adolescent males. In general, boys with stomach or duodenal ulcers are immature and have remained very dependent: They do not share the common drive of adolescents to gain emancipation from the family. Rather, they are conflicted about a desire for emancipation and their need to retain a dependent relationship.

> Charles, a 14-year-old with a 2-year history of peptic ulceration, said he liked being with peers. But, in reality, he looked forward most of all to his divorced mother's day off, when he stayed home from school and helped her clean house.

Patients like Charles have definite and specific intrapsychic conflicts (see chapter 8). An Oedipal conflict is clearly present in this case, with Charles assuming the role of his missing father. One might infer from this brief vignette that the mother also has a conflict, in that she permits him to stay home; it seems to be a symbiotic relationship, each person depending on the other for emotional nourishment. In other cases, the child may have difficulty handling angry feelings.

Children with peptic ulcers are not difficult to treat, though a combined medical and psychological approach is necessary. The medical treatment is straightforward, aimed at reducing acid production in the stomach. Psychotherapy is facilitated by the patient's need for dependence, since he will relate quickly to the therapist as long as no attempt is made to break up his dependent relationship with his mother. Reducing dependency can be a worthwhile secondary treatment goal but should not be attempted prematurely. At first, the reason for the reluctance to mature and gain independence should be explored.

Ulcerative Colitis

Ulcerative colitis is characterized by abdominal pain and bleeding inside the colon, producing a bloody, mucoid diarrhea. The disease may start suddenly and follow a rapid, fulminating course ending in death. More often it begins gradually and continues chronically. Children with ulcerative colitis, usually adolescents, are also passive and overly dependent. The mother is usually the dominant parent, with the father often submissive and retiring. The families are sometimes described as "bowel oriented," possibly conditioning the child's colon to respond to psychological conflict with the increased activity and inflammation.

Since death can occur, the child must be involved in a medical and psychological treatment program. One must be very careful in psychotherapy, for confrontations which are premature or stressful may exacerbate the colitis and disrupt treatment.

Idiopathic Celiac Disease

Another disorder of the gastrointestinal tract is idiopathic celiac disease. It is characterized by a large, pale, foul-smelling stool and is apparently due to an enzymatic defect that makes it hard to digest the gluten of wheat. It can occur in infancy and run a chronic course, with periods of remission and exacerbation. It is usually controlled by eliminating gluten from the diet, though emotional stress is often followed by another episode of diarrhea. Sometimes gluten can be reinstituted in the diet without producing an exacerbation, when there is no emotional stress. Thus, it seems that we have another example of a genetic defect that is necessary for the disease to occur but insufficient to cause the disease; an emotional or psychic factor is also needed.

Obesity and Anorexia Nervosa

Eating disorders have received considerable public attention in recent years, for the most part due to the marked increase in their prevalence. Research studies have failed to eliminate controversy as to their etiology. The view propounded by Bruch in the 1950s and 1960s—namely, that eating disorders are based primarily on the mother-infant relationship and early feeding patterns—remains valid. Family relationships are important factors in both obesity and anorexia nervosa, and sociocultural values are also significant in the latter. The interrelationship between the biological and psychosocial, between nutritional needs, eating habits, and emotional needs, however, remains controversial.

The eating disorders are discussed in detail in chapter 15.

Bronchial Asthma

Bronchial asthma is more common in boys than in girls. The basic defect seems to be a particularly sensitive bronchial tree, sensitive to allergens, irritants, and physical and emotional stressors. In children with this hereditary predisposition, attacks may be triggered by fear of parental loss, open conflict between child and parent, and marital problems. Coughing spells may also precipitate attacks, a fact that enables the child to consciously bring on an attack when the price is right. That is, if he stands to gain sufficiently, he can use the illness as a means to an end.

The attitudes of physicians and parents are most important in the management of this condition, since each experience affects future experiences. Medical treatment by an understanding pediatrician who helps the parents through these frightening attacks is usually sufficient. In refractory cases, psychotherapy is indicated.

CHRONIC DISEASE

Any chronic disease in children carries with it major problems adjusting to the treatment regimen, the social isolation, the feeling of being less than whole, and the feeling of being special. Hemophilia, diabetes mellitus, juvenile rheumatoid arthritis, eczema, and any physical deformity (even as mild as prominent ears) are examples of disorders that carry a risk for the development of secondary psychiatric problems. Very often, a feedback mechanism develops wherein the secondary emotional problem adversely affects the initial problem. Psychological stressors can precipitate attacks of arthritic pain, cause a child to scratch his eczema, and prolong recovery from corrective surgical procedures.

> Karen, a 12-year-old diabetic, was hospitalized almost monthly with her diabetes out of control. After 2 years, she was admitted to a psychiatric hospital. While there she began to explore, with her therapist, the feelings she had in fourth grade when she was told she had diabetes. Since then she often wished to die and used her disease as a means to reach this goal—refusing to take her insulin or purposely rubbing the syringe in dirt before injecting herself. Although her course in the psychiatric facility was stormy, the outcome was quite satisfactory.

Most families have considerable difficulty dealing with the birth of a deformed child, though some do amazingly well. They may very well gain support from their church, extended family, and friends. Whatever the source of their faith, the result is sometimes nothing less than fantastic.

> A child born without legs was helped to cope successfully. He wanted to play golf in high school so he made a plaster cast of his rump and fastened it to the top of a stool. He rode in a golf cart, placed the stool near his ball, and, using his arms and shoulders,

hoisted himself up onto the stool. He hit the ball from this perch and continued on his way. At last report, he had finished his education and had established himself in a professional career.

His family must have been incredible! Such an outcome is not to be expected in the majority of cases.

Parents of children with seizure disorders are frequently afraid to spank them for fear of causing another convulsion. They may also feel compelled to overprotect their child, not permitting him to swim, climb trees, or cross busy streets, for fear that even a mild seizure will result in a serious injury. When the cause and treatment of a chronic disease are unknown, as is the case with juvenile rheumatoid arthritis, parents often blame themselves and also feel compelled to try a variety of treatment approaches. One mother was advised by a well-meaning stranger to soak her child's legs in sauerkraut juice, to cure arthritis. She warmed a large vat of juice on the stove, enough to cover her 6-year-old's legs, on the same day that the doctor instituted treatment with adrenocortical steroids. She knew using sauerkraut juice was foolish but simply could not resist.

Complicating, secondary psychiatric problems often accompany chronic physical illness, sometimes worsening the somatic symptomatology.

CONVERSION REACTIONS

The last group of problems that involve both physical and psychological components are referred to as conversion reactions, meaning that the anxiety associated with the psychological conflict is *converted* into a physical symptom. One of the remarkable things about this mechanism is the fact that it solves the psychological conflict immediately and completely—substituting a physical symptom that appears, to the outsider who hasn't experienced the patient's emotional pain and anxiety, infinitely more debilitating.

Tommy, an 8-year-old, lived in a crowded, high-rise apartment building. His bed was right next to a fourth-story window, so his mother had always warned him of the dangerous fall that could occur if he jumped on his bed. She had also warned him of the dangers of the neighborhood.

He did well in first and second grade; his mother always walked to and from school with him. He was transferred to another

> school for third grade, a school that had previously been devoted to use by crippled children. Many of the crippled children had been transferred to other schools in the interest of mainstreaming, but some remained. When Tommy entered the building, he was confronted with the sight of wheelchairs, crutches, and physically handicapped children, a sight that immediately reminded him of his mother's warnings to "be careful." The wish to avoid the frightening sight was greater than his concomitant desire to attend school. A conversion reaction took place, with Tommy's anxiety converted into the only symptom that could solve the problem, blindness.

Tommy had developed an hysterical blindness. His eyes were anatomically and physiologically normal, but he saw nothing. With psychotherapy focused on the conflict over freedom and danger, his vision returned gradually to normal.

Situations such as this are rare, but children can and do develop paralyses of their legs or arms, hysterical seizures, and other symptoms. The findings on physical examination do not follow true anatomical patterns but, rather, patterns determined by the child's belief and understanding of anatomy and physiology. For instance, a young child recently complained of double vision, a symptom that occurs when the eyes are not properly synchronized; an object is viewed slightly differently by each eye and a double image recorded in the brain. The child was asked what she saw when one eye was covered; she "saw" two images with her right eye but only one with her left. Since two images with a single eye cannot occur, the child apparently had an hysterical diplopia.

SUMMARY

In this chapter we have discussed a number of conditions in which both psychological and physical symptoms are present. The mechanisms by which the symptoms are produced vary, but the theme underlying the chapter should be apparent. During initial contacts, the child should be believed, no matter how unlikely the circumstances seem. Only when certain should one accuse the child of imagining the symptom or of outright fabrication.

BIBLIOGRAPHY

Prugh DG: *The psychosocial aspects of pediatrics.* Philadelphia, Lea & Febiger, 1983

Renbourn ET: Body temperature and pulse rate in boys and young men prior to sporting contests. A study of emotional hyperthermia: With a review of the literature. *J Psychosom Res* 4:149-175, 1960

Chapter 15

EATING DISORDERS: ANOREXIA NERVOSA AND BULIMIA

KATHARINE N. DIXON, MD

The increasing incidence of anorexia nervosa and bulimia reflects our cultural preoccupation with thinness, dieting, and food. Dieting is currently normative behavior for middle and upper social class adolescents, even though they may be of normal weight. Eating-related problems among high school and college women are taking on the contagious flavor of drug abuse in the late 60s. Anorexia and bulimia are observed most frequently in those countries where achievement and technology are important, thin women are admired, and food is abundant.

While these changing values do not cause an eating disorder, they contribute significantly to the development of anorexia or bulimia in vulnerable women. Such individuals tend to have been "good" children. In adolescence and adulthood their achievement-orientation, high need for approval, and perfectionism place them at risk to develop a food- and weight-related disorder characterized by extreme overcontrol and/or undercontrol.

Not unexpectedly, 95% are women. It is likely that male anorexics have associated gender identity problems, while little is known about male bulimia. Since muscle development is a focus for male adolescents, it could be speculated that excessive body building is the male counterpart of anorexia nervosa. Male athletes who need to maintain a certain weight (eg, wrestlers and jockeys) are known to use vomiting occasionally for weight control, but it is not known whether many of these athletes develop a full-blown eating disorder.

While anorexic and bulimic individuals are contrasts in eating restraint, they have similarities in personality traits and social class. Approximately one half of bulimic women were previously anorexic, while the remainder began as severe or chronic dieters.

Classic anorexia nervosa is a voluntary semistarvation in the relentless pursuit of thinness. Often beginning with a goal to lose just a few pounds, the anorexic eventually loses the ability to control continuing weight loss or to appreciate her thin appearance.

She resists others' efforts to restore her weight. Hunger, threats, and forced feeding do not discourage the anorexic from a compulsion to rid her body of fat.

At the other end of the continuum, bulimia, or "ox-hunger," is characterized by alternate binge-eating and purging (via vomiting, laxatives, or diuretics) or by fasting. Bulimics are usually of normal weight, depending on their eating and purging patterns.

Although anorexics and bulimics differ in their eating behaviors, they are similar in their preoccupation with food, thin body ideal, perfectionistic personality traits, poor assertion skills, and reliance on external approval. Bulimics are more likely to be outgoing, spontaneous, and impulsive; they have problems with depression, alcohol, or drugs and are less able to tolerate hunger.

The first half of the chapter will deal with diagnosis, medical aspects, psychological features, and treatment of anorexia nervosa. Similar areas of emphasis in regard to bulimia will be covered in the remainder of the chapter.

ANOREXIA NERVOSA

Diagnosis

A confident diagnosis requires that both attitudinal and physical aspects of the disorder be present. Criteria for diagnosis are listed in Table 15-1. At times, the anorexic's denial, withholding, or skill in masking psychological symptoms may hinder evaluation, but careful interviewing and parents' history will usually clarify the clinical picture. With skillful interviewing, a diagnosis can be made and treatment can begin before severe weight loss has occurred. If the patient has weight loss without characteristic anorexic attitudes, another cause should be suspected — eg, depression or medical disease.

Medical Aspects

Malnutrition itself produces many of the physical changes, laboratory abnormalities, and psychological symptoms seen in the severely restricting anorexic. Common physical signs and symptoms are loss of menstrual periods (amenorrhea), fine body hair (lanugo), slow heart rate, low blood pressure, yellowish skin color

TABLE 15-1
DIAGNOSTIC CRITERIA FOR ANOREXIA NERVOSA

An intense fear of becoming obese, which does not diminish as weight loss continues.
Disturbance of body image, eg, claiming to "feel fat" even when emaciated.
Weight loss of at least 25% of original body weight. (If under 18 years of age, weight loss from original body weight plus projected weight gain expected from growth charts may be combined to make 25%.)
Refusal to maintain body weight over a minimal normal weight for age and height.
No known physical illness that would account for the weight loss.

(carotenemia), cool extremities, and constipation. Abnormal laboratory findings include anemia, low white blood cell count, low cholesterol, increased cortisol secretion, and low thyroid function. These abnormalities usually will return to normal with improved nutrition and weight gain.

The most common causes of death in anorexia nervosa are infection, suicide, and complications of starvation (eg, electrolyte imbalance). Hospitalization is indicated if the anorexic's weight is 25% below her ideal body weight. Since malnutrition interferes with the anorexic's ability to use psychotherapy, progress as an outpatient is usually unsatisfactory. A psychiatric facility able to provide adequate medical services is preferable to hospitalization on a medical unit.

Psychological Features

Since the anorexic usually experiences hunger until the final phase of starvation, the term "anorexia" is misleading. The anorexic goes to great lengths to deny and suppress hunger feelings, including drinking large quantities of liquids and diet pop, exercising, and calling on willpower.

Thought process impairment in the starving anorexic can make even ordinary conversation difficult. Obsessive thinking revolves around food, weight, calories, and how to avoid weight gain. Anorexic "attitudes" include an inability to recognize the increasing emaciation, an irrational wish to be thin even when already severely underweight, and even denial of illness. The fear of gaining weight leads to desperate and manipulative behaviors to avoid food intake or get rid of calories consumed. The previously obedient daughter becomes irritable and perhaps explosive, when her parents pressure her to eat more normally.

Major depression with insomnia, guilt feelings, low self-esteem, hopelessness, and suicidal ideation may complicate the course of anorexia and delay recovery. Depression needs to be distinguished from "empty" anorexia, with its rigidity, lack of spontaneity, and restricted fantasy life.

Treatment

Anorexic adolescents are among the most challenging psychiatric inpatients with whom to work therapeutically. They lie, cheat, manipulate, divide staff personnel, and in other ways create intrastaff tension and conflict. Successful treatment requires meticulous attention to intrastaff teamwork and communication and must speak to both nutritional and psychological aspects of the disorder.

Medical management. The initial phase of hospitalization should be directed toward medical assessment and restoration of nutrition. Particular care must be taken to monitor the patient's physical condition and to correct dehydration and electrolyte imbalance. An occasional severely starved or recalcitrant anorexic may need intravenous therapy or hyperalimentation, but the majority will respond favorably to a behavioral program or firm encouragement to eat sensibly. Careful explanation of the need for gradual but steady weight gain, with staff reassurance of support to prevent overeating, will be adequate for some patients to initiate sensible eating patterns. Failure to improve eating within a few days of admission indicates the need for a more structured behavioral plan.

Milieu management. In the Adolescent Psychiatry Inpatient Unit at Ohio State University, a graph is drawn projecting the anorexic's weight gain at a quarter pound per day (Figures 15-1 and 15-2). The graph is posted where the patient can see her weight progress. If the patient can demonstrate the capability for steady self-determined weight gain, she is allowed to take responsibility for her own nutrition and weight restoration. On the other hand, if, after several days of observation, the anorexic is unable to initiate a steady gain, she is placed on a behavioral management plan (Table 15-2) until her weight gain is judged to be progressing satisfactorily and she is capable of assuming responsibility for her nutrition.

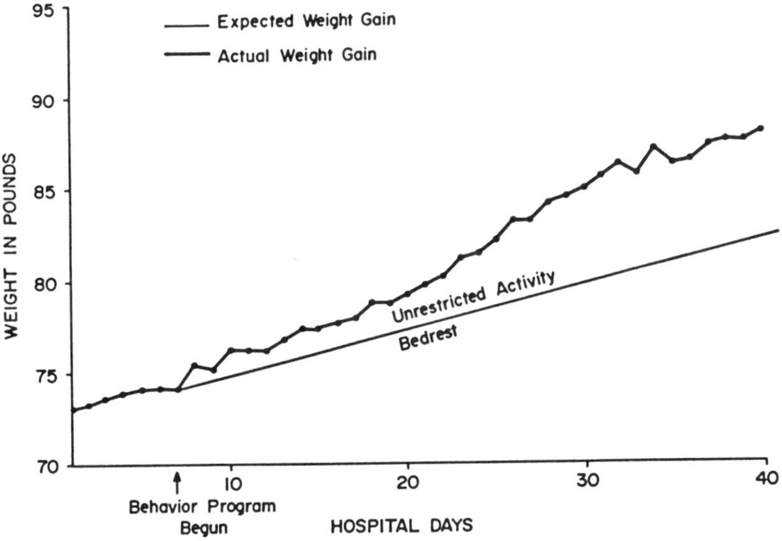

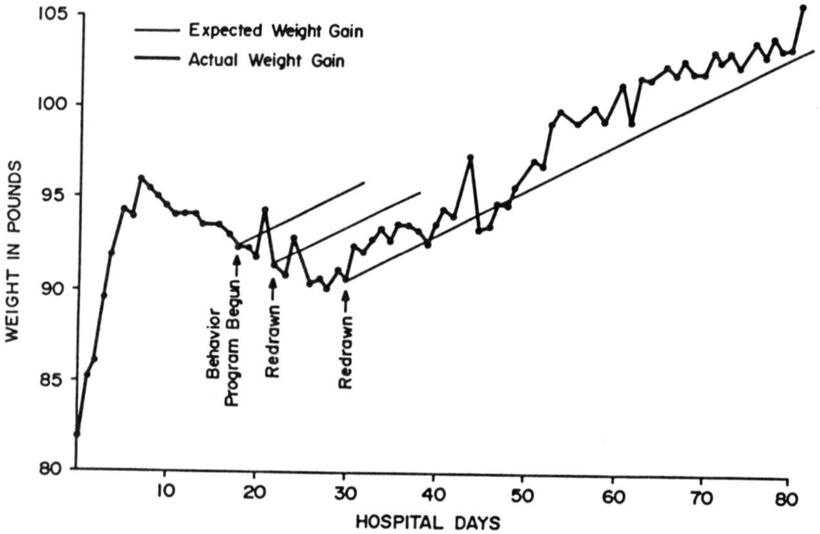
105
100
95
90
85
80
WEIGHT IN POUNDS
Expected Weight Gain
Actual Weight Gain
Behavior Program Begun
Redrawn
Redrawn
10
20
30
40
50
60
70
80
HOSPITAL DAYS

TABLE 15-2
BEHAVIORAL APPROACH FOR THE HOSPITALIZED ANOREXIC*

Objective	*Potential Problem*	*Plan*
A. The patient will have dietary intake adequate to produce ¼ lb gain/day.		Plot the patient's expected daily weight gain on a calibrated graph. (See Figures 15-1 and 15-2)
	1. Failure to gain required weight.	The patient is weighed each morning before breakfast. If the patient's weight is on or above the line of expected weight gain, the patient is rewarded with normal activity without restrictions for that day. If not, she is placed on bedrest, in pajamas, for the remainder of the day. Bathroom privileges are supervised and the patient does not have access to radio, reading materials, or peer contacts.
	2. Patient falsely manipulates daily weight.	The patient remains in bed until 7:30 AM when nursing escorts her to the bathroom, closely observes voiding and changing into designated pajamas, and weighs her.
B. The patient will eat a balanced diet and establish normal eating patterns.	1. Patient does not make appropriate food choices.	A dietician reviews food preferences with the patient. The patient selects food prefences daily from a provided menu.
	2. Patient unable to tolerate normal-sized meals.	Initially, the dietician will provide 2000 calories/day in 6 small meals. Caloric value of food consumed is calculated and reported to the staff after each meal. Daily calories are increased as needed to provide

TABLE 15-2 *(Continued)*
BEHAVIORAL APPROACH FOR THE HOSPITALIZED ANOREXIC*

Objective	*Potential Problem*	*Plan*
		steady weight gain, and feedings are consolidated into 3 main meals when tolerated. The patient eats prepared meals in dining room with peers when not on bedrest. When on bedrest, she eats in bed.
C. Patient will eat entire meal and/or drink all of supplement without any subtle negative reinforcement for not eating.		Staff provides 1:1 supervision during meal time and does not allow the patient to manipulate conversation about the program or food. Staff confirms meal items on tray using the diet slip and observes that the patient does not toss any foods off the tray. After 30 minutes, the tray is removed without comment. The tray is checked for food eaten and hidden food.
	1. Patient leaves part or all of meal uneaten.	Calories not consumed at a meal are replaced with equivalent caloric value of a liquid supplement (Ensure, Sustacal, etc). Limit the amount of liquid supplement given at one time (eg, 200 cc of Ensure), since excessive amounts can produce diarrhea. Staff provides 1:1 supervision while patient drinks entire amount of supplement. If liquid supplement is refused, the patient remains on her bed until next mealtime.

TABLE 15-2 *(Continued)*
BEHAVIORAL APPROACH FOR THE HOSPITALIZED ANOREXIC*

Objective	*Potential Problem*	*Plan*
	2. Patient attempts to vomit consumed calories.	Patient is provided with 1:1 staff supervision 30 minutes after meals, liquid supplements, and medications.
	3. Overeating.	Staff sets limits on excessive eating at meals and snacks. Family and friends are not permitted to bring food for the patient. Off-unit privileges are monitored.
D. The program will remain constant while anger and feelings of ineffectiveness are acknowledged.	1. Anger at staff over loss of autonomy. 2. Patient attempts to manipulate the program.	One nurse and/or physician will answer all questions or respond directly to comments about the program or issues of weight and food. Auxiliary staff will focus on identification and elaboration of feelings while providing support.
E. The patient will have appropriate physical activity to promote and increase muscle mass and tone.	1. Loss of muscle mass and tone, due to starvation.	Physical therapy is initiated when the patient's nutritional status has improved sufficiently.
	2. Exercises to burn off calories.	Limits are set on exercising and other recreational activities according to doctor's orders.
F. The patient will identify and experiment with healthy coping skills.	1. Limited coping skills.	Nursing staff assists the patient in identifying feelings, verbalizing them assertively, and coping with daily life situations in healthy ways. Assertiveness training classes are encouraged.

*The author gratefully acknowledges Jerilyn Bunofsky, R.N., Head Nurse of the Ohio State University Adolescent Psychiatry Inpatient Unit, who outlined the behavioral approach for the hospitalized anorexic.

The anorexic's personality characteristics and weight gain pattern may provide clues to her potential for becoming bulimic. Figure 15-1 illustrates the steady, controlled weight gain of a rigid, extremely self-disciplined adolescent, unlikely to develop symptoms of bulimia. In contrast, Figure 15-2 shows the initial rapid weight gain and frequent fluctuations in a low-weight anorexic adolescent with bulimic symptoms, including laxative use. Her initial dramatic weight gain reflects fluid retention commonly seen when laxative abuse is stopped. This adolescent was spontaneous, outgoing, and impulsive in contrast to the purely restricting subgroup of patients with anorexia nervosa illustrated in Figure 15-1.

Particular care must be taken to prevent overeating or binge-eating by the recovering hospitalized anorexic who hopes to "eat" her way out of the hospital or who shows signs of becoming bulimic. Prolonged bed rest as part of the anorexic's behavioral program needs to be avoided. Should the anorexic's weight lag significantly behind her needed weight gain, it is sometimes advisable to redraw a fresh line to avoid discouragement and giving up. An explanation and firm direction will minimize the likelihood that she will view this maneuver as subtle permission to continue at a low weight (Figure 15-2).

The importance of staff teamwork cannot be overemphasized. Not only is the desperate anorexic capable of manipulating and dividing staff; she may also attempt to bring her parents and therapist into the melee. A balance of firm, consistent staff authority and parent self-direction holds most promise for a smooth course of treatment.

Straightforward discussion between the attending physician and nursing staff is crucial for dealing with staff anxiety about the low-weight, and perhaps medically unstable, anorexic. Unless this issue can be dealt with openly, the treatment team may not be able to develop a consistent and rational plan for patient management. Premature or unnecessary hyperalimentation or tube feeding can be precipitated by the physician's failure to provide sufficient direction and support for the therapeutic team.

Psychotherapy. Ideally, individual psychotherapy and management of the milieu should be provided by different members of the treatment team. Therapists highly experienced in treatment of eating disorders can sometimes perform both functions effectively.

As a general rule, separation of therapist and environmental authority roles reduces the time spent during therapy attempting to bargain, negotiate, and manipulate programming and allows the therapist to focus on psychological issues.

This does not imply that the therapist should prohibit discussion about eating and weight issues, particularly the anorexic's feelings in this area. On the contrary, the therapist needs to help the patient understand the association between her feelings, life circumstances, and her eating disorder.

Even supportive psychotherapy can be difficult until nutrition is restored to a level where rational thinking returns. As the anorexic's thought processes improve, therapy can be directed toward helping the patient understand her symptoms in the context of her total life situation, while encouraging her to develop healthier, nonfood or weight-related coping alternatives.

Family therapy during hospitalization is crucial for maintenance of the recovering anorexic's progress after discharge. Even when the family's contribution to the anorexic's illness has been minimal, the daughter's anorexia has had an impact on the family. It is not unusual for one or both parents to share in the daughter's denial. Even parents who have read extensively about the disorder may focus on refusal to eat as their daughter's only problem.

Drug therapy. Since no drug is available for the treatment of anorexia nervosa itself, chemotherapy is directed toward alleviation of secondary symptoms. Multivitamins, electrolyte replacement, stool softeners, and oral nutritional supplements may be used to remediate malnutrition symptoms. Although an anorexic may refuse food but readily drink a prescribed nutritional supplement, prolonged use of liquid supplements should be avoided. The staff should encourage an early transition to obtaining all calories through food intake.

Antidepressants can be helpful in the anorexic with depressive features, but dosage, vital signs, and cardiac function should be monitored closely. Appetite stimulants (eg, marijuana or steroids) and antipsychotics have not been useful in the treatment of primary anorexia nervosa.

BULIMIA

Diagnosis

Bulimia, recurrent episodes of binge-eating followed by purging and/or fasting to avoid weight gain, is a fairly common problem among adolescents and young women. Recent media attention and dissemination of information by national self-help organizations have encouraged increasing numbers of bulimic women to identify themselves to the health-care profession. As a result, bulimia is beginning to present as a greater problem than the restricting type of anorexia nervosa. Diagnostic criteria for bulimia are listed in Table 15-3.

Onset of bulimia usually occurs in late adolescence or young adulthood, in contrast to the early or midadolescent onset of anorexia. About one half of bulimics have progressed from restricting anorexia to the full-blown bulimic syndrome. In this "mixed" disorder, the individual is usually of normal weight, though she previously had severe weight loss and amenorrhea as a restricting anorexic. Both the bulimic and anorexic overvalue a thin body ideal, but the bulimic is unable to maintain the anorexic's rigid dieting.

TABLE 15-3
DIAGNOSTIC CRITERIA FOR BULIMIA

Recurrent episodes of binge-eating

At least three of the following:

- Consumption of high-caloric, easily ingested food during a binge
- Inconspicuous eating during a binge
- Termination of binge by abdominal pain, sleep, social interruption, or self-induced vomiting
- Repeated attempts to lose weight by severely restrictive diets, self-induced vomiting, or use of cathartics or diuretics
- Frequent weight fluctuations greater than ten pounds

Awareness that the eating pattern is abnormal, and feeling out of control when eating

Depressed mood and self-deprecating thoughts following binges

Cause not anorexia nervosa or any physical disorder

She begins to binge-eat, usually on sweet or salty foods, with subsequent vomiting, laxative or diuretic use, or fasting to get rid of calories consumed during binges. Whether a "mixed" or a pure bulimic who has never been anorexic, the individual who learns to purge decreases her need for eating with self-restraint, and binge-eating becomes a habitual method to relieve stress. Food is used primarily to meet emotional rather than nutritional needs.

Medical Aspects

Medical complications of bulimia, relatively unstudied compared to those of anorexia nervosa, are primarily caused by the particular purging method used. Electrolyte imbalance from vomiting, laxatives, and diuretics may produce symptoms of weakness, fatigue, and dizziness. Salivary gland swelling and erosion of dental enamel commonly occur in the vomiter. Death can result from cardiac arrest or stomach rupture.

Psychological Features

Like anorexia, bulimia is an emotional disorder with accompanying secondary physical signs and symptoms. While bulimic behaviors may be the most striking aspect of the clinical picture, it should be recognized that these eating behaviors are merely symptomatic of underlying personality problems and psychopathology. The bulimic resembles the restricting anorexic in her inadequate assertiveness, reliance on external approval, perfectionistic traits, and feelings of ineffectiveness. She is more likely than the anorexic to have problems with depression and substance abuse.

The bulimic uses food to avoid painful feelings and direct confrontation with personal and interpersonal issues. Although the binge-purge-fast behaviors may have begun as a maladaptive reaction to a stressful event or life period, the pattern continues as a chronic and universal response to everyday anxieties and feelings of ineffectiveness.

The bulimic has to be a master of denial and rationalization to allow the destructive, health-eroding, binge-purge pattern to continue. Examples of the bulimic's faulty thinking include:

"I won't be a binge-vomiter long enough to sustain damage to my body."

"I know I'll keep thinking about food this evening; I may as well binge so I can concentrate on other things."

"If I binge, I won't feel so depressed (anxious, lonely, angry)."

"I've already overeaten. I may as well enjoy myself now, since I know I'll have to vomit anyway."

Shame and self-disgust cause the bulimic to hide her abnormal eating behaviors, even from family members, and she becomes increasingly socially isolated. Obsessive thinking may interfere with concentration on studies or work performance.

Treatment

Recovery from bulimia involves elimination of the habit of binging and purging, restoration of sensible eating patterns, and a self-awareness of attitudes, personality traits, and thought patterns that contribute to bulimic behavior. These therapeutic goals are achieved most effectively and efficiently by a combination of psychotherapeutic and behavioral approaches. The bulimic patient is less likely than the anorexic patient to require hospitalization; treatment most often occurs on an outpatient basis. Indications for hospitalization are failure to produce significant change while in outpatient psychotherapy or deterioration in physical health.

Behavior therapy. The bulimic's tendency to apply "all-or-nothing" thinking to the recovery process produces a cycle of unrealistic resolutions to be completely binge-free, followed by relapse into former binge-purge patterns and self-reproach. Behavior techniques allow the bulimic to begin control of her disordered eating in small increments.

A food diary—with recorded information about time of day, length of eating time, eating in response to hunger vs. feeling state, activity and location of eating—can help delineate eating and purging patterns. From this, then, specific interventions can be devised to interrupt the usually predictable binge-purge pattern. For example, if binge-eating is associated with arriving home from school to an empty house, the bulimic adolescent can plan after school activities or time with friends to postpone eating until other family members arrive home. Additional interventions include removing or avoiding the usual stimuli for binge-eating, avoiding eating with other solitary activities (watching TV, cooking), postponing eating while in a binge mood, and planning alternatives for stress management.

Strategies to decrease binge-vomiting episodes need to be directed toward prevention of the binge itself. Once a bulimic feels she has overeaten, she is almost always compelled to purge or fast. Elimination of binge-vomiting must be accompanied by beginning to eat sensibly at regular mealtimes. Otherwise, the bulimic who is decreasing binge episodes may fall back into the anorexic pattern of fasting.

Weekly goal setting in terms of specific interventions to reduce the likelihood of binge-eating and to increase days free from binge-vomiting provides structure and incentive for steady progress. For best results, the bulimic needs to integrate behavior techniques with an understanding of the relationship between feelings, underlying motivations, and eating behaviors.

Psychotherapy. Bulimic adolescents are good psychotherapy patients since they are usually intelligent, verbal, attractive, and spontaneous. Since they tend to experience more distress from their disorder, they are more motivated than restricting anorexics to seek treatment on their own. However, need for approval can impair their ability to be self-disclosing with a therapist, and they may drop out of therapy early.

The bulimic's normal eating behaviors are perpetuated, in part, by a wish to achieve or maintain an unrealistically low weight while being unable to adhere to the necessary continuous and restrictive diet. They may approach psychotherapy with the unrealistic expectation that they will be able to rid themselves of the unwanted binge-vomiting, while achieving or maintaining the thin body ideal. Without resolution of this issue, the bulimic may drop out of treatment or fail to make progress with her eating symptoms.

Utilization of family therapy will depend on the age of the bulimic, family cooperation, and the degree to which the family contributes to the patient's illness. Parent guidance can prove helpful in reducing parents' guilt feelings and in freeing parents of responsibility for their adolescent's eating problems. Group therapy incorporating both behavioral and psychotherapeutic techniques has proven an effective adjunctive treatment modality for bulimia.

SUMMARY

Anorexia nervosa and bulimia are sister disorders sometimes occurring sequentially in the same individual. They produce symptoms so striking that underlying psychopathology may be overlooked or neglected by both parents and professionals. Treatment of these disorders requires a multidimensional therapeutic approach that addresses both attitudinal and behavioral aspects of the illness. Outcome will be influenced not only by the extent of psychopathology but also by the knowledge, experience, and expertise of the treating mental health professionals.

BIBLIOGRAPHY

Bruch H: *The golden cage: The enigma of anorexia nervosa.* Cambridge, Harvard University Press, 1978

Casper RE, Eckert ED, Halmi KA et al: Bulimia. *Archives of General Psychiatry* 37:1030-1035, 1980

Ferguson JM: *Learning to eat: Leaders manual.* Palo Alto, Bull Publishing Co, 1975

Garfinkel PE, Moldofsky H, Garner DM: The heterogeneity of anorexia nervosa. *Archives of General Psychiatry* 37:1036-1040, 1980

Garner DM, Garfinkel PE: *Anorexia nervosa: A multidimensional perspective.* New York, Brunner-Mazel, 1982

Garner DM, Garfinkel PE, Bemis KM: A multidimensional psychotherapy for anorexia nervosa. *International Journal of Eating Disorders* 1:3-46, 1982

Geller JL: Treatment of anorexia nervosa by the integration of behavior therapy and psychotherapy. *Psychotherapy and Psychosomatics* 26:167-177, 1975

Minuchin S, Rosman BL, Baker L: *Psychosomatic families: Anorexia nervosa in context.* Cambridge, Harvard University Press, 1978

Sours J: *Starving to death in a sea of objects.* New York, Jason Aronson, 1980

Wooley OW, Wooley S: The Beverly Hills eating disorder: The mass marketing of anorexia nervosa. *International Journal of Eating Disorders* 1:57-69, 1982

Chapter 16

DEVELOPMENTAL DISORDERS WITH PHYSICAL SIGNS: STUTTERING, ENURESIS, ENCOPRESIS, SOMNAMBULISM, AND SLEEP TERRORS

KATHARINE N. DIXON, MD

This chapter concerns itself with developmental disorders which present with physical signs. Included in the discussion are sections on stuttering, encopresis, and such sleep "arousal" disorders as enuresis, somnambulism, and sleep terrors.

STUTTERING

Stuttering is a disorder of speech fluency in which the individual repeats or prolongs sounds and words or has frequent, unusual hesitations and pauses while speaking. Preschool children commonly have periods of dysfluent speech, but most preschool-age stuttering resolves spontaneously. It is believed that undue parental attention and criticism directed at the child's speech create anxiety in the child about communication and contribute to the perpetuation of the problem.

The onset almost always occurs between the ages of 2 and 9, with boys outnumbering girls by about four times at all ages. Only 50% of *severe* childhood stuttering will resolve by adulthood. There is often a strong family history of dysfluency.

Even though stutterers do not have characteristic personality patterns or emotional disorders, persistence of stuttering into adolescence and adulthood is often accompanied by low self-esteem and self-confidence, avoidance of social and public situations, lack of assertiveness, and anxiety about communication. As the child grows older, the struggle and distress involved with speaking increases, possibly due to intensified anticipation of dysfluency. When under pressure to communicate, the stutterer may show associated motor features, such as head-jerking, tics, eye blinks, or lip tremors. Stuttering tends to be episodic and is more likely to occur under specific and predictable circumstances—for example, in new situations, before a class, or on the telephone. The stutterer may be entirely free of dysfluency while whispering, singing, communicating with one person or talking to a pet.

Treatment

A variety of treatment approaches has been advocated for stuttering; these include relaxation training, traditional psychotherapy, and hypnosis. The most comprehensive and effective approach concentrates on the speech behavior itself and, secondarily, addresses those emotional patterns that accompany or contribute to the stuttering. A speech therapist is most qualified to work with the child on improving his fluency; others in the environment can assist by listening with full attention, not hurrying the child's speech, and refraining from comments that focus attention on the child's verbal production. Allowing the child to speak without interruption lessens the pressure he may feel to speak rapidly. A prearranged hand signal can be given to remind the child to speak more slowly. Most treatment approaches have as their emphasis to slow speech to the point where the stutterer can be consistently fluent.

The airflow technique advocated by Schwartz teaches the stutterer to begin speaking while exhaling in a relaxed fashion, much like sighing. This method prevents the stutterer's vocal block by decreasing vocal cord tension. This technique can be used for young stutterers.

A multidimensional approach advocated by Burns and Brady uses a combination of techniques. Speech is metronome paced to the highest rate at which the stutterer can still speak fluently. A miniature electronic metronome worn over the ear allows the stutterer to generalize his paced, fluent speech to everyday situations. As the stutterer gains confidence in his fluency, the metronome device is gradually withdrawn. In addition, the therapist helps the stutterer understand the illogical, self-defeating thinking that has developed around his stuttering, particularly the anticipation of failure. Assertiveness training techniques are taught to improve the social skills of the timid, passive, or unassertive stutterer. This approach is more appropriate for older stutterers.

ENURESIS

Persistent, involuntary wetting beyond the age of 3 is abnormal. The term "enuresis" has come to be used for nighttime wetting, but wetting may occur both day and night in a small percentage of children. The child with diurnal (daytime) enuresis is more likely than the nocturnal (nighttime) enuretic to have associated emotional problems. Bedwetting occurring in children who have never sustained a period of nighttime bladder control is referred to as "primary enuresis"; the recurrence of bedwetting in a child who has attained nighttime continence for at least 3 months is called "secondary enuresis." Of all enuretics, 80% have primary enuresis.

Enuresis is the most frequent childhood sleep disorder, with an incidence of 10% in 5-year-old girls and 15% in 5-year-old boys. Most enuresis will subside spontaneously during middle childhood, but about 3% of all 12-year-olds continue to be bedwetters. Secondary enuresis accounts for a larger number of children at age 12 than it does at a younger age. Of 18-year-olds, 1% continue to be enuretic. The incidence of enuresis is higher for institutionalized children. Family members often have a history of enuresis.

Maturational delay is believed to be a significant factor in most primary enuresis. The enuretic child may have other developmental sleep behaviors, such as sleepwalking, sleeptalking, or night terrors, or have signs of neurological immaturity. In addition, faulty or permissive toilet training may play a role in the child's failure to develop consistent bladder control. Transient secondary enuresis can appear after illness, birth of a sibling, or other life event, as an indicator of regression to an earlier stage of emotional development. Diurnal or persistent secondary types of enuresis in children are more likely to have a medical cause, such as diabetes, seizure disorder, or urinary tract malformation.

The association of enuresis with specific sleep stages is still unsettled. The enuretic event may take place only during nondreaming (NREM) stages of sleep—either deep sleep, as an "arousal" event when the child is arousing from a deep to lighter stage of sleep, or light sleep. The adolescent enuretic is thought more likely to wet in lighter sleep stages, while enuresis in the young child generally occurs in deep sleep. Enuresis occurs most often in the first third of the night, but it may happen anytime during the period of sleep.

Formerly, bedwetters were likely to be referred to a mental health professional, because of the belief that enuresis represented a sign of emotional disturbance. It is now known that enuresis most often exists without other behavioral or emotional problems and, in most cases, will stop eventually without professional intervention. There is, however, a greater incidence of psychopathology among latency-aged and adolescent enuretics than nonenuretic children of the same age. Enuresis is not associated with a typical behavior or personality pattern; rather it is seen across the spectrum of psychiatric disorders in children. Bedwetting can produce guilt, shame, and anxiety and serve as a focus for adult criticism and adult-child conflict, even in the child who does not have an associated emotional disorder.

Treatment

Treatment planning should take into consideration two important factors. First, in view of the high rate of spontaneous remission in early and middle childhood, the treatment itself may not be responsible for producing nighttime dryness. Second, treatment should be undertaken only with confidence that organic disease is not causing the symptoms. Almost all enuresis is functional, but a physical examination, urinalysis, and urine culture can quickly rule out the rare organically-caused enuresis.

Behavioral techniques, counseling, and medication are the principal therapeutic approaches to the enuretic symptom. All therapy should be directed toward having the child take age-appropriate responsibility for bedwetting, while protecting his self-esteem. The younger child should be expected to assist with changing and laundering wet sheets, while the older child can be expected to take full responsibility for these duties. Approaching the child's nighttime wetness or dryness in a nonjudgmental, matter-of-fact fashion avoids focusing undue attention on the enuretic symptom. Parents or child-care workers should avoid critical or subtly negative comments about the child's bedwetting.

Counseling and simple behavioral techniques should be the first approach to the child's enuresis. A baseline record of wet and dry nights provides an objective measure of the child's progress toward bladder control. The child's active participation in recording and treatment planning will elicit greater cooperation. Keeping a star chart of wet and dry nights may be sufficient for some children to gain bladder control. Additional positive reinforcement can be provided by a reward for a pre-determined number of consecutive dry nights. Fluid restriction and awakening the child early in the night usually have little impact on the bedwetting.

One of the most effective approaches for bedwetting is conditioning with an alarm and pad device. The system can be purchased at a retail store for under $50. The pad is placed in the child's bed and connected to a bell or buzzer system that sounds when the child urinates on the pad. The alarm should be placed at such distance that the child must get out of bed in order to turn it off. To be effective, the child must awaken completely after wetting, go to the bathroom to finish voiding, change or help change the wet sheets, and reset the alarm. Usually, this procedure requires adult supervision. A response can be expected within three weeks, but a 3- to 4-month trial is necessary before considering the technique unsuccessful. The system should be used until the child achieves consecutive dry nights for three weeks. Relapse after termination should be expected in about 25% of cases and can be managed by prompt resumption of the system.

The most widely used antienuretic drug is imipramine (Tofranil), a tricyclic antidepressant. Its mechanism of action in enuresis is unclear. Imipramine is given in a single dose one hour before bedtime, beginning at a dose of 25 mg for children under 12, or 50 mg for children over 12. It should not be used for children under 6 years of age. If necessary, the dose can be increased to 50 mg for the younger child, and 75 mg for children over 12. Drug holidays every three months will determine if bedwetting is still a problem. Although often immediately effective, imipramine therapy should be reserved for those children who are very distressed by their enuresis or for whom other treatment approaches have been unsuccessful. A high relapse rate after termination of drug therapy is the general rule.

ENCOPRESIS

Encopresis is repeated fecal soiling past the age of 4 years, not due to organic causes. The toddler can be expected to gain control of his bowel sphincter muscle between the ages of 1 and 3, with a period of partial control preceding consistent bowel control. Adult attitudes — particularly if permissive, harsh, or overly meticulous — can influence the course of toilet training and subsequent bowel control.

Compared to enuresis, fecal soiling is a fairly rare symptom. Encopretic boys outnumber girls five to one. About one third of encopretic children are also enuretic, often with daytime enuresis. Of encopretics, 25% are retentive—that is, they retain feces and may be impacted. The chronically constipated encopretic may leak mucus or fecal material around the hoarded feces.

The several varieties of encopresis need to be distinguished in order to determine a treatment approach. Encopresis can be divided broadly into two categories, primary and secondary. In primary encopresis the fecal soiling has been continuous since infancy, while in secondary encopresis bowel control was consistently present for at least 6 months. The term "encopresis" technically excludes fecal soiling with an organic cause; however, the clinical pictures of organic and nonorganic soiling may be indistinguishable.

Children with primary encopresis, most often inadequately toilet trained, usually come from chaotic families or poorly staffed institutions. Sometimes referred to as "dirty" encopretics, their inadequate social training may also be reflected in poor hygiene, deficient self-discipline, and violation of other social norms. Even though the children were not taught consistent and appropriate bowel habits, their parents or caretakers may react to the soiling with anger, punishment, or abuse. Organic disease, such as Hirshprung's disease (congenital defect in nerves to a section of the intestine), may produce inability to gain bowel control. Mental retardation, particularly if severe, is commonly accompanied by delay in gaining bowel control.

Secondary encopresis is almost always emotionally caused. In aggressive encopresis, the child unconsciously uses fecal soiling as a means of negative expression. The mother often is meticulous, compulsive about cleanliness, and controlling. Soiling, then, becomes a manifestation of the power struggle between the child and his compulsive, bowel-conscious mother. Expression of aggression normally expected from children may not have been allowed from this encopretic child. He may retain his feces or deposit them inappropriately in his clothes or around the house, not unusually in the parents' bedroom. Referred to as a "clean" encopretic, he may be neatly dressed and may otherwise follow the usual social norms.

In other cases, secondary encopresis, like secondary enuresis, may be a transient adjustment reaction following a stressful life event.

Treatment

Most encopresis will eventually resolve on its own, but meanwhile the symptom can be disruptive to interpersonal relationships and a chronic source of parent-child conflict. As a general rule, when the child is both enuretic and encopretic, control of fecal soiling should be addressed first. While a simplistic formula cannot be applied to every fecal soiler, the therapeutic approach can be guided by the following questions:

(1) Is there an organic cause?

Every encopretic child needs a physical examination. Bowel x-rays will demonstrate the presence of Hirshprung's disease or megacolon, enlargement of the bowel secondary to chronic fecal retention.

(2) Is the child a chronic fecal retainer?

Fecal retention can be determined by rectal examination, bowel x-rays, or can, at times, be felt through the abdomen. Chronic fecal retention deadens the bowel nerve sensitivity and causes the bowel wall to be flabby. The child may not experience the usual physiologic sensation to defecate. Retained feces should be removed using suppositories, enemas, or laxatives, but excessive use of enemas should be avoided. Stool softeners given regularly for a few weeks help the bowel regain normal function. A glycerine suppository can be used just before sitting the child on the toilet if he lacks the sensation to defecate. Whichever method is used, the child should receive a careful explanation of the procedure, in advance of its use.

(3) Did the child have faulty toilet training?

Both the primary encopretic, whether "dirty" or retarded, and the aggressive fecal soiler, especially the fecal hoarder, may need bowel retraining with a behavioral program. A behavioral approach not only teaches appropriate deposition of feces but also attempts to utilize the normal physiologic bowel response to food ingestion. Within 20 to 30 minutes after a meal, especially breakfast, the child sits on the toilet for 10 minutes. If he has a bowel movement, he is given a reward or verbal praise. If unsuccessful, the toilet sitting time is terminated without judgmental comment, and he tries again after the next meal. A bedtime laxative, such as Senekot, may be helpful for a few weeks to stimulate a postbreakfast bowel movement. As an example, a 9-year-old deaf, encopretic, and severely behaviorally handicapped boy had never been able to learn from ordinary toilet training methods. Consequently, he was both enuretic and encopretic. He responded readily to consistently receiving a wheelchair ride immediately after successful deposition of feces or urine in the toilet.

Enemas or suppositories are not recommended for the encopretic who does *not* retain feces. These are used to remove retained feces from the fecal hoarder in the initial phase of treatment. Regular enema use is not justified in the treatment of encopresis. As with enuresis, the fecal soiler should be expected to take age-appropriate responsibility for cleaning himself and his environment after an encopretic episode. Continued personal hygiene assistance given by the mother or female caretaker to an older child may provide sexual stimulation and prolong the child's encopretic problem.

Success of behavior techniques with the encopretic depends on the caretaking adult's ability to follow a prescribed program consistently over a period of weeks. Lack of consistency with a behavioral program is a common cause for therapeutic failure. In addition, the adults in the child's environment must be able to change old attitudes and interactions which contributed to the child's symptoms. In monitoring baseline and treatment symptoms, both encopretic episodes and appropriate toileting should be recorded. When only encopretic episodes are monitored, the child can appear to decrease soiling when—in actuality—he is merely increasing retention.

Toilet training with the severely mentally retarded individual poses special problems. A comprehensive program described by Foxx and Azrin recommends repetitious practice with toilet behaviors, combined with thorough cleaning after every accident.

(4) Do parental or caretaker attitudes contribute to the child's symptoms?

Parent guidance is indicated for the parents of the younger child, while family therapy should be considered for the older encopretic. The permissive or inconsistent parent will need to offer consistency and structure, with regard to the child's toilet habits and with his adherence to other social norms. The parents of the aggressive soiler need to permit the child healthier alternatives for expression. The presence of these attitudes in the child's caretakers should be explored if the child is living in a residential facility.

(5) Is the child stressed or emotionally disturbed?

The stressed encopretic child should improve spontaneously with increased environmental support. In those children with more serious psychopathology, the underlying emotional problems and family issues must be addressed, along with the encopretic behaviors. Traditional psychotherapy alone is not likely to change soiling behaviors. Psychotherapy can be offered to improve the self-image of the fecal soiler whose problem is organically caused.

SOMNAMBULISM

Somnambulism is one of a group of childhood sleep "arousal" disorders. One of the disorders, enuresis, has already been addressed in this chapter. Others include sleeptalking and sleep terrors. Table 16-1 documents commonalities which the "arousal" disorders share.

Somnambulism (sleepwalking) is primarily a childhood phenomenon, with 15% of all children having sleepwalked at least once and 1% to 6% sleepwalking with regularity. The onset is between the ages of 6 and 12 and can be expected to diminish and disappear with maturation. A sleepwalking event is more likely to occur when the child is fatigued or under stress. It can be precipitated in both normal and sleepwalking-prone children by standing them on their feet while they are in deep sleep. Although sleepwalking is associated with a higher incidence of sleep-related

TABLE 16-1
CHILDHOOD SLEEP "AROUSAL" DISORDERS
(Enuresis, sleepwalking, sleeptalking, terrors)

Occur during the 1st third of night
Males more frequent than females
Familial trend
Diminish or disappear with central nervous system maturation
Except for enuresis, not more likely associated with psychopathology

events, such as enuresis and sleeptalking, it is not often associated with psychopathology.

Sleepwalking occurs during nondreaming deep sleep. The sleepwalking child's clumsiness and low level of awareness predispose him to injury by falling over objects, climbing out of windows, or falling down stairs. The episode may be limited to sitting up in bed, perhaps accompanied by picking at bedclothes or sleeptalking, or may proceed to getting out of bed. The child has a glassy look, appears confused, and is difficult to awaken fully. He may perform complex behaviors, such as getting dressed or going to the bathroom. Aggressive behavior is uncommon. The episodes may last a few minutes to a half an hour, with amnesia for the episode next morning.

Treatment

Since sleepwalking poses a serious safety problem, every effort should be made to eliminate potential hazards in the environment. This might include clearing the floor of clutter, minimizing access to the outdoors, assigning the lower bunk, and changing to a ground-floor bedroom. Explanation of the behavior should be given to other children in the environment and the sleepwalker assured of his safety. Efforts should not be made to awaken the sleepwalking child; generally, he can be gently guided back to his bed. Sleepwalking can be helped with a bedtime dose of diazepam (Valium), but a medication approach should be reserved for severe sleepwalkers or those whose environmental hazards cannot be eliminated.

SLEEP TERRORS

Sleep terrors, formerly called night terrors, commonly occur in children between ages 3 and 5 but may continue into later childhood. Sleep terrors generally disappear before adolescence, but a few adults will continue to experience terrors.

The sleep terror needs to be differentiated from a dream anxiety attack, formerly called a nightmare (see Table 16-2). Sleep terror occurs during deep sleep in the first third of the night. The child sits up in bed with a panicky scream and signs of intense autonomic activation, including sweating, dilated pupils, rapid breathing, and rapid pulse. He appears terrified and inconsolable. The

TABLE 16-2
SLEEP TERROR VS. NIGHTMARE

	Sleep terror	*Nightmare*
Sleep stage	Nondreaming sleep	Dreaming sleep
Time of night	First 1/3	Latter 2/3
Recall	Visual image	Dream sequence
Autonomic arousal	++++	+
Confusion	++++	Clear sensorium
Associated "arousal" problems	Yes	No

episode lasts from one to ten minutes, but may last as long as twenty minutes. He may get out of bed and begin to sleepwalk. If he can be fully awakened, he may describe a feeling of terror, frightening visual images, or chest heaviness.

In contrast, nightmares occur during dreaming sleep in the latter two thirds of the night. There will be some anxiety and autonomic arousal, but not to the extent as with a sleep terror. The child will often have some recall of the nightmare's content the next morning, reporting a dream sequence rather than a single visual image.

Treatment

Frequent or severe night terrors can be disruptive to others in the child's environment. When this is the situation, diazepam (Valium), 5 to 10 mg at bedtime may be helpful as a preventative. Usually, however, no treatment is necessary once the parents understand the benign nature of the syndrome.

In the final section, sleep terrors were differentiated from dream anxiety attacks. Most children have fewer terrors with maturation. Suggestions were offered to deal with disruption to others in the environment caused by the sleep terrors.

BIBLIOGRAPHY

STUTTERING

Burns D, Brady JP: Stuttering and speech disorders. *Psychiatric Clinics of North America* 1:335-348, 1978

Schwartz MF: *Stuttering solved.* Philadelphia, JB Lippincott, 1976

ENURESIS

Kolvin I, MacKieth R, Meadows S (eds): *Bladder control and enuresis.* Philadelphia, JB Lippincott, 1973

Leventhal JM: Enuresis, in Gabel S (ed): *Behavioral problems in childhood: A primary care approach.* New York, Grune & Stratton, 1981

Sours JA: Enuresis, in Wolman BB, Egan I, Ross AO (eds): *Handbook of treatment of mental disorders in childhood and adolescence.* Englewood Cliffs, NJ, Prentice-Hall, 1978

ENCOPRESIS

Foxx RM, Azrin NH: *Toilet training the retarded.* Champaign, IL, Research Press, 1973

Gabel S: Fecal soiling, chronic constipation, and encopresis, in Gabel S (ed): *Behavioral problems in children: A primary care approach.* New York, Grune & Stratton, 1981

Young GC: The treatment of childhood encopresis by conditioned gastroileal reflex training, in Graziano AM (ed): *Behavior therapy with children.* Chicago, Aldine Publishing Co, 1975

SLEEP DISORDERS

Anders TF, Weinstein P: Sleep and its disorders in infants and children: A review. *Pediatrics* 50:312-324, 1972

Ferber R, Rivinus TM: Practical approaches to sleep disorders of childhood. *Medical Times* 107:71-80, 1979

Chapter 17

STEREOTYPED MOVEMENT DISORDERS

R. DEAN CODDINGTON, MD

In this chapter we will deal with behavior in which movement is a prominent feature and in which the movement is repeated in the same way each time. The fighting and restlessness seen in hyperactive children is quite varied and not at all stereotypic and will, therefore, not be considered here. Stereotyped movements can be divided into two types, those under voluntary control at least at the outset and those involuntary movements referred to as tics. This division is somewhat arbitrary since a movement such as nail biting may become so habituated as to be, for all practical purposes, involuntary. Moreover, even involuntary tics can be suppressed for a few minutes or hours, though only with considerable effort. But, while somewhat arbitrary, the division is nonetheless a convenient one.

VOLUNTARY MOVEMENTS

Odd or unusual voluntary movements are not uncommon in children. Normal infants may practice head rolling or head banging when placed in their beds to sleep. Such behavior can persist for months, even years, and is seen quite often in older, retarded children. These movements, by definition, are stereotyped because they are carried out in the same way each time. But they are quite clearly voluntary and may be pleasurable in some strange way; it would be difficult, otherwise, to understand why the child maintains the habit. Other movements appear to be painful, as, for instance, head banging. It may be that the rhythmical characteristic of the movement is sleep inducing and even—in some way—gratifying.

Lest the reader get the impression that these are simple, mild movement patterns that should cause no concern, a few vignettes will be presented to clarify the situation.

A 2-year-old boy stood in his crib and rocked rhythmically, hard enough to walk the crib across the room. The father bolted the crib to the wall only to have the bolts torn from their sockets. The creaking noise produced by the movement of the crib disturbed the sleep of every family member.

***

The parents of a 1-year-old are concerned about the bald spot on the baby's head, caused by the stereotypic rolling of his head from side-to-side.

***

A large, indurated, and scarred area developed on the forehead of a baby who habitually banged his head on the end of his crib.

When an otherwise normal child exhibits voluntary stereotyped movements, we needn't be overly concerned, though we would do well to investigate the situation. Does the child seem to be happy at other times? Were other alternatives (eg, being rocked by the parents) available when the movements began? Was the infant left alone a lot? Was he allowed to cry himself to sleep? If we can gain an understanding of the genesis of the behavior and if the situation has since changed for the better, we can be fairly safe in reassuring the family that the movements will eventually subside.

If, on the other hand, the movement is becoming more and more of a problem, we should begin looking for signs of mental retardation or a severe disintegrative process, as in the pervasive developmental disorders or psychoses (see chapters 11, 18, and 19). If no other diagnosis can be made, the appropriate classification would be atypical stereotyped movement disorder.

Some habits are characterized by stereotyped movements. Thumb sucking, masturbation, nail biting, and hair twirling—pulling with or without eating the hair—are the most common examples.

Thumb Sucking

Thumb sucking is related to age and need, and should not be considered abnormal before age 4 or 5 or even later, depending on sociocultural factors. All babies need the oral stimulation provided by sucking, even after being weaned from the breast. They should be allowed to suck on pacifier or thumb without concern, at least until age 4 or 5. Pedodontists agree that no permanent damage is done to the dentition before that time. On the other hand, it is reasonable to ask ourselves why the 4-year-old has not given up the habit. If we fail to find some cause for concern, as, for instance, maternal deprivation for whatever reason or associated lack of weight gain, we can rest assured that it will be given up in the near future.

Masturbation

Masturbation is also a normal form of self-stimulation. Very young infants find their genitalia. Very young males seem to get pleasure out of what appears to the onlooker as painful pulling on the penis; at this age it is casual, irregular behavior that only becomes stereotypic by age 4 or 5. Boys discover the pleasure of rhythmic manipulation of the penis and the resulting erection it produces. Little girls will squeeze their thighs together rhythmically or handle their genitalia. Masturbation in both sexes is perfectly normal and only becomes problematic when performed more or less openly or publicly. It embarrasses the child's parents and their friends but goes unnoticed by other children under age 7 or 8. When children masturbate openly, apparently unaware of the effect their behavior is having on adults and older children, we must consider two possibilities: (1) Their drive to provide pleasurable stimulation is abnormally strong, almost irresistible, indicating underlying pathology. (2) They are at least momentarily out of touch with reality, unaware of the external environment. In either case, this form of stereotyped movement warrents a psychiatric appraisal.

Nail Biting and Habits Involving the Hair

Nail biting and habits involving the hair should be considered signs of anxiety; such habits may exist for years before the family seeks medical help. As a matter of fact, hair pulling may be discovered only during an investigation of alopecia (a bald spot).

> A 5-year-old girl with a poor appetite was examined by an alert pediatrician who found a palpable mass in the upper abdomen. He suspected she was a hair puller and eater whose habit had produced a "hair ball" in her stomach, even though her parents were unaware of such habits. X-rays confirmed the diagnosis; when a surgeon removed the baseball-sized mass that filled her stomach, the youngster's appetite improved dramatically. Once the parents became aware of the habit, they were able to deal with it successfully, preventing a repetition of the problem.

INVOLUNTARY MOVEMENTS

Tics, the hallmark of all three of the more classical stereotyped movement disorders, are defined as *involuntary* rapid movements of a muscle group or the *involuntary* production of noises or words. There is no sign of pleasure attached to the movement and, above all, the child has little control over the action. Tics disappear during sleep. Sometimes, a tic appears to an observer as a movement which had a purpose when it first occurred but which has now become a deeply entrenched habit, without purpose. For instance, one of the most common tics is a sudden twisting of the head to the right (or to the left, but in one direction only), as if the patient were looking over his shoulder to see what's behind him or, alternatively, as if the patient wishes to avoid seeing something right in front of him.

Another very common tic is the eye blink. Facial, neck, and shoulder tics are far more common than tics of the body or lower extremities. Sudden contracture of the diaphragm may produce grunting noises or coughs; when one stops to think about it, these movements are reminiscent of the startle reactions seen in babies and young children. This similarity—coupled with the early age of onset and the fact that other symptoms of immaturity such as thumb sucking, enuresis and speech defects are often present in children with tics—has led some authors to view tics as a distortion of some underlying physiological (ie, normal) process, which then becomes a learned habit.

Only 5% to 7% of patients at child psychiatry clinics have tics. Since other members of their families have sometimes experienced similar symptoms, there may be some genetically determined predisposition that makes these children more likely to develop tics in certain situations. Thumb sucking and other symptoms of immaturity are far more common than tics, so we cannot attribute tics simply to immaturity. The onset of these disorders, in many cases, seems to follow some frightening or otherwise stressful event or situation, and all forms of tics become more pronounced during times of stress. Thus, we have three factors that must be considered as contributors to the cause of movement disorders: a weak genetic predisposition, a significant degree of immaturity in personality development, and some frightening or stressful event or series of events.

The three more typical involuntary movement disorders include transient tic disorder, chronic motor tic disorder, and Tourette's disease.

Transient Tic Disorder

As one might expect, this is the least severe, the easiest to treat, and the one most similar to the normal startle response of infancy. The child is able to consciously suppress the movement for a few minutes to an hour or so, but usually becomes quite fatigued by the effort. The intensity of the tic may vary from week to week or month to month and it may disappear spontaneously.

The movement must be present for at least one month in order to warrant the diagnosis but, if it lasts more than a year, the diagnosis must be changed to one of the other types.

When the onset is between 6 and 8 years of age, the chance of spontaneous remission is greatest, though other psychiatric symptoms may remain. If the tic first appears in a younger child, it may disappear, only to recur in adolescence in a more severe form. Similarly, when the onset is in adolescence, the underlying psychopathology tends to be more severe. This is not to say, however, that the tic itself is less intense or less dramatic in a younger child, but only that the prognosis is better.

The treatment of choice of this transient tic disorder is psychotherapy, along with a relatively simple explanation of the relationship of the tic to external events. Treatment can effectively shorten the expected course of the illness.

Chronic Motor Tic Disorder

Chronic motor tic disorder should not be diagnosed unless the symptoms have persisted for a year. The intensity of the tic is less variable, being quite constant for weeks or months, though the patient is still able to suppress the movements for minutes to hours. Two or three separate muscle groups may be involved.

It is clear that this disorder is more severe than the transient, highly variable symptomatology described above. It stands to reason that psychotherapy alone may not be sufficient but needs to be augmented with haloperidol (Haldol), chlorpromazine (Thorazine), or diazepam (Valium). It is not certain just how these drugs work: by their antianxiety effect or, in the case of haloperidol, directly on the dopamine system, by blocking dopaminergic pathways in the brain.

Tourette's Disease

Gilles de la Tourette's disease is undoubtedly the most striking of the stereotyped movement disorders, characterized as it is by a combination of vocal and motor tics, involving multiple muscle groups. It, too, is a chronic disorder lasting more than a year, though symptoms may vary from time to time and may be voluntarily suppressed for a period of time, from minutes to hours.

The vocal tics may be sniffs, grunts, barks, yelps, coughs, or words; in more than half the cases, the words are obscene. Involved muscle groups may include the arms, torso, and the legs.

Tourette's disorder usually begins during the elementary school years, with only 10% starting in the preschool years. The age of onset is between 5 and 10 years in about 68% of the cases. A simple motor tic commonly ushers in the disorder, with the addition of a vocal tic around age 9 or 10 and coprolalia (the use of obscene language) in early adolescence. The course of the disorder is characterized by remissions and exacerbations of varying duration. There is often an abatement of symptoms in late adolescence.

The cause of Tourette's syndrome is unknown, but a combination of two factors seems to be necessary in most cases: an inherited organic predisposition and a family environment overly concerned with the suppression of aggression. A few cases have been reported in which a parent and a child both suffered from the disorder, but this is very uncommon. The fact that the disease responds to haloperidol (Haldol) also supports the concept of an organic factor; also supportive of organicity is the recent finding of an association with the hyperactivity often seen in cases of the attention deficit disorders. On the other hand, the occurrence in almost half the cases of intrafamilial conflict over the expression of aggression, with emphasis on suppression, points to a psychogenic factor. The likelihood is that both factors are present, one at times more prominent than the other.

Many forms of therapy have been tried in the past, each with some success, perhaps due partly to spontaneous remission or decrease of symptomatology and partly to the treatment itself. Nevertheless, haloperidol has been widely used now for over a decade and produces improvement in almost 90% of affected children.

Tourette's disease has been known for more than a century, but progress in its diagnosis and treatment has occurred only in the last twenty years. Parents of children with this rather rare syndrome were so frustrated by the ineffectiveness of the medical profession that they formed the Tourette Society to encourage research and better understanding on the part of teachers, physicians, and society in general. Children with the disorder are often excluded from classrooms because of their disruptive symptoms and are ashamed of their own behavior. They become the brunt of jokes and develop very low self-esteem. Consequently, treatment must also be aimed at ameliorating these secondary problems.

SUMMARY

In this chapter the full spectrum of stereotyped movement disorders has been discussed, from the normal rocking of young infants and common thumb sucking to the rare but psychologically devastating Tourette's disease. The etiology in all cases seems to involve a psychogenic element, sometimes minimally, but usually as a major factor. Except for the most normal behaviors, there are always psychologic sequelae. The presence of an organic factor in Tourette's disease was emphasized; this disorder is probably never purely psychogenic.

Since psychologic sequelae follow most stereotyped movement disorders, the need for early diagnosis and treatment is obvious.

BIBLIOGRAPHY

Corbett JA, Mathews AM, Connell PH, et al: Tics and Gilles de la Tourette's Syndrome: A follow up study and critical review. *Br J Psychiatry* 115: 1229-1241, 1969

Corbett J: Tics and Tourette's Syndrome, in Rutter M, Hersov L (eds): *Child psychiatry: Modern approaches.* Oxford, Blackwell Scientific Publications, 1977, pp 674-687

Lucas AR: Tic: Gilles de la Tourette's Syndrome, in Noshiptz JD (ed): *Basic handbook of child psychiatry.* New York, Basic Books, 1979, vol 2, pp 667-684

Chapter 18

PERVASIVE DEVELOPMENTAL DISORDER: INFANTILE AUTISM

MOLLIE M. WALLICK, PhD

Before the early 1960s, autism was recognized by few professionals and was essentially unknown to the general public. Since the 1970s, the disorder has been discussed widely in the media—on TV and radio, in newspapers and magazines. As a result, most people know of its existence, even if their understanding of it is very vague.

The intent of this chapter is to sharpen the reader's comprehension of the syndrome of autism. The chapter contains a concise historical perspective, an exploration of clinical features of the disorder, and sections on etiology, treatment approaches, and long-term outcome.

HISTORICAL PERSPECTIVE

The new interest in autism may suggest that it is a new problem. Actually, descriptions of persons apparently autistic are found in articles and books written long ago. Perhaps the most fascinating is an account first published in 1799, *The Wild Boy of Aveyron*, by a French physician, Jean-Marc-Gaspard Itard. Given charge of a young adolescent found wandering and living wild in the woods, Itard was filled with the enthusiasm for new ideas current at the time of the French Revolution. He saw his charge whom he named Victor as the prototype of the natural savage, a human completely untouched by education, raised—he thought—by wolves. To the modern reader there is no doubt that the boy displayed most of the diagnostic features of autism. It may be that Victor was autistic because he was abandoned in infancy. But it seems more likely that he was abandoned by his parents in the troubled times following the revolution *because* he was autistic and difficult to manage.

Although isolated cases were reported earlier, it was not until 1943 that a child psychiatrist at Johns Hopkins, the late Leo Kanner, formally identified children with autism as a special group.

Kanner based his findings on 11 children and chose the label "early infantile autism" because he believed that early aloofness and social withdrawal were his patients' most significant attributes.

But even after Kanner named and described the children, it was almost 20 years before the general public began to hear of them. Today there is much more widespread interest, partly because attitudes toward handicaps have changed, partly because of Public Law 94-142 (The Education of All Handicapped Children Act of 1975), partly because more researchers are working to find a cause, but perhaps most of all because of NSAC, the National Society for Autistic Children. Founded in 1965, NSAC has grown from a small but dedicated group of parents to a truly national society with an active membership of parents and professionals. The stated purpose of NSAC is to bring into being programs of legislation, education, and research for the benefit of all children with severe communication and behavior disorders. While retaining the acronym NSAC, the organization changed its name in 1981 to the National Society for Children and Adults with Autism.

Studies in the US, England, and Denmark have reported approximately four or five children of every 10,000 with classical Kannerian autism. Using broader criteria, NSAC estimates the incidence at about 15 of every 10,000 youngsters. Boys are affected about four times more often than girls. Apparently, autistic persons can be found all over the world.

CLINICAL FEATURES OF AUTISM

The complexity of the autistic syndrome has led to confusion and even disagreement in diagnosis. Kanner's choice of label (from the Greek "autos," meaning "self") was unfortunate in that the same word had been used earlier to depict withdrawal into fantasy by schizophrenic patients. Rather than movement *from* relationships and an elaborate ability to fantasize, Kanner clearly described a failure to develop relationships and a characteristic lack of imagination. Further, while delusions and hallucinations are the sine qua non of schizophrenia, they are not believed present in autistic children and develop only rarely when the children reach adulthood.

A review of the panoply of traits attributed over the years to autistic children and their families may help us reach a mutual understanding of the disorder.

Family Background

In his early classic article and a decade later after evaluating his first 100 cases, Kanner described the parents in almost as much detail as the children. While using many other descriptors, he characterized them as upper-middle class, intelligent, well educated, and frequently of Jewish extraction. Many early studies supported the findings of higher educational and occupational levels, but most recent investigators have found autistic children in families of all socioeconomic, occupational, educational, intellectual, religious, and racial backgrounds. The early correlation of Kanner's syndrome with higher educational and occupational levels may have been a spurious one: Considering the cost of private evaluation procedures (before PL 94-142 mandated free evaluation and treatment), it seems reasonable that families in upper economic brackets could better afford to persist in obtaining a diagnosis. Similarly, the bias toward higher social class may have been an artifact due to selective referral of cases.

Universal and Specific Features

By referring to autism as a syndrome, Kanner suggested that certain behaviors cluster together and differ from those in other disorders. But in spite of commonalities, each autistic child is unique and in many ways different from other children with the same diagnosis—in part because the condition may be present in any degree from very mild to very severe, but perhaps more so because each child's individuality comes through somehow, despite his handicap. Michael Rutter of the London Institute of Psychiatry considers three features pathognomonic of autism: 1) a profound failure to develop social relationships, 2) severe language retardation and deviation, inconsistent with intellectual level, and 3) stereotypic play, abnormal preoccupations, and resistance to change—what Kanner called "an anxiously obsessive desire for the maintenance of sameness."

> The mother of a 9-year-old autistic boy engaged four men to move a piano from the living room to an adjacent solarium. That night while the family slept, the boy returned the piano to its original location. Deep scratches in the hardwood floor provided mute testimony to his absolute insistence on sameness in his environment.

Age of Onset and Early Development

For the diagnosis of autism, symptoms must be present prior to 30 months of age. Some children who become autistic are reported as having developed normally for the first year or two; however, careful questioning may reveal that, as babies, they lacked affective ties and displayed little interest in the environment. Others give their parents cause for concern almost immediately—with feeding, sleeping, and elimination problems and a subtle lack of awareness of the mother's presence.

Most parents confirm Kanner's early observation that autistic children fail to lift their arms in anticipation of being picked up and do not adjust their bodies to the posture of the person holding them. They may spend an unusual amount of time scratching and tapping with their fingernails (perhaps for the sound or sensation). Typically, autistic children avoid direct eye contact by using peripheral vision or by looking through people, rather than at them.

While developmental milestones are occasionally accelerated, delay is much more common. Frequently reported during the preschool years are disturbed sleeping patterns, obsessive food preferences, and ritualistic eating and bedtime habits. Other behaviors noted include fear of harmless things (concomitant with unawareness of real danger) and immature and socially deviant actions. Self-injury—eg, head-banging or wrist-biting—is fairly common. Often unusually attractive, the autistic child appears aloof and unaffected by the world; but if a familiar routine is disturbed, the quiet remote child becomes a bundle of fury until his tantrum expires—as quickly as it started, much as if a faucet had been turned off.

Response to Stimuli

Autistic children may be fascinated by a special sound, apparently oversensitive to others (covering their ears as if in distress), and at the same time unresponsive to sounds in general and to conversation directed toward them in particular. Self-absorption is often so extreme that the children appear deaf. Itard wrote of Victor, "The sound of a cracking walnut or other favorite eatable never failed to make him turn around ... yet ... [he was] ... insensible to the loudest noises and the explosion of firearms."

Often, autistic children respond as atypically to visual stimuli as to sounds. They may ignore objects of great interest to a normal child but appear fascinated by something quite trivial, such as a piece of string or a scrap of shiny paper. They may gaze entranced at a street lamp but avoid looking at a light used for photography. Usually, the children react less to stationary objects than to mobile ones—eg, toy vehicles with wheels for spinning.

Like the deaf-blind, autistic children compensate for their handicaps by exploring the world through their senses of touch, taste, and smell—long after the infant and toddler stages have passed. Also like the deaf-blind, many autistic children make bizarre movements: they whirl round and round, walk on tiptoe, flap their arms and legs, twist and turn their fingers (most often at the periphery of vision), and make facial grimaces. Spinning and rocking may reflect pathologic retention of infantile reflexes or may represent an attempt to make sense of the sensations in the environment.

It should be stated that normal children display many of these behaviors as they move through various phases. The difference is that autistic children engage in most of them for years on end.

Language

Occasionally a child with Kanner's syndrome develops a few words and then, after a few months, loses them. In the early years, the autistic child screams or grunts until someone determines what he wants; later, the child grabs an adult's hand and leads the adult to the desired object. Slightly more than half of the children eventually learn to use at least a few words, but their speech usually lacks communicative intent and is clearly abnormal. Poor pronunciation, volume control, and pitch are typical; voice quality is atonal and arrhythmic, with inflection either inappropriate or absent.

With the emergence of speech, the autistic child often repeats words spoken by other people, especially the last word or closing phrase of a sentence; in this parrot-like echoing, called "echolalia," the exact accent of the speaker may be copied, as well as the intonation and inflection of his voice. A recent study suggests that immediate echolalia may serve a variety of functions: Besides indicating a "yes" answer or a request, the echoic utterance may serve as a rehearsal strategy ("thinking out loud") to aid in comprehension, or may help the speaker regulate his own behavior. Echoes may be a form of labeling or may serve to maintain social interaction. A related phenomenon, indicative of excellent rote memory, is "delayed echolalia," in which the children repeat words, phrases, or sentences heard in the past, sometimes weeks or months earlier.

At a more advanced stage, the child may use copied phrases to obtain something he wants. For example, he may remember his mother asking, "Do you want a cookie?" Now, when he wants one, he characteristically exhibits pronominal reversal, saying, "You want a cookie," his "you" of course referring to himself. It was originally thought that avoidance of the pronoun, "I," was related to the child's inadequate sense of self; considering the phenomenon of echolalia, pronominal reversal may be a function of word order in English, since "I" rarely occurs at the end of a sentence.

Words which are commonly paired are frequently used in reverse by autistic children, who, for example, may identify a sock as "a shoe." Literalness often precludes an understanding of synonyms and of words with multiple meanings. The peculiar metaphors of autistic children are of particular interest; eg, when asked the sum of 4 plus 4, a 5-year-old replied, "As many sides as an octagon." Also of note is the unusual choice of words, some apparently nonsensical but, perhaps, with private meaning:

> The family of a 9-year-old autistic boy entertained a visitor from out-of-town for a day. At the end of the evening, the youngster shook the guest's hand and—in an apparent attempt to convey how much he liked her—blurted out, "chocolate chip double fudge ice cream." He had paid the guest the highest compliment in his repertoire.

Special Abilities

Often the autistic child has some skills—all nonverbal (eg, musical, mechanical, or visuospatial)—which contrast sharply with his deficits. Remarkable is the rare autistic savant, in whom isolated outstanding abilities coexist with generalized cognitive arrest. These islets of brilliance may involve unusual feats of memory and of calendar calculation, as well as highly developed artistic and computational skills. A more common manifestation is rote reading, which may develop precociously even in the absence of formal instruction; unfortunately, reading is only infrequently accompanied by comprehension.

> A 7-year-old with perfect pitch habitually flicked objects to vibrate them and determine their tone. One day he approached a large-busted woman in a busy department store, flicked the crystal pendant suspended on her chest, and proclaimed loudly, "A sharp!" The same youngster played an entire Bach prelude flawlessly, having heard it only once.
>
> ***
>
> At an informal NSAC session, an 18-year-old casually mentioned his calendar calculative ability, and invited questions from the audience. I told him the dates of birth of my three children, and he in turn announced the corresponding days of the week when the births occurred—all different days and all correct.
>
> ***
>
> The director of the Autism Services Center showed a videotape of her 22-year-old son's mental math calculations: When asked to multiply such numbers as 893 X 765 and 2,345 X 862, he determined the products accurately in his head—before a competent adult could do so on a calculator.

IQ

A discussion of the rare autistic savant leads naturally to a consideration of IQ. Early on, in spite of the low functioning of his patients, Kanner was impressed by what he called their "strikingly intelligent physiognomies"; he was convinced of their endowment with good cognitive potential. We now know that the IQ score in the case of autistic youngsters—as in normal or retarded children—is sufficiently stable to predict later educational attainment with reasonable accuracy. It is not at all unusual for autism and mental retardation to coexist: it has been reported that approximately 60% of autistic persons have IQ scores below 50, 20% between 50 and 70, and only 20% above 70.

Adulthood

Follow-up studies have shown that the behavior of autistic children changes appreciably as they reach adolescence and adulthood. They tend to become much more affectionate, although they lack empathy. Generally, their handicaps preclude mature relationships: it is extremely rare for an autistic person to marry, and their is but a single published report of an autistic person having given birth to a child.

As an example of social and obsessive difficulties in adulthood —in the extreme—read Herman Melville's short story, "Bartleby," written in 1853. Melville's hauntingly tragic account of the compulsive scrivener, or law-copyist, is poignantly suggestive of an autistic adult (albeit undiagnosed and untreated) who shuns all personal contact and retreats into utter impersonality.

ETIOLOGY

Emotional Causation

The climate of opinion in 1943 favored emotional causation, since most psychiatrists at the time thought that early experience explained all mental illness. Even though Kanner called attention to *inborn* disturbances of affective contact, he nonetheless alluded to parental obsessiveness, lack of warmth, emotional detachment, and preoccupation with abstractions. Bruno Bettleheim, then principal of a residential facility for psychotic children at the University of Chicago, expounded on the "refrigerator mother." In his book, *The Empty Fortress*, Bettleheim proposed as the precipating factor in autism "the parent's wish that his child should not exist." He therefore prescribed a "parentectomy" and prolonged separation, with psychotherapy as the treatment of choice.

With regard to parental personality, it appears that Kanner and Bettleheim reported personal impressions which could easily have been biased. Accumulating clinical evidence indicates that neither the parents as a group nor their family dynamics are significantly different than parents of normal children and their dynamics. Parents of autistic children comprise a continuum of personality types and differ from other parents only in the incredible amount of stress to which they are subject; most have in common genuine love, sensitivity, and concern for their offspring.

The theory of emotional causation is refuted in the literature by studies dealing with children brought up in totally deprived settings, none of whom became autistic, and by the Harlow experiments with monkeys raised by unsympathetic and even cruel and rejecting mothers, in which the monkeys' standard reaction was a persistent attempt to elicit the mothers' attention, and not autistic isolation. Furthermore, while an international registry established in 1980 has identified 74 families with multiple incidence of autism, most parents of children with Kanner's syndrome—including many of the 74 multiple-incidence families—have normal offspring, as well.

Neurobiologic Causation

Early arguments in support of organic etiology—all, not incidentally, by professionals having an autistic child—include the fact that the syndrome occurs so very early in life, the high male-female ratio, the strong suggestion of an abnormality in the central nervous system by virtue of the perceptual and speech difficulties, and the fact that a third of mentally retarded autistic youngsters with no early indication of neurological disorder nevertheless develop epilepsy in later childhood. Increasing evidence of a biological basis has accumulated in recent years, although there is still no single hypothesis to explain the mechanism underlying the deficits. It is generally believed that eventually many causes will be found, each accounting for one subgroup of children presently classified together.

Retrospective data on 78 autistic children and an equal number of matched controls indicate that the parents of the children with Kanner's syndrome had a much greater exposure to chemicals in the preconception period (20 of the 78, compared to only one control family) and a higher incidence of hypothyroidism (five fathers and 11 mothers, compared to one father and three mothers in the control group). When the same subjects and controls were examined for the presence of minor physical anomalies, three stigmata—low-set ears, wide-set eyes, and webbed fingers or toes—were significantly more frequent among the autistic population.

In an ongoing investigation using a frame-by-frame microanalysis of film to study the effect of sound on body movement, it was found that autistic persons lack the precise synchronization of movement to speech displayed by nonhandicapped persons; in addition to a delay on the right side, multiple orienting responses to sound were detected. In other research, results of auditory nerve and brainstem evoked responses of 15 autistic youngsters, when compared with nonhandicapped children, indicate a longer response latency of the auditory nerve and a delayed brainstem transmission.

A decade ago, the brain formation of 17 children with Kanner's syndrome was measured. Although none of the subjects displayed a specific symptom of neurological disease, apparent in 15 of the 17 children were an enlarged left lateral ventricle and an even more prominent enlargement of the left temporal horn. It should be acknowledged that the histories of the children were inadequate; in some cases, autism was apparently secondary, rather than the primary diagnosis.

A turnabout quote by Kanner himself in a 30-year follow-up report demonstrates how far the pendulum has swung from psychogenic to organic etiology: "Parents are beginning to be dealt with from the point of view of mutuality . . . not as etiological culprits, nor merely as recipients of drug prescriptions and of thou-shalt-not rules, but as actively contributing cotherapists." But demonstration of organic etiology does not negate the influence of environmental factors on the developmental course of autistic persons.

TREATMENT APPROACHES

Most clinicians have attested to the ineffectiveness of psychotherapy as a treatment modality. Many have emphasized the significance of behavioral intervention and the experience of schooling. In addition, several biochemical approaches are in current experimental usage.

Experimental Biochemical Approaches

A recently discovered genetic defect called the "fragile X chromosome" has been linked to several cases of mental retardation and to at least a few cases of autism. Several centers in France and in the US are using folic acid to decrease the number of fragile X chromosomes; limited improvement in speech, eye contact, and social smile has been reported.

When compared with normal persons of the same age and sex, approximately 40% of autistic persons have elevated blood serotonin. Hypothesizing that CNS serotonin may also be elevated in the same subgroup, several UCLA researchers attempted to manipulate serotonin with a drug, fenfluramine (Pondimin), known to lower brain serotonin in animals. Preliminary results were reported in 1982 of successful reduction of blood serotonin in three young autistic boys, along with corresponding improvement in behavior and cognitive functioning. Both the specificity and generality of the responses are unknown; also not yet known is whether prolonged drug therapy is necessary and how long improvement will maintain when treatment is discontinued. Minor side effects of fenfluramine have been reported; carefully controlled research conditions are required for its administration.

In a recent study using double-blind methodology with 52 autistic children, the efficacy of combined magnesium-vitamin B-6 administration in reducing autistic symptoms was demonstrated. Both behavioral and biological effects were reported. The research team concluded that clinical improvement "may be related to brain dopamine metabolism."

Educational Therapy

Education has come into its own as the treatment of choice for autistic children. Eclectic and pragmatic, special education draws upon techniques used in psychotherapy, operant conditioning, sensory integration, and speech therapy. Through tactile and vestibular stimulation, sensory integration attempts to facilitate sensory processing and, thereby, to better organize behavior. The use of simultaneous communication, which combines sign and verbal language, has offered nonverbal children an alternative mode of communication and, thus, has helped reduce their tremendous frustration; it has also afforded many mute children confidence to attempt speech.

The best curriculum for autistic children is a flexible one that can be constantly adapted to changes in developmental level and behavioral and learning patterns. Most workers in the field agree that autistic persons require predictability, structure, and limits in their training, as they do in their lives in general. Effectiveness of treatment depends largely upon clarity of structure and generalization. Therapeutic gains are reversible, unless conditions are maintained in the everyday environment, be it home, group home, supervised apartment, or residential setting. With children, using parents as therapists is one way of assuring generalization of skills; for maximal effectiveness, active parental participation throughout the treatment process is essential.

LONG-TERM OUTCOME

While many autistic persons are institutionalized as teenagers and adults, the outcome of others is more fortunate, apparently largely dependent upon IQ. Follow-up studies have indicated that autistic children with IQs above 50 display greater variability in prognosis, depending on education and experience. Approximately half of autistic persons with normal intelligence — and almost none with IQs less than 70 — are either exposed to higher education or are in regular paid employment.

It is only in the past decade, largely since PL 94-142, that public schools have accepted the mandate to provide comprehensive educational services to all handicapped persons. Currently, most delivery systems involve segregated programs in self-contained schools or institutions. However, the pendulum is swinging toward an integrated model in which handicapped — and even severely handicapped — persons function along with nonhandicapped students, to facilitate their subsequent productive interaction as adults.

CONCLUSIONS

Four decades after its recognition by Leo Kanner, early infantile autism remains a pervasive developmental disorder. Ability to influence the course of the disability is limited, although progress has been made. The current understanding of autism is subject to ongoing revision as new insights into causation, prevention, and treatment become available.

BIBLIOGRAPHY

Bemporad JR: Adult reflections of a formerly autistic child. *Journal of Autism and Developmental Disorders* 9:179-197, 1979

Coleman M (ed): *The autistic syndromes.* New York, Elsevier, 1976

Creedon MP: *Appropriate behavior through communication: A new program in simultaneous language for nonverbal children.* Chicago, Michael Reese Medical Center, 1975

DeMyer MK: *Parents and children in autism.* New York, Wiley, 1979

Des Lauriers AM, Carlson CF: *Your child is asleep: Early infantile autism.* Homewood, IL, Dorsey Press, 1969

Fenichel C: Special education as the basic therapeutic tool in treatment of severely disturbed children. *Journal of Autism and Childhood Schizophrenia* 4:177-186, 1974

Furneaux B, Roberts B (eds): *Autistic children: Teaching, community and research approaches.* London, Routledge & Kegan Paul, 1977

Kanner L: Autistic disturbances of affective contact. *Nervous Child* 2:217-250, 1943

Kanner L: Follow-up study of eleven autistic children originally reported in 1943. *Journal of Autism and Childhood Schizophrenia* 1:119-145, 1974

Lovaas OI, Schreibman L, Koegel RL: A behavior modification approach to the treatment of autistic children. *Journal of Autism and Childhood Schizophrenia* 4:111-129, 1974

Oppenheim R: *Effective teaching methods for autistic children.* Springfield, IL, Charles C Thomas, 1974

Rimland B: *Infantile autism.* New York, Appleton-Century-Crofts, 1964

Ritvo ER, Freeman BJ, Ornitz EM, et al: *Autism: Diagnosis, current research and management.* New York, Spectrum, 1976

Rutter M, Schopler E (eds): *Autism: A reappraisal of concepts and treatment.* New York, Plenum Press, 1978

Wallick MM: An autistic child and books. In Baskin BM & Harris KH (eds): *The mainstreamed library: Issues, ideas, innovations.* Chicago, American Library Association, 1982

Wilcox B, Thompson A (eds): *Critical issues in educating autistic children and youth.* Washington, DC, US Department of Education, Office of Special Education, 1980

Wing L (ed): *Early childhood autism,* ed 2. Oxford, Pergamon, 1976

Chapter 19

CHILDHOOD SCHIZOPHRENIA

R. DEAN CODDINGTON, MD

In the recent past, the childhood psychoses were divided into (1) early infantile autism, (2) symbiotic psychosis, and (3) childhood schizophrenia. Autism is now included among the pervasive developmental disorders and is discussed in chapter 18. Some cases that would have been classed previously as symbiotic psychosis are also included there.

In this chapter we will deal with serious disturbances that may reflect difficulty during the separation-individuation (symbiotic) phase but that may not become readily apparent for three or more years. Because it is important to get seriously disturbed children into treatment early, the focus will be on early signs of the psychotic process.

SEPARATION-INDIVIDUATION

The developmental process in which the child begins to separate from his mother and to become autonomous is known as the separation-individuation phase. The change from infancy to childhood, marked as it is by saying "no," by becoming toilet trained, by wanting to go "bye-bye," has been described by Margaret Mahler as the *psychological birth* of the infant:

> We refer to the psychological birth of the individual as the *separation-individuation process:* the establishment of a sense of separateness from, and relation to, a world of reality, particularly with regard to the experiences of *one's own body* and to the principal representative of the world as the infant experiences it, the *primary love object.* Like any intrapsychic process, this one reverberates throughout the life cycle.... But the principal psychological achievements of the process take place in the period from about the fourth or fifth month to the thirtieth or thirty-sixth month, a period we refer to as the *separation-individuation phase.*

The reason this material is included in a discussion of psychotic process in childhood is this: the fundamental problem seen in psychosis is a break with reality, a perceptual problem wherein the individual seems to have difficulty separating reality from fantasy. The schizophrenic patient has difficulty distinguishing what is outside his body from what is inside. It's as if he fails to perceive clear boundaries between self and the inner representation of others. Thus, the failure to obtain object constancy in the process of separation-individuation is considered the core problem in psychoses and borderline states. A case in point may serve to clarify this concept.

> A 12-year-old girl was referred for admission to the hospital because of two symptoms. On several occasions, once or twice in the middle of the night but also in broad daylight and in her mother's presence, she perceived the disappearance of objects held in her hand—a fork on one occasion, a plate on another. As she watched, the object disappeared and then returned; she would not be swayed by her mother's arguments. The other symptom was inappropriate laughter which she explained by saying a voice told her to laugh. On one occasion she laughed uproariously in her doctor's office and then denied it. He diagnosed her as schizophrenic and sent her to the hospital.
>
> The mental status examination at the time of admission failed to reveal any sign of psychosis with the exception of her insistence that the objects had actually disappeared. She presented as a rather frail, thin, prepubescent girl. She cried over having to leave her mother for the first day or two in the hospital and was visibly afraid of those adolescents who were a little older. She had not begun to menstruate and had no interest in boys. She looked for all the world like a girl with anorexia nervosa, but her appetite had always been poor and she had not lost any weight.
>
> Her mother had herself been taken to a mental health center at the age of 12, was raped at gunpoint at 14, and had several psychiatric hospitalizations at ages 17 and 18. She was an attractive woman who was proud of her appearance but who, when discussing her marriages, emphasized her complete disinterest in sex and in her husband. She had no complaints about her husband; she simply wasn't interested in men. "I wish he'd leave. I'd much rather be alone with my children." The closeness between mother and daughter was readily apparent and both were obviously upset by the separation necessitated by the hospitalization. And there is the interesting coincidence that mother and child both developed symptoms at age 12.

This girl was discharged, to be followed as an outpatient with a diagnosis of hysterical dissociative episode, rather than schizophrenia or a schizophreniform disorder. The reason for the presentation here, however, is to illustrate the close association between what appeared to be an incomplete separation-individuation of child from mother and the onset of a perceptual disorder; although of short duration, the perceptual disorder is reminiscent of schizophrenia. The mother is not schizophrenic, so one might well predict that the child will also escape serious illness. On the other hand, unless the child can be helped to function as a more autonomous individual, the prognosis is, at best, guarded.

Some children develop imaginary playmates with whom they spend much of their time. Many hours may be spent in conversation and play, just as if another child were present. The use of such a mechanism is of little concern in most instances, but on occasion this phenomenon, too, seems almost hallucinatory. One 10-year-old girl played with "a green alligator man" but gave him up almost immediately upon admission to the hospital. As it turned out, her mother was subject to bizarre delusions but was so intelligent that she could make her delusions sound almost logical. It was very difficult for this little girl to separate reality from fantasy while at home, but she did so quite readily in a structured hospital setting in which there was only one psychotic girl.

The need to assist children through the separation-individuation phase is as important as helping them through the dependency of early infancy. It is imperative that the child relate to the caregiver, incorporating both the "good mother" and the "bad mother," but equally imperative that the child separate from the mother and develop clear boundaries between self and reality.

THINKING DISORDERS

The most basic symptom of adult schizophrenia is some form of thought disorder. The incoherence, distorted grammar, echoing, loosening of associations, and delusions of adults are both less frequent among children and adolescents and more difficult to discern because of the child's incomplete development and limited education. One must be expert in the ability to communicate with children and, even then, must repeatedly digress from the topic at hand to ask for clarification. Whereas, when one is unable to follow the thought content or flow of an adult, a psychosis must be considered, it is often difficult to follow the thinking of normal children due to their expressive immaturity.

Adult schizophrenics often present both clear-cut hallucinations and delusions that have existed for weeks or months. A thorough history often reveals some alienation from peers and family members in adolescence and the development of certain eccentricities or peculiarities which, in retrospect, appear to have been the early or, perhaps, premorbid symptoms of schizophrenia. With a gradual, insidious onset, the symptoms may have gone unnoticed by the family or may have been attributed to the individual's personality structure. If these early symptoms are serious enough—or if the family is discerning enough—to bring the young adolescent to a mental health professional, the diagnostic ability of the interviewer will be severely tested.

Rapport may be difficult to establish, due to the patient's withdrawal into his own world. One may get the feeling that he is confused at times, particularly when alone or in darkness, when ties to reality are less apparent. Blocking and loss of the ability to concentrate may be evident. But it will take an experienced child psychiatrist to detect these symptoms in a young schizophrenic. The inability to concentrate is a common complaint in latency-aged children and in adolescents, often demonstrated by the plummeting of school grades. Ordinarily, this symptom is *not* due to schizophrenia; but if another explanation cannot be found, the child should be referred to the most experienced professional in the community.

When hallucinations are the presenting symptom in any child or young adolescent, a toxic or other organic cause should be considered first and then ruled out *before* considering schizophrenia. Fever can cause terrifying visual and tactile hallucinations in young children, while street drugs are the most common cause in adolescents. Pediatric consultation is imperative. As indicated earlier, imaginary playmates will be described in very real terms by children, making it difficult to know whether they represent a true perceptual disorder or merely a figment of the child's imagination. Hysterical phenomena may also appear to be hallucinatory.

Delusions, too, may be difficult to ascertain in children, due to honest misconceptions. A fifth-grade boy was once explaining how food progressed through the stomach, to the small intestine, to the large intestine, later to be excreted as waste via the anus.

Liquids, he asserted, entered the blood, then the kidneys, *and finally the large intestine, to be excreted along with solid waste.* This was what he was taught in school, or so he said. Although this child was quite healthy, such a belief was, by definition, quite delusional. When he was confronted by the examiner's surprise, he reported that the information came directly from his health book. The book was brought in as evidence and, indeed, a picture of the inside of the body was just as he had described. The genitalia and the urinary bladder were omitted, blurred into the background; the ureters led from the kidneys to a point immediately adjacent to the colon. No conclusion could be formed other than that arrived at by our "patient."

Another healthy boy, 8 years of age, was describing the birth of a litter of pups, which he had witnessed. He described the amazing process in great detail, including the fact that "*the mother's belly button opened up like a zipper, and the pups came out one by one; then it closed up again.*"

Unfortunately, a number of children are misdiagnosed as schizophrenic every year, even by competent general psychiatrists, and are either admitted to a hospital or placed on an antipsychotic medication. The emphasis here on the need for a child psychiatrist is not based on the author's professional bias but on the fact that one must be very competent in interviewing children if one is to obtain valid information. Anyone can make the diagnosis once the data have been obtained, but not everyone can communicate effectively with children.

> A 10-year-old hospitalized girl was describing her plan to bring a baby giraffe, whose birth she had witnessed in the nearby woods, into the dormitory so other girls could see it. She told of seeing the giraffe eat paper from the trash and described the giraffe as very friendly. This little girl had a peculiar appearance with rather odd mannerisms, but was clearly of average intelligence.

While most of those present at the staff meeting were wondering about the diagnostic implications of her thought processes, a psychiatric aide (the lowest paid person there) quietly found two pictures in an encyclopedia of a giraffe and a raccoon. The reader can guess which one the child was talking about; she was as surprised to find out what a giraffe looked like as we were to discover our ineptitude.

SOCIAL RELATIONSHIPS

It has already been suggested that an early symptom of schizophrenia is the withdrawal into one's own world. There may be the development of some rather bizarre behaviors that tend to make other children want to avoid the "odd" child for fear of embarrassment. The patient may begin to talk to himself or may become rather emotionally unresponsive. His affect may be described as blunted—that is, showing little expression. On the other hand, he may laugh inappropriately and may even choose to explain this behavior by claiming that he heard a voice telling him to laugh. This may be a true auditory hallucination, or it may be a confabulation designed to make the inappropriate laughter seem more rational.

Not only will peers tend to avoid associating with the "odd" child; they may also make fun of him. This, of course, stimulates further withdrawal. When alone, rumination occurs, with increasing confusion and disordered thinking.

TREATMENT

Hospitalization is most often a necessary part of the treatment program. Sometimes, an accurate diagnosis cannot be made without the systematic observations of a well--trained and experienced staff; especially useful are observations of patient interrelationships. Then too, the structure of the hospital milieu helps the child organize his thoughts. Removal from the daily ward routine can be very confusing to the schizophrenic child.

At times, antipsychotic medication provides a rapid improvement in thinking processes and, in effect, has a remarkably calming influence. However, neuroleptic pharmaceuticals must be used cautiously in children, since they may bring about symptomatic relief before a full understanding of the child's thought content has been reached; this relief may block subsequent efforts towards further understanding. The treatment of specific target symptoms (eg, hallucinations) is definitely indicated and should be given high priority.

Special educational services are a must; experienced teachers within a standard hospital milieu can accomplish a great deal over a 3-month to 9-month period. The additional judicious use of medication can enable the child to get maximum benefit from the friendly, protective, but controlled environments of ward and classroom, alike.

Individual psychotherapy can be effective, but requires a highly experienced therapist willing to devote a year or more to the child, while receiving little gratification in return. One of the fastest ways to discourage a young, eager therapist is to assign a schizophrenic patient for three-times-a-week sessions and provide little supervisory support. This is not to say that individual psychotherapy is contraindicated; but it is certainly not the treatment of choice. One can learn a lot about a schizophrenic child in the playroom, much that can be useful in the treatment of other children later on. The cost, however, far outweighs the benefit for the child.

On the other hand, group therapy of an activity nature (eg, an occupational therapy group), rather than insight-oriented therapy, may be very beneficial. Physical activities, adapted physical education, and sports requiring gross motor coordination should also be included in the treatment program.

Schizophrenic children with serious difficulty relating to other people have been found, on some occasions, to relate more readily to pets. Certain breeds of dogs are known for their tolerance and for their ability to move away quickly when threatened. Horses, too, are apparently attractive to some children who avoid interpersonal relationships.

SUMMARY

Although childhood schizophrenia is a rare condition, it should be correctly diagnosed as early as possible, so that treatment can be instituted. Any single symptom can occur in nonschizophrenic children. The important issue is the constellation of symptoms—especially, aberrant thought processes. The presence of a definite thought disorder can be considered pathognomonic of schizophrenia.

The true cause of schizophrenia is still unknown, but there is known to be an inherited factor that either causes the disease or, more often, predisposes the child to the development of the disease. It is also felt that a problem in the separation-individuation process predisposes the child to schizophrenia. This does not exclude the possibility that some inherited, biochemical defect causes both the separation-individuation problem and, later on, schizophrenia. Diabetes mellitus is an example of a known metabolic disorder that does not become symptomatic for many years and, perhaps even then, only under certain circumstances.

A slow, gradual process has been described as the natural history of schizophrenia, with an emphasis on the need to recognize symptoms quite early. There are times, however, when the disorder presents very suddenly during adolescence, sometimes along with the use of mind-altering drugs or in association with a severe stressor. The proper diagnosis would be toxic psychosis if a drug were considered the etiologic agent; nevertheless, on occasion, the psychotic symptoms may persist for months or years. In such an instance, it is usually thought that an incipient schizophrenic process pre-existed the use of the drug and that the properties of the drug served merely to precipitate the full-blown disease.

The prognosis in acute-onset schizophrenia is better than in the insidious-onset variety; indeed, the two forms of schizophrenia may turn out to be different diseases.

Once again, we have pointed out the need for caution in making the diagnosis, while underscoring the desirability of early intervention. Schizophrenia can be treated effectively, most often through a team approach. The childcare worker, nurse, teacher, and occupational therapist are indispensable members of the team that establishes the therapeutic milieu.

BIBLIOGRAPHY

Mahler M, Pine F, Bergman A: *The psychological birth of the human infant.* New York, Basic Books, 1975

Rothstein A: Hallucinatory phenomena in childhood: A critique of the literature. *J Child Psychiatry* 20:623-635, 1981

Chapter 20

SUBSTANCE ABUSE IN ADOLESCENTS AND CHILDREN

Elsa Rae Pool, MSW, MHA
Douglas S. Pool, MD

The use and abuse of psychoactive drugs is not a new phenomenon in our society. However, in the late 1960s an unprecedented increase was noted in substance abuse, primarily among adolescents. Although the alarm has quieted somewhat since that time, the use of these potentially harmful drugs continues.

The aim of this chapter is to expand the reader's understanding of the problem of substance abuse among youth. A discussion of chemical use and abuse will be followed by an exploration of personality, environmental, and psychological factors that may predispose an adolescent to become involved in drugs. The effects of the more popular drugs will be discussed, to make their use more easily recognizable. Some treatment approaches will be explained, although at this time there is little agreement regarding the degree of effectiveness of any particular approach.

CHEMICAL USE AND ABUSE

Some psychoactive drugs are available and legal. These drugs are divided into four categories. The first group are prescription drugs which require the authorization of a physician and include sedatives, tranquilizers, and stimulants. The next group are over-the-counter drugs which are intended to be used according to accompanying instructions and, if properly used, are considered safe; the instructions, however, are frequently ignored. The next group are the socially acceptable drugs: alcohol, nicotine, and caffeine. The last group includes those agents that are neither produced nor sold for the purpose of human consumption, such as airplane glue and gasoline.

Generally, when the term "drug abuse" is used we think of the illegal group of psychoactive drugs, such as marijuana, heroin, cocaine, and hallucinogens, including LSD, mescaline, and peyote.

Legally prescribed drugs (eg, stimulants, tranquilizers, and sedatives) fall into the category of substance abuse when they are used improperly and illegally.

The actual socioeconomic and potential biological consequences of drug abuse among youth in this country have prompted many studies of the problem. Results reveal some interesting and, perhaps, useful information about some of the factors that predispose adolescents to use drugs.

Predisposing Factors

Availability of drugs is the first prerequisite for drug abuse, followed by the opportunity to use the drug. In general, a person does not seek his first drug experience; instead the opportunity to use a drug or multiple drugs conveniently presents itself. The reduced stigma of drug use—particularly cigarettes, alcohol, and marijuana in the adolescent culture—has added to its increase in popularity; indeed, in many groups these drugs are not only accepted but considered a status symbol.

In the past, the prevailing opinion was that marijuana and personality problems were closely related. This line of thinking may be in error. No consistent relationship between the use of marijuana and the presence or absence of personality disorders has been found. Thus the stereotypic image of an abberant individual who is a social isolate no longer fits with the reality of today's adolescents who use drugs. In fact, there is, apparently, no fixed profile of an adolescent drug user. Instead, studies show a variety of predictive factors; it is possible that all, some, or none apply to the individual adolescent abuser. A multidimensional view of this behavior seems the most reasonable approach.

PERSONALITY, ENVIRONMENTAL, AND PSYCHOPATHOLOGICAL FACTORS

As a means of defining the facets of the problem of substance abuse, we will consider three factors that affect the individual patient's involvement. They are: (1) personality, (2) environmental, and (3) psychopathological factors.

Personality Factors

The personality system as discussed here will refer to a combination of values, attitudes, and behaviors. Adolescents who use drugs tend to be less successful in adapting to their educational environment. This is reflected in lower grades and a high rate of truancy. Results of studies indicate that most adolescent drug abusers are average to above average in IQ. This information is consistent with the values expressed by those youths involved in drugs; that is, these students tend to place greater value on independence than on academic achievement.

A significant correlation between adolescent drug use and the activities engaged in by these individuals has been noted. Students who spend many evenings outside the home involved in recreational activities are at higher risk for drug involvement. Earlier and more frequent dating patterns are linked with drug use. Essentially, those individuals who spend most of their time socializing rather than engaged in more age-appropriate and conventional activities —such as homework, sports, and family activities—tend to exhibit a higher rate of drug involvement.

Adolescents who work a greater number of hours per week seem prone to more drug abuse. Working may, in part, reflect the high value of independence held by those involved with drugs. The amount of time spent working obviously deprives the adolescent of time to participate in more suitable activities. Instead, the youth may associate with his/her fellow employees, at least during working hours and frequently after work. It is highly probable that these fellow workers are older and consequently involved in activities that are less acceptable for an adolescent, such as drinking, smoking, and staying out late. This combination of factors seems to be related to an attitude of rebelliousness and nonconformity; unfortunately, whether this is a cause or an effect is unclear. It has been speculated that the amount of time worked relates to drug abuse by contributing to a higher income which provides a means for buying drugs.

Evidence gathered from research indicates that drug users reflect a greater tolerance for deviant, nonconforming behavior than do nondrug users. Nondrug users, on the other hand, tend to be more conventional; predictably, they value and seek adult approval, participate in more traditional behavior, and associate with others who feel and act similarly. This attitude of traditionalism among nonusers extends to the political views held by this group. Studies have shown a definite correlation between those students who place themselves on the conservative end of the political continuum and those less likely to use drugs. Religious commitment seems to be one of the strongest predictors of the risk for drug involvement. Those most involved in religion, including beliefs and/or activities, are far less likely to be involved in any sort of drug use.

Environmental Factors

The second system, environmental, refers to family and peer influence and various demographic factors. While reviewing the demographic data, it should be noted that variations occur with specific drug use, frequency of use, and degree of involvement.

Race, sex, and age distribution. In the past, drug abuse was viewed as a problem primarily seen in minority populations, with males being the most likely candidates. Although many still believe this to be the case, statistical evidence does not support this finding. The use of marijuana is approximately equal across racial lines. More Caucasians seem to use pills and psychedelics, while more blacks are found among heroin users. The differences in drug use between the sexes is rapidly diminishing: males still exceed females in the use of alcohol; however, in regard to cigarette smoking, females exceed males. The use of illicit drugs usually occurs between the ages of 13 and 25, with the period of highest risk for initiation into marijuana use between 15 and 17.

Region of US. There seems to be little correlation of drug use with region or urbanicity. There does appear to be above average use of drugs in the Northeast United States and below average usage in the South.

Socioeconomic factors. Socioeconomic factors do not predict a preponderance of use at any one level, nor is there a correlation between parents' educational attainment and children's drug use. However, it is obvious that the family is extremely influential in determining the developmental path of each child. There are certain parental characteristics that have been identified as predictors of drug use; these characteristics can serve only as guidelines. Far more research is needed before a comprehensive description of environmental influences can be offered.

Parental role. Parents serve as the primary role models for their children; thus, parental use of hard liquor and/or medical or illegal drugs portends the same behavior by the exposed offspring. Lack of closeness between parents and children markedly increases the risk of drug use. Lack of maternal emotional involvement in the child's activities appears to predispose the child to use. Absent or insufficient discipline, which frequently characterizes families lacking in closeness or involvement, has also been identified as a predictor. Lastly, low parental educational aspirations for children have been correlated with drug abuse.

Peer influence. To gain further perspective concerning the environmental system, the contribution of peers must be considered. Among adolescent drug users, compatibility between parents and friends seems minimal, with friends being the more influential. Friends may not only approve of drug-taking behavior, but frequently are models for engaging in such behavior. The sequence of involvement with drugs seems to proceed from beer and wine to cigarettes and hard liquor, followed by marijuana and, finally, other illicit drugs. However, a particular individual may stop at any stage in the sequence and not progress further.

Psychopathological Factors

The third system to be considered is the individual's psychological makeup. Results of studies have shown little evidence of severe psychopathology among most adolescent drug abusers. The adolescent involved in drug use to avoid psychological problems or to free himself from the pain of experiencing these problems appears to be the exception, rather than the rule. If an adolescent uses drugs in isolation instead of with a peer group, it may indicate that he/she is suffering from some fundamental discomfort. In the less common case of heroin or amphetamine addiction, psychopathological causes are relatively likely, but cases of such extreme involvement reaching addictive proportions in adolescents are rare.

There are several psychological factors that warrant mention here, in that they may have some predictive value. Adolescents using drugs may display a rather pessimistic view of the future. This is a symptom of their overall depressed mood, which may lead to self-destructive behavior. Low self-esteem and self-defeating attempts to achieve gratification also seems to correlate with adolescent drug abuse. Rebelliousness from early childhood is predictive of drug abuse in adolescents. In general, the self-confident, contented, and secure adolescent does not seem to need or desire to become involved with drugs, while the dependent, unfulfilled, depressed person is much more likely to participate in drug abusing behavior.

DRUG EFFECTS

In order to recognize individuals who may be involved in drug abuse, a brief description of the physical, affective, and cognitive symptoms produced by popular drugs will be presented.

Alcohol

When a person appears to be under the influence of a drug, alcohol intoxication should be considered first, since alcohol is the most widely abused drug. A person intoxicated from barbiturates or barbiturate-like drugs, also easily obtainable, presents a clinical picture very similar to that of an individual intoxicated with alcohol. Alcohol is unique in that it requires no digestion and is quickly metabolized in the body, thus causing rapid behavioral changes.

Each individual will react differently to alcohol, just as he/she will vary in behavior whenever any drug is consumed. A mildly intoxicated person is generally happy, friendly, and talkative, while those more intoxicated may become disoriented, fearful, or withdrawn. In cases where extremely large amounts of alcohol have been consumed, a person may be in a stupor or may lose consciousness. The early motor effects include slurred speech, lethargy, and possible respiratory depression. Initially, an intoxicated individual may feel euphoric; generally this is replaced later by feelings of depression and insecurity. In the cognitive area, problems become evident in loss of social judgment, progressing to an inability to answer simple questions, poor memory, and complete disorientation.

Marijuana

Physiological changes accompanying marijuana use include increased pulse rate, bloodshot eyes, and dryness of mouth and throat. Generally, initial restlessness is followed by a feeling of detachment. At low doses, there are illusionary experiences (eg, shadows seem to be real objects). With higher doses there are rapidly changing illusory images, fragmentation of thought, and a sense of increased insight and tranquility. Hallucinations may appear at higher doses.

LSD/Mescaline

LSD or mescaline intoxication may be characterized by such cognitive changes as altered time sense and disturbed judgment. Hallucinations and illusions of changing colors and shapes may occur, creating a feeling of fear, dread, and—on occasion—panic. Physical effects include mild dry mouth, dilated pupils, and a transient or mild increase in pulse rate and blood pressure. Frequently there is increased motor activity.

PCP

Effects of phencyclidine (PCP) occur rapidly after the drug has been ingested. At low to moderate doses, physical signs include slurred speech, mild loss of coordination, rapid heart beat, and vomiting. With larger doses, additional signs include hypertension, purposeless movement, violent outbursts, and muscular rigidity. Coma may occur. Cognitive effects may include alteration in body image and sensations of the body contracting or elongating. These effects may not occur for several days. The immediate effect is euphoria, followed by anxiety, loneliness, feelings of isolation, and depression. At higher dosages, hostility and rage may progress to apathy, convulsions, or catatonia. The slow onset and slow decline of these altered behaviors should suggest the ingestion of PCP.

Stimulants

With stimulant intoxication the physical signs include increasing heart rate and elevated blood pressure, mild to moderate hypertension, muscle twitching, sweating, and dilated but reactive pupils. The affects vary from anxiety or elevated mood at low dosages to irritability and aggressive behavior at higher levels. Cognitive changes include increased alertness and accelerated thought processes, possibly accompanied by pressured speech and mild confusion. There may be a slight increase in task performance.

Solvents

Acute solvent intoxication generally produces the physical sensation of blurred vision and ringing or buzzing in the ears. Affectively, the individual is generally giddy; however, in more severe intoxication, stupor or coma may result. The patient appears disoriented.

Narcotics

The adolescent intoxicated with a low dosage of narcotics, such as morphine or heroin, exhibits the following physical signs: drowsiness, nausea, lethargy, and inability to concentrate. At low dosages, affect ranges from euphoria to dysphoria; anxiety and care appear suppressed. This carefree feeling increases the individual's desire to obtain more of the drug in order to maintain his euphoric state. Cognitive impairment per se appears to be mild. With higher doses, the patient may exhibit nausea, vomiting, sleepiness, constricted pinpoint pupils, and respiratory depression.

Over-the-counter Medications, Prescription Drugs, and Plant Alkaloids

Anticholinergic drug intoxication may occur from ingestion of over-the-counter cold or sleep medications, antihistamines, some prescription drugs, and plant alkaloids such as belladona. Physical signs include elevated heart rate and temperature, blurred vision, widely dilated pupils with flushed face, and possible difficulty in urinating. In spite of a lack of sweating, extreme anxiety is the norm. Psychological symptoms include disorientation and visual, auditory, and tactile hallucinations, along with psychomotor agitation.

TREATMENT APPROACHES

Treating the drug abusing adolescent is obviously no easy task. There are many unanswered questions that may make the job even more difficult than dealing with adult drug abusers. Among these are: What are the differences/similarities between a substance abusing child and a substance abusing adult? Since current use of alcohol and marijuana is so widespread among youth, when does substance use become a mark of pathology rather than normality? Is the use of different drugs indicative of different problems, each requiring a specialized approach? Or is drug abuse like a rose by any other name? Research is being conducted to obtain answers. It is hoped that the answers will lead to more effective methods to treat the self-destructive behavior of drug abuse.

A brief discussion of treatment approaches will reflect the broad spectrum of techniques used in dealing with the adolescent drug abuser. Programs can be categorized roughly into three phases: preventative, treatment, and rehabilitative.

Prevention Programs

Preventative programs are geared toward those individuals who are potential or infrequent drug users. The aim of these programs is to prevent these individuals from becoming regular drug users. Generally, the primary prevention programs are educational in nature. People involved in these programs may learn about drugs and their dangers, but this component is but a minor portion of such a program. Results have indicated that programs limited to education in the area of drug use are somewhat ineffective. However, it is important to note that those students who have received drug education prior to drug use generally are less likely to become frequent or heavy drug users.

An apparently more effective educational approach involves not only drug education, but also includes clarification of values and learning—or relearning—communication skills, decision making, and helping relationships. In some programs, students complete a "course" and then are promoted to the level of teacher, instructing other students. The holistic approach to behavior along with peer teaching seems to produce positive results. Similar programs are used in the prevention of cigarette smoking, as well as alcohol and drug abuse.

Treatment Programs

Modalities. Treatment programs available to an adolescent who has been assigned the label of substance abuser vary greatly. As discussed earlier, most programs include an educational component. Therapy with families is frequently required, since the adolescent is generally functioning as part of a family system which affects and is affected by the adolescent's behavior. Group therapy seems to be a useful means of dealing with the substance abuser, since peers are often aware of each other's strategies to avoid blame, mask emotions, and justify inappropriate behavior. Professional therapists may guide the sessions, or groups may be composed of only substance abusers, both present and past. Individual therapy may be the approach of choice if the substance abuse behavior is seen as a result of psychopathology. Occasionally, medication is used therapeutically: antabuse may be prescribed for alcoholics, and methadone dispensed to heroin abusers. It is relatively rare for an adolescent's addiction to be severe enough to warrant this type of pharmacological approach.

Setting. Treatment may take place in various environmental settings. Some programs will allow the adolescent to remain at home and to continue at school, thereby preventing any major disruption in the youth's routine. The adolescent would attend regularly scheduled meetings and therapy sessions.

There are various residential programs for the adolescent substance abuser. Some programs are patterned after the Synanon concept, where the residents are all abusers and the therapists are "recovered" abusers. Frequently these programs have no professionals per se. Some offer the gamut of therapies. Additionally, they require that each resident have certain assigned responsibilities in the maintenance of living quarters. Advancement in status is based not only on absence of drugs but also on improvement of attitude and behavior.

Other residential facilities are located in psychiatric hospitals. Such programs usually include a state-approved school, so that adolescents can maintain their academic status while in treatment. Drug education, generally family and group therapy, and occasionally individual therapy are part of the treatment regimen. Professionals—eg, psychiatrists, psychologists, social workers, and nurses—are employed to implement the program, to which adolescents may be admitted voluntarily or judicially.

Rehabilitative Programs

Rehabilitative programs are not necessarily separate and distint from treatment programs. There may be a shift in emphasis in a rehabilitative program, such that therapy time is decreased and time spent in attending public schools, vocational training, or on-the-job training is increased. The theme here is to facilitate the individual's ability to accept responsibility and to provide education and training that will be useful once he/she is independent.

In many programs for adult substance abusers, the goal is to "control" the individual. In the past, and—unfortunately—frequently in the present, the same programs are being used for adolescents. These programs are inappropriate since, in the case of adolescents, a "cure" may be possible. Since young substance abusers represent an entirely different population with unique characteristics, it seems obvious that programs designed for adults are not appropriate for them.

CONCLUSIONS

There is a great deal more to be learned about the substance abusing adolescent; currently, research is increasing in this area. The mystery remains of who these adolescents are and why they are abusing chemicals. Attitudes exist from one end of the continuum to the other, from the contention that any use of drugs represents pathologic behavior to the belief that the use of alcohol, cigarettes, and marijuana is reasonable, acceptable, and normal behavior. Theoretical constructs are still being sought. The primary concern is to prevent any behavior that will lead to destruction of the great potential which our adolescent population represents. If drug abuse is indeed a danger to an individual's healthy growth, methods must be found to deal with it so that the individual, as well as society, will not suffer.

BIBLIOGRAPHY

Bachman JG, Johnston LD, O'Malley PM: Smoking, drinking and drug use among American high school students: Correlates and trends, 1975-1979. *Am J Public Health* 71:59-69, 1981

DiSclafani A, Hall RCW, Gardner ER: Drug-induced psychosis: Emergency diagnosis and management. *Psychosomatics* 22:845-855, 1981

Dorus W, Senay EC: Depression, demographic dimensions, and drug abuse. *Am J Psychiatry* 137:699-704, 1980

Farley GK, Eckhardt LO, Hebert FB: *Handbook of child and adolescent psychiatric emergencies.* Garden City, NY, Medical Examination Publishing Co, 1979

Fisher EB Jr: Progress in reducing adolescent smoking. *Am J Public Health* 70:678-679, 1980

Huba GJ, Wingard JA, Bentler PM: Incentives to use drugs among adolescents: A longitudinal analysis. *International J Addictions* 16:331-339, 1981

Jessor R, Chase JA, Donovan JE: Psychosocial correlates of marijuana use and problem drinking in a national sample of adolescents. *Am J Public Health* 70:604-613, 1980

Kandel DB: Epidemiological and psychosocial perspectives on adolescent drug use. *J Child Psychiatry* 21:328-347, 1982

Kim S: How do we know whether a primary prevention program on drug abuse works or does not work? *International J Addictions* 16:359-365, 1981

McAlister A, Perry C, Killen J, et al: Pilot study of smoking, alcohol and drug abuse prevention. *Am J Public Health* 70:719-721, 1980

McCafferty C, Clive D, Jordan J: Issues in the psychiatric approach to substance abuse in the adolescent. *Psychiatric Annals* 11:53-59, 1981

Nystrom KF, Bal AL, Labrecque V: Substance abuse, in Noshpitz JD (ed): *Basic Handbook of Child Psychiatry.* New York, Basic Books, 1979, vol 2

Pandina RJ, White HR: Patterns of alcohol and drug use of adolescent students and adolescents in treatment. *J Stud Alcohol* 42:441-456, 1981

Pederson LL, Baskerville JC, Lefcoe NM: Change in smoking status among school-aged youth: Impact of a smoking awareness curriculum, attitudes, knowledge and environmental factors. *Am J Public Health* 71:1401-1404, 1981

Ray O: *Drugs, society, and human behavior.* St. Louis, CV Mosby Co, 1978

Robbins LN: The natural history of drug abuse. *Acta Psychiatrica Scandinavia* 62:7-20, 1980

Woodruff RA, Goodwin DW, Guze SB: *Psychiatric diagnosis.* New York, Oxford University Press, 1974

Yankelovich D: Drug users vs drug abusers: How students control their drug crisis. *Psychology Today* 9:39-42, 1975

Chapter 21

OTHER DISORDERS

R. DEAN CODDINGTON, MD

Discussed in this chapter are five specific entities in which there seems to be a problem in the child's relationship with his mother or with society as a whole. The entities are included together because of this similarity, not because of a common etiology. Moreover, the reader should not assume that these are the only disorders in which maternal relationships suffer or in which the adolescent is at odds with society; both conditions are true of many syndromes. We will begin with the youngest children and progress up the developmental ladder.

REACTIVE ATTACHMENT DISORDER OF INFANCY

As the name implies, this disorder involves an infant's failure to form an attachment to his mother. The term is reserved for those cases that are due to lack of maternal care and excludes persons with infantile autism and those who fail to form attachments because of a congenital anomaly. In the reactive disorder of infancy, the infant is reacting to gross emotional neglect or to isolation in an institution. The onset of the disorder is before 8 months of age.

Rene Spitz was the first to describe institutionalized infants who experienced very little visual or auditory stimulation and insufficient handling by a caretaker. There was no rocking, caressing, cooing, singing, or playing on the part of the nurse. The infants became less and less active; because they lay still for long periods of time, hollows were formed in their mattresses. They showed less and less interest in their adult caretakers and seemed depressed! Spitz measured their developmental progress and found them severely retarded by 6 to 12 months of age. Since some of the mothers were in a nearby prison, Spitz was able to bring them in to care for their babies, rather than having one nurse care for eight infants. With this extra attention and stimulation, the infants brightened and began to catch up developmentally.

Under emotionally deprived conditions, infants fail to thrive. They are more liable to catch viral and bacterial infections and may even die. The reactive attachment disorder is not limited to institutionalized children but can occur at home when the mother is unable, for reasons of her own, to provide a stimulating, growth-promoting environment. (The reader may wish to review chapter 1 to fully understand normal mother-infant attachment.) Depressed, schizophrenic, and alcoholic mothers are examples of mothers with severe affective limitations that may preclude their relating normally to their babies.

Treatment can be very effective if the therapist is able to alter the situation. Hospitalization is often necessary for infants who have gained little weight; when provisions are made for one nurse or nurse's aide to devote herself to the child, a dramatic change may follow in a week or two. At the same time, the mother's condition must be treated to avoid recurrence of the problem. If the treatment is too time-consuming or if the mother is not motivated to change, referral *must* be made to child protective services and foster placement arranged.

> At 4 months of age, Sarah began vomiting whenever her mother fed her. Despite several short hospitalizations in which she did well, the vomiting recurred immediately upon discharge. At 9 months of age, Sarah weighed less than her birth weight.
>
> Further history revealed that Sarah's mother, a young nurse, was concerned when the onset of labor was delayed. She predicted that the baby's head would be molded out of shape due to the prolonged pressures placed on it, and reassured her husband that it would soon return to normal; and so it did. It seemed to the therapist that this early concern and the detailed notes about developmental progress reflected unusual concern over the baby's neurological functioning. The therapist asked what the mother thought was the worst possible condition that could be the cause of Sarah's vomiting. "Bowel obstruction" was her immediate response. The therapist reacted, "No, that's not your worst fear; you're afraid of brain damage." With that, the mother cried, went immediately to Sarah to cuddle her, and then seemed to relax. It was as if at last she could talk to someone about her dreadful fear. She knew that a bowel obstruction could be treated surgically, but she considered brain damage untreatable.
>
> Her anxiety was so great that she was unable to relax, even during feedings. The muscular tension was transmitted to Sarah, causing

her to vomit. With relief of the anxiety after one or two family sessions, Sarah's vomiting ceased and she developed normally.

Cases like this impress one with both the fragility and plasticity of infants. They react quickly to insufficient care and just as quickly in the other direction when care is given. The ability to bounce back provides us with an excellent measure of the child's well-being; something is wrong if a healthy baby fails to respond to good maternal care. If the mother can't bring about a change in a reasonable period, it's time for the father to step in. When neither is effective, the child is probably unwell and it's time to call the pediatrician.

OPPOSITIONAL DISORDER

It would not be an exaggeration to say that almost all 2- and 3-year-olds are oppositional some of the time; some of them are oppositional most of the time. As they complete the separation-individuation phase of development, they become very demanding (see chapters 1 and 2). They clearly have a mind of their own and want to exercise it. A child may indicate that he's hungry, but then refuse to climb up in his high chair when food is offered. He says "No" to almost any suggestion, even though he may clearly enjoy the activity in question. This normal oppositional behavior gradually wanes so that the majority of 5-year-olds are pleasant, cooperative, and fairly compliant. It is only when the oppositional behavior persists or recurs at a later age that we must begin to consider the diagnosis of oppositional disorder and investigate causative factors.

A mother presented her 9-year-old son as incorrigible; she couldn't do a thing with him: he was very demanding and did just about whatever he pleased. She was advised on the first visit that children need a certain amount of structure, meaning that parents must set limits on their behavior. As mother and son left the building they passed some vending machines; the boy asked for and received an Eskimo Bar. By the time they reached the car in the parking lot, he had consumed the treat and demanded another. Unable to resist, his mother agreed to a return to the vending machine. Once again, the boy finished the Eskimo Bar by the time they reached the car, and once again he cried out for another. She remembered that the doctor had advised her to set limits, and

> said "No!" They got in the car in the midst of a full-fledged temper tantrum and started home. A few blocks from the office, the boy spotted a Howard Johnson's restaurant, whereupon he ceased screaming long enough to demand more ice cream. The distraught mother pulled across a lane of traffic and collided with another car, in an attempt to quiet her demanding son.

How does such oppositional behavior evolve? Why does any parent permit such demanding behavior? In an attempt to answer these and other questions, both mother and child were hospitalized in a psychiatric hospital. The boy behaved appropriately with every other patient (adults) on the unit but constantly disobeyed his mother. When he disobeyed, she, on the other hand, seemed unable to discipline him in the most basic way. For example, it was suggested that she stand him in the corner, facing the wall, for fifteen minutes. She could not do it! In three weeks she signed out of the hospital, unimproved. What had been learned about the evolution of this remarkable state of affairs?

The mother, it was discovered, had had a very disturbed childhood in which, on a number of occasions, her father had locked her in a small room. Every time the staff locked the unit door, she relived her childhood experience.

It was also learned that she married a man 20 years older than she and, very quickly, became disenchanted with him. She asked his cooperation in dissolving the marriage, but he refused. She decided that the only way to get out of the marriage was to antagonize her husband by becoming pregnant out of wedlock, and she proceeded to do just that. Her son was the product of such an affair, but her strategy failed: she gained an unwanted son but still had her unwanted, and now furious, husband. The marriage was worsened, and she had an additional burden of guilt. She and her son moved out and lived alone.

The psychodynamics are now clear: The woman had a disturbed attitude toward men, which included an introjected image of a bad father who locked her in a small room as punishment. She married a man her father's age, perhaps with some inner hope of reliving her childhood in a more comforting manner. When it became apparent that her hopes were unrealistic, she behaved badly (according to her own standards) and conceived a child out of wedlock. She grew to hate the child when his presence failed to achieve her goal (also, perhaps, because he was a male). She may well have wanted to punish the boy severely—irrationally, for simply existing—and may have reacted against her murderous wish by not punishing at all. The child was in complete control: a demanding, disobedient, oppositional boy, who served as living proof that "all men are bastards."

Fortunately, most examples of this disorder are not as dramatic. Many children express their aggressiveness in a much more passive manner, without open defiance. These are the children who apparently obey all the rules but are late in doing so: they obey the letter of the law but not the spirit. They get ready for school but forget their schoolbooks. They do their homework but too late. They take the teacher's note to their parents' home but accidentally misplace it, so that it is never discovered. Their disobedience is not open; they avoid punishment, since it's hard to punish a forgetful child who seems to be trying to conform.

Unlike the extreme example given, it is difficult in most cases to obtain sufficient data to permit a clear formulation as to cause. The problem begins in the normally oppositional period, continues rather unnoticed for 2 or 3 years, and then becomes generalized as the child's personality begins to form. The behavior is recognized, of course, but the parents frequently resign themselves to having an oppositional child in the family. He may never be brought to the attention of a psychiatrist until the behavior results in poor school performance and the teacher recognizes that he is not measuring up to his potential.

Treatment is difficult and must involve some form of psychotherapy, either individual or family therapy, over a rather long period of time. By age 8 or 9 when the referral is made, the condition has existed for 6 or 7 years and is well ingrained into family dynamics. All kinds of compensations and compromises have been made for years and are not easily unlearned. The therapist will find a number of battles going on within the family, very likely producing coalitions between pairs of family members. Individual therapy is often indicated by the fact that the child's behavior is carried over into the classroom and will result in secondary educational and interpersonal problems, if not corrected.

ELECTIVE MUTISM

Elective mutism is a very descriptive term: some children choose not to talk to certain individuals. Or, to put it another way, they limit all verbal communication to one, or very few, individuals. Usually the child talks to his mother and siblings, and often to the father, too, but not to very many others. The syndrome begins in the preschool years, with the child appearing to be shy—a situation sometimes viewed as "cute" and reinforced by parents. As with the oppositional disorder discussed above, elective mutism becomes problematic in school.

> Susan had progressed through six grades without uttering a single word in school. It seems unlikely, to be sure. However, she communicated nonverbally sufficiently well to get by. She was also a friendly child, well liked by adults and peers, and may have been given a "social promotion" or two.
>
> When admitted to the adolescent unit of a psychiatric hospital, she established a nonverbal communication system with peers within 24 hours. She would sit upright in a chair with her hands by her sides and raise one index finger an inch or two to indicate "yes," the middle finger to indicate "no," and the ring finger for "I don't know." The other children undoubtedly contributed to the development of this system, making her a very special kid who was center stage for awhile as people watched for her signals.

Susan had a very close relationship with her mother and looked forward to her visits and, particularly, to a home visit. This relationship was used effectively in developing a behavior modification program. She could earn time with her mother by increasing verbal communication with some member of the staff. She earned her discharge in this manner in about six months. Believe it or not, she joined the debating squad in high school two years later.

The psychodynamics involved in elective mutism often include a very close, symbiotic relationship with the mother and the use of mutism as a form of aggression. Remember that rapid language development is occurring concurrently with the child's separation from the mother in the individuation process. As a case in point, consider a set of twins who spoke only to one another and to their mother. They never spoke to their father! (Nor did they speak to the therapist.) A careful history revealed considerable marital discord: the mother's method of handling her disapproval of her husband was *to avoid talking to him.* It is evident that her little girls were carrying on their mother's battle. When it was suggested that they be hospitalized, the mother broke off all contact with the therapist *without a word!*

Unlike the case of these twins, treatment is usually successful. A behavior modification approach is the treatment of choice, but family therapy can also be used quite effectively.

IDENTITY DISORDER

Adolescents today seem to have considerably more difficulty defining themselves than did those of yesteryear. Consequently, identity disorders are more common than they used to be.

An identity disorder is defined as severe subjective distress over uncertainty about such issues as long-term goals, career choice, friendship patterns, sexual orientation and behavior, religious identification, moral value systems, and group loyalties. If an adolescent suffers from uncertainty in at least three of these areas and is impaired in his social or educational functioning for at least 3 months, identity disorder is a likely diagnosis. Just how common the disorder is is unknown, but there is no doubt that society has changed in a way that presents multiple options to the teenager.

In the 1930s and 40s, the high school student had no car and a rather circumscribed social life and was expected to accept his parent's religious and political views and to attend the college of *their* choice. Things were much simpler. Most adolescents can accept today's less structured society with equanimity, but some are unable to do so and become anxious, confused, and depressed. They seem unable to make the necessary decisions, unable to decide on a career, and unable to pursue the career decided upon. They ruminate over moral issues and examine different religions in an endless effort to find themselves.

The adolescent is normally seeking emancipation from family, but this process in those with identity disorders is characterized by transient experimental periods of rather widely divergent behavior, as if the adolescent were trying a role to see how it feels. Not only does our society provide many more options than it did in the past; it also encourages deviance from the norm through movements aimed at legalizing marijuana, assuring the civil rights of male homosexuals, and accepting a variety of life-styles. It is much more difficult to be an adolescent today!

The treatment of an adolescent with an identity disorder is, to say the least, difficult. The psychiatrist may be rejected because he is part of the establishment. On the other hand, a cultist may be accepted because he is not so associated. However difficult it may be, psychotherapy is indicated and may, at first, consist of merely establishing rapport. Therapy may be broken off by the patient but reinstituted a few months or years later when the adolescent, himself, feels the need.

SCHIZOID DISORDER OF CHILDHOOD OR ADOLESCENCE

Children with this disorder lack the capacity, or have a severe defect in the capacity, to form social relationships. They have no close friends of their age except, perhaps, another similarly isolated child. Unlike the avoidant disorder (chapter 6) in which the child has a desire for social relationships, the schizoid child has no such desire. He gets no apparent pleasure from contact with peers and has no interest in clubs or teams. The condition is much more common in boys and can be diagnosed as early as age 5.

Careful evaluation reveals good reality testing and no difficulty distinguishing ego boundaries; that is, a child with a schizoid disorder separates self from others without difficulty. Family relationships may be unremarkable, leading us to believe that the disorder does not arise from a symbiotic mother-child attachment. Unlike childhood schizophrenia, there is no evidence of a thought disorder.

Sometimes children with a schizoid disorder become very interested in some esoteric subject or concentrate on a hobby that can be pursued in isolation. From this point of view they are sometimes rather interesting people, though they don't reciprocate with interest in another's activities.

In all likelihood children with this disorder will continue to develop along the same lines and will be diagnosed as having a schizoid personality disorder after age 18. Little is known about treatment, but long-term psychotherapy and psychoanalysis are the only modalities that may be effective.

SUMMARY

Five syndromes have been discussed which have in common a problem between mother and child or, for older children, a problem between society or peers and the child. The first, reactive attachment disorder, begins in infancy and is due to the inability of the mother to relate to her baby in a manner conducive to attachment. The second, oppositional disorder, begins in the preschool period and can be traced to an overly understanding and tolerant mother, who is unable to set appropriate limits. Children with elective mutism, also 3 to 4 years of age at the time of onset, seem closely identified with their mother, who may be pleased that her children choose to talk to her alone.

The schizoid disorder may begin during the preschool period but may also start later in life; it is characterized by an almost complete lack of interest in peers or their activities. In this respect, it is not unlike elective mutism; the child retains an interest in his family and in his hobbies.

The adolescent with an identity disorder has trouble making decisions, usually those decisions that have to do with emancipation from the family. Once again, we see strong family ties although, in this instance, there seems to be a normal desire to be independent.

Thus, there is similarity in the psychodynamics involved, or more precisely, in the interpersonal relationships within the family. As we learn more about these disorders and more about their causes, we may be justified in classifying them elsewhere.

Index

A

B

C

F

G

H

I

J

K

L

M

O